THE PAGEANT
OF AMERICA

R.K.

Independence Edition

VOLUME III

THE PAGEANT OF AMERICA

A PICTORIAL HISTORY OF THE UNITED STATES

RALPH HENRY GABRIEL

EDITOR

HENRY JONES FORD   HARRY MORGAN AYRES

ASSOCIATE EDITORS

OLIVER McKEE

ASSISTANT EDITOR

CHARLES M. ANDREWS   ALLEN JOHNSON
HERBERT E. BOLTON   WILLIAM BENNETT MUNRO
IRVING N. COUNTRYMAN   VICTOR H. PALTSITS
WILLIAM E. DODD   ARTHUR M. SCHLESINGER
DIXON RYAN FOX   NATHANIEL WRIGHT STEPHENSON

ADVISORY EDITORS

DAVID M. MATTESON

INDEXER

TOILERS OF LAND AND SEA

BY

RALPH HENRY GABRIEL

For Reference

Not to be taken from this room

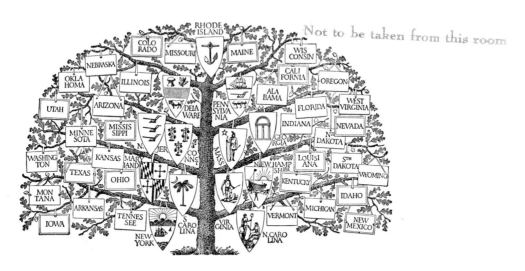

NEW YORK

UNITED STATES PUBLISHERS ASSOCIATION

TORONTO · GLASGOW, BROOK & CO.

1976

TABLE OF CONTENTS

THE AMERICAN FARMER

IN the seventeenth century news of the continent of America began filtering into the country villages and out-of-the-way manors of England. The English peasant, shaking off a little of his inherited lethargy, tried to picture to himself what the new country must be like. He heard vague tales of places with strange names, Virginia, New England, Maryland. He heard of friends who had made the long journey to one of the English seaports to take ship for America. Here and there a peasant, more venturesome than his fellows, said farewell to the familiar village where his ancestors had lived for generations and embarked upon the great adventure.

Seventeenth-century England was not always a happy place for the country villager. The old manor system of mediæval days where the feudal lord was linked to his villeins in a communal enterprise was steadily breaking down. Here and there the arable fields of a manor were no longer cultivated but left to grow up to grass for sheep pasture. The families who had once derived their sustenance from those fields were compelled to move away. There were also political and religious troubles which sometimes, as in the case of the Scrooby folk, uprooted whole communities. For one reason and another Englishmen began to go to America. Some came from the cities — from London or Bristol — artisans, clerks, merchants and members of the gentry. Some came from the sleepy country villages. Settlements like uneven beads on a string began to dot the western shore of the Atlantic. English townsfolk and peasants came suddenly face to face with a strange forest that stretched endlessly westward, while the ocean, battering a desolate coast, cut off retreat. In desperate earnest they mustered up that traditional knowledge of husbandry which had served long generations in England and found it ill adapted to the untamed wilderness of America. Near them curled the smoke from the squalid lodges of their new neighbors, the Indians.

The redskin had plants peculiar to America and a rude system of cultivation adapted to his life in the forest. In the spring, when the oak leaves were the size of a mouse's ear, his squaw began to scratch the earth and in due time planted the corn and beans and squashes. In the autumn, when the forest was a blaze of color, she harvested the crops and put aside the winter stores. The Indians traded seeds to the white intruders for gewgaws and taught them the simple principles of their culture. Sheer necessity drove into the stolid peasant minds of Europe the basic ideas of a new, if savage, husbandry. Out of the marriage of Indian and English farming came the first solution of the problem of the food-quest and the beginnings of American agriculture.

The tenseness of the first critical years relaxed as pioneer axes chopped away the forest farther and farther from the sea. Along the river banks of New York, Maryland, and Virginia and in the warm coastal lowlands of Carolina large estates appeared, great areas marked out in the primeval woods. It was the beginning of the plantation. Here was the owner's house, aspiring to a crude, provincial grandeur. Near it, in the Hudson River region, were the tenants' cabins or, in the South, the slaves' quarters. In Virginia a wharf on an estuary of the James or the Rappahannock, where ships from across the sea tied up, kept contact with the civilization that had been left behind. These plantations marked the transfer of the age-old ideal of a landed gentry to the new country of America. The provincial gentlemen strode the boards of their diminutive colonial stage with something of the manner of the lords of England. Feudal aristocracy found the wild continent beyond the Atlantic a favorable environment, and agriculture in the New World, as in the Old, gave it root.

But in New England the American reflection of the European feudal lord was seldom seen. Amid the stony hills of Connecticut and Massachusetts little groups of plain people, usually a church congregation, jointly took up tracts of land and huddled their cabins into tiny villages. As a group they cleared away the woods and laid out the fields. Here was the arable, there the meadow, and yonder the common pasture where the cow-keeper drove the village herds. It seemed as though an English vill, reduced to its simplest terms, had been set in the American forest. But there was a vital difference. No over-lord had title to the land from whom the villagers held by various tenures. In this new country men owned the acres they tilled.

Years passed and land-hunger, born of this opportunity for ownership, drew ship-loads of people from the static feudal communities of Europe to the great gamble in America. There were Germans and Scotch-Irish as well as English. These eager new-comers passed through the older settlements on the seaboard to a frontier rapidly receding from the ocean. Over rough and hardly distinguishable "traces" and across bridgeless streams they plunged into the back-country — and found themselves isolated from the world. Amid the stumps of their little clearings they built their rough shanties, sometimes grouped together in tiny hamlets, but more and more frequently alone in the open spaces of the woods. The wind moaning through the trees in winter and the night howl of the wolves reminded man of his solitude.

In such surroundings the husbandman and his wife, dividing the tasks between them, faced practically alone the struggle for life. Thrown back upon themselves, they developed in their forest clearing the self-sufficient American farm. From their meager acres they secured for family need the food and fuel and materials for shelter and clothing. The pioneer, looking out over the fields reclaimed by his own hard labor — absolute master of them — could justly feel a sense of pride and independence. In such frontier communities where men stood on an equal footing American democracy was begotten. Democracy and aristocracy in the western continent were both born of husbandry. Fruitful indeed the calling that could mother such offspring.

But the restless frontier kept moving. The families of the back-country that had so bravely and with such high hope chopped out a foothold in the woods saw it move beyond them westward over the Appalachian mountains. Between these isolated farmsteads and the seaboard markets lay scores of miles of almost useless roads. Self-sufficiency suffered with the failing soil. When the forest had been felled and burned and the stubborn stumps uprooted, the pioneer by constant and unintelligent cropping had greatly reduced fertility. The rich mould, the fruit of the rains of a thousand summers and the falling leaves of a thousand autumns, was dissipated within a generation. As the years passed, the farmer of the interior, often with a dull shiftlessness, settled down to the dreary task of wrestling from steadily deteriorating fields the essentials of life. The excitement of the frontier gone, the lethargy of the peasant reasserted itself. Over these isolated backwoods communities crept the dark shadow of excess; in brawling local tavern or at neighborhood still they found almost the only escape from the monotony of life. With incentive gone and isolation become impenetrable, the back-country slowly and steadily fell into decay. More and more men became involved in debt with small prospect of getting clear. As the eighteenth century drew to a close, it grew plain that the people who chose to remain east of the mountains must take thought.

So it came about in the years following the Revolution, when the marching of armies had ceased, that a few men in America began to turn their thoughts to the betterment of agriculture. They were of the landed aristocracy, north and south. Having leisure for study and experimentation, they chose to serve their fellow countrymen through the gospel of better farming. They kept in touch with the great agricultural developments in England in the days of Arthur Young. They organized societies, wrote papers and books. They inaugurated the science of American agriculture. But to the small farmer of the interior came scarcely an echo of the new movement.

He had little incentive to improve his acres when his increased crops must rot in his barn for want of a market. New methods held little hope for him. Moreover, the conservatism of the peasant and the individualism of the backwoods democrat insulated him from the influence of the lordly aristocracy. He went into politics and in the days between the Revolution and the Constitution secured control of state after state. In Massachusetts he failed and Shays' rebellion was the result. He deluged the country with cheap paper money and passed stay laws impeding his creditors in the collection of their debts. But his power was only for a day. The new Constitution set up a government which he could neither control nor successfully oppose. The futile Whiskey Insurrection of 1794, in western Pennsylvania, brought to an end his threat of force.

Then a strange thing happened. An aristocrat, a planter of Virginia, became the political leader of the discontented small farmers of the interior. With the aid of lieutenants, many of whom were also of the aristocracy, Jefferson welded them into the Democratic-Republican party and in 1800 stormed and captured the citadel of the central government. But before the party of the debtor-farmer assumed control of the nation the crisis in his affairs was passing. In the seventeen-nineties the turnpike era had dawned and improved highways pushing into the interior were galvanizing stagnant communities with that new life which only contact with a market can bring. The canal followed the turnpike. The early decades of the nineteenth century saw the back-country east of the mountains crossed and recrossed by the travel routes reaching out from the coast to the broad stretches in the new West.

Throughout the first half of the nineteenth century the United States of America remained, in the main, a nation of farmers. The small cities of the seaboard grew larger; commerce and industry increased; but the great bulk of the people still lived close to the soil. West of the Appalachians the rich central lowland, watered by the Mississippi, rapidly filled with people. As the years passed, the land policy of the central government tended more and more to stimulate settlement. The new Cumberland Road built at national expense across the mountains was jammed with the Conestoga wagons of settlers trekking westward; keel-boats and flat-boats on the Ohio carried the flood of people on into the continental interior. This westward advance of the frontier meant an expansion of the farming country of America. Into the valley of the Mississippi came the two types of agriculture that had been developed east of the mountains, the small farm and the plantation. Each was the foundation for a developing culture, democracy in the North and aristocracy in the South. The stage was being set for one of the great dramas of our history.

Largely forgotten is that humble farmer folk of the North who followed the skirmish line of the frontier, consolidating what had been won and claiming it for civilized life. Yet these people in the first half of the nineteenth century fought a great battle for freedom. In the broad valleys of the Ohio and the Mississippi were duplicated on a vast scale the causes that had produced the debtor-farmer in the East. There was isolation, the desperate struggle for existence with a naked, untamed environment, the same improvident, soil-destroying husbandry. It was the struggle of the mind against the blunting influence of social loneliness and long continued manual labor. Beside the farmer, while for weary days he followed the plow and harrow, stalked the specter of the European peasant from whose loins he had sprung and to whose level the hard conditions of life in the New World seemed pressing him down. Like Jacob with the angel he wrestled with this ghost of the past. From this struggle, up and down the broad areas of the American countryside, the farmer emerged in the first half of the nineteenth century still rough and uncouth, still conservative and suspicious of innovation, a "hoosier" or a "rube" perhaps, but no longer a peasant; an independent, self-reliant, and confirmed individualist. Yet the greatest victory did not lie with the husbandman.

In the days when roads were few and intolerably poor and unremitting toil necessary for bare subsistence, loneliness and heavy labor burned deep into the heart of the farmer's wife. For her, as the children came, isolation was a cruel, a killing thing. Frail creatures, like Nancy Hanks, lingered a day till the flickering spark went out. The women who survived gave to America most of the great men of the next generation. They divided with their husbands the tasks of supporting life. The family group became the important economic unit. The little evening circle about the blazing logs in the rough stone fireplace of the isolated shanty was evidence that the family was also the most important social unit. Here the mother of the back-country, whose early fading beauty told the hardness of her life, kept aglow the simple idealism and aspiration which runs through that true song of this people, *Home Sweet Home*. Under such circumstances, though ignorance and conservatism remained, the farmer of America could never sink back into the status of the peasant.

The very vastness of the farming country that lay around him called for progress, for new methods and new tools. Out of the East came echoes of the agricultural awakening which had begun to stir at the end of the last century. New farmers' societies with their country fairs and new-born agricultural press of the 'twenties and 'thirties brought across the mountains the new gospel of better farming. Here and there, particularly in the East, appeared the beginnings of agricultural education. But most important of all, in the fields of East and West alike was heard in the 'thirties and 'forties and 'fifties the noise of new machines, the reaper, the mower, and the thresher, lifting the husbandman above the hand-to-hand struggle with nature. The coming of the new tools marked the advent of a new era. The plow-boy whistling down the lane seldom drove in from pasture the plodding, general-service ox; the specialized and more efficient horse was displacing the beast that had served for so many centuries. Meantime King Cotton was claiming the South for his domain.

Whitney's gin, invented in 1793, had made cotton growing profitable. The colonial staples of rice and indigo gave way before the new crop. White cotton fields pushed westward into the black belt of Alabama, the lowlands of Mississippi and Louisiana, and on into the broad warm plains of Texas. With them went the negro and the plantation system. The new soil was fertile, cotton was profitable and labor scarce. Slavery which had seemed on the decline in the late eighteenth century sprang into new life.

Even the ideal of aristocracy which had wavered in Jefferson's day was steadied by triumphant cotton and the expansion of negro slavery.

Civilization in the heart of the South was based on agriculture. Cotton planters, in the midst of smaller landholders, became a cultivated gentry worthy of the best traditions of aristocratic England. In their fine old homes moved a society out of which the crudities of the New World had been refined while much of its strength had been preserved. With dignity and courtesy they ruled the affairs of their local communities. Knights they were and their women-folk ladies, the crowning glory of their civilization. How different from the horny-handed folk north of the Ohio!

It was a strange fate that created in the young republic two distinct civilizations, both based largely on agriculture. For people of a later time there is a tragic fascination in looking back upon the parallel developments of these two peoples leading them inevitably into conflict. The tradition of democracy and free labor made war on that of slavery and aristocracy. When the smoke of battle had cleared away, the South, with all its culture, lay in ruins like an alabaster vase struck from its place. It was a dear price to pay for ridding the nation of the incubus of slavery. But, when the war had passed, it was clear that the old dualism in agricultural development had come to an end. The passing decades saw, slowly but surely, the conquest of the defeated section by the economic methods of the victor.

While the war was yet young an old dream of the northern farmer, long blocked by the political power of the planter, was suddenly realized. The Homestead Act of 1862 threw open free, to the men and women who would use and improve them, the unsettled lands of the West. Democracy's ideal of equal opportunity was at last a fact. Under the stimulus of this opportunity the homesteader, the new pioneer, built his sod hut and ran his barbed wire fences farther and farther westward, across the lowlands of the Mississippi, step by step up onto the High Plains, and on across them into the rain-shadow of the towering Rockies. The bison melted away before him and the Indians defeated in their last desperate stand against the advance of the whites were penned up like caged animals on reservations. At last the sun had set for the red man; in all the broad lands of which he had once been master there was now none he could claim for his own. His tipi of buffalo skins was rolled up to make place for the rough shack of the cattle man or the farmer. As the war-whoop of the Indian died away the homesteader, high up on the western plains, heard from the eastward, dimly at first, then more and more clearly the hum of factories, and the ceaseless pounding of great machines.

Industrialism swept America in the years following the war. Giant cities, vast towers of Babel, were rising above the meadows and the cornfields from which their sustenance came. In the region of the northeastern United States a new civilization was taking shape. The old days when most Americans had won their living from the soil were passed; the wage earner and the white-shirted capitalist had appeared. The farmer, planting his crops as he had always done, began dimly to feel that he belonged to a group apart. He was not at home amid the dazzling lights of the new cities; he was suspicious of the foreign looking laborers crowding into the factory gates, speaking strange tongues; he both feared and hated the new capitalist who built up fortunes by methods he could not understand and who took scant notice of the farmer's needs or rights. He attempted to organize for his protection and there resulted the Grange in the 'seventies, the Alliances and the Agricultural Wheel in the 'eighties, and the Populist party in the 'nineties. But, one after another, his efforts failed. The intense individualism born of a half century of single-handed struggle with nature and with loneliness thwarted the one thing now need-ful — co-operation. The victory of one generation had become the defeat of the next.

Quietly, during those fateful decades when the frontier was disappearing and when America was passing swiftly through her great industrial revolution, groups of men in centers of learning here and there were preparing for the day that was inevitably to come. In the same year with the Homestead Act, the Morrill Act had called the land grant college into being. Within the walls of these new institutions and of older colleges and universities scientists turned their minds to the task of creating a science of agri-culture. Little sympathy they got from the wage earner or the capitalist, and the farmer, conservative still, looked at their soft hands and citified ways and sneered. Nevertheless, aided by the state and the national governments, they persisted and, by the end of the century, the foundations of their great work had been securely laid. Their problem became how to spread the new body of knowledge beyond the halls of the colleges and set it at work on the fields of the nation. The opening years of the twentieth century saw this problem solved in a way which few anticipated.

For years before that century opened, it had seemed as though the industries and the cities of the new civilization would rob the countryside of its best brains and blood. The most energetic farm boys were drawn to the great urban centers where could be found bright lights, pleasure, social contacts and power for any who were strong enough to seize it. The sons of the mothers who had survived the dread ordeal of the frontier became cap-tains of industry and masters of capital. Then, as a spring wells up in the rainy season and overflows the lowlands, the civilization of the new day flowed out of the cities and overspread the countryside.

To the farms came the material comforts, the telephone, the improved highway, the automobile and the electric light. The rural free delivery bringing the metropolitan daily and the journals and magazines, the crossroads circulating library bringing books for the winter evenings, the music machine, the movie and the radio all combined to carry to the farmer the pleasures, the ideas and the culture of the new day. For the husbandman it was and is the period of intellectual awakening. The lethargy and the conservatism of the peasant are sloughing off. The agricultural scientist speaks to an audience as wide as the nation.

But industrialism has reshaped American life. The men and women actually living on the farms have become a minority in the population of the nation. More and more the city rather than the countryside directs national policies. Group consciousness born of the nation-wide division of labor among the capitalist, wage earner, and farmer has grown and intensified. Organization brought into existence gigantic industrial and financial enterprises. The farmer found himself dealing single-handed with a race of Brobdingnags. He has begun to organize. Out of Rural America a new giant has come. But the city, the center of thought and of economic power, retains its pre-eminence. The farmer must adjust himself to it. Slowly and painfully he is realizing that not all of urban civilization is adaptable to his scattered communities. He is becoming aware that, if the agricultural life of the nation is to remain sound, a peculiar rural civilization must arise comparable in its rewards of satisfaction to that of the town and city. Saddled with a heritage of ignorance and conservatism not yet entirely shaken off, blinded by the lights of a new world into which he has suddenly come, the farmer of the twentieth century stumbles into the future.

RALPH H. GABRIEL

CHAPTER I

ANCESTORS OF THE AMERICAN HUSBANDMAN

IN the fourteenth century, as Chaucer tells it in his *Canterbury Tales*, a band of pilgrims rode at easy pace, and with much dalliance by the way, across feudal England to the shrine of Becket, sainted as Thomas of Kent. They, and many bands like them, passed through miles of robber-infested moor and fen and heather which opened every now and then into a manor where lived the typical English folk of the Middle Ages. Again and again the little cavalcade, emerging from the forest, looked out over one of these manors clothed in the new green of spring, and its people just shaking off the lethargy of winter. There was the lord's house, sometimes a castle for defense against enemies. Near by was the church with its little plot of graves. In the shadow of the sanctuary huddled the cottages of the vill (village). Perhaps there were a dozen, possibly two score or more, such humble habitations in which frequently the cattle and chickens shared the "hall" with the good man and his family. Beyond the little village street stood the mill, owned by the lord and operated for him by the proverbially prosperous and equally proverbially dishonest miller. And near the vill were the broad arable fields through which the highway ran. Beyond them lay the common pasture dotted with thistles and scrubby bushes. Even the cheerful Chaucer, watching the heavy-witted peasants leave for a moment their spring tasks to gape at the well-mounted and travel-stained Knight or the broad hat above the ruddy cheeks of the Wife of Bath, must sometimes have held but a poor opinion of them. Uncouth they were, yet they had a rugged strength and a certain fineness of quality. Many times from the village street the party could see, rising in the distance, a cathedral tower on which, perhaps, the builders were still at work. That, too, was part of the mediæval picture.

Three centuries later, another band of pilgrims left one of these old manors to go to Holland and, ultimately, to America. The span of years had brought change but not so much as might be expected. There was still the lord's house, the church, and the vill. But the mediæval system of serfdom had been abandoned and the independent peasant now rented his land from the lord. In feudal days the manor had been a co-operative farming enterprise, its people working together to get subsistence from the land; and many co-operative features still remained far into modern times. The seventeenth-century husbandman still looked in most cases for his best guide to the ways of the fathers; three centuries had changed but little his methods, crops, or tools. The tenant farmer was as much a peasant as his forefather who had been a villein. And conservatism was the very warp and woof of his life. It went with him to America.

7

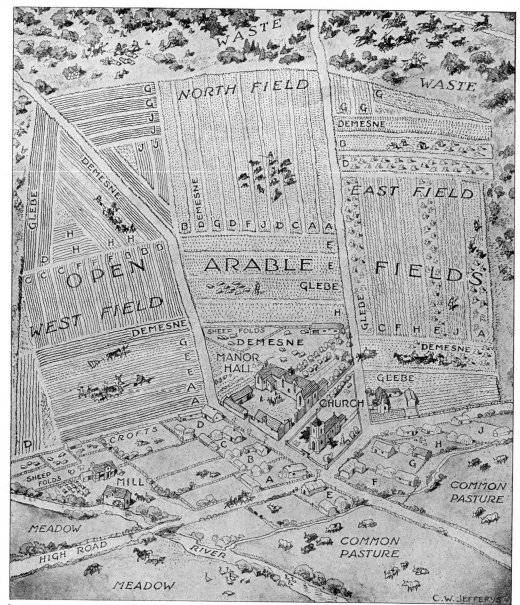

1

Drawn expressly for *The Pageant of America* by C. W. Jefferys (1869–)

THE MEDIÆVAL MANOR

THE manor of Chaucer's time was a self-sufficient unit, comparable in acreage to a small American township or a large ranch, where lord and peasant worked together to get their living. Few supplies were brought in from the outside and equally few the products sold. From the encircling "waste" came the bundles of twigs and branches that were used for fuel, the posts for fences and the cottage beams. Over the "common" and, sometimes, in the waste grazed the animals of the vill tended by the oxherd, the swineherd and the shepherd. From the "meadow," beside the stream which drove the mill, was cut the hay stacked neatly in the hayrick in the "croft," the little enclosed plot beside the peasant's cottage. The crops grew on the "arable" which was sometimes divided into two but usually three great fields, each in turn cut into a number of strips. The lord's individual holding, known as the *demesne*, was sometimes a single large piece of land but more often was made up of strips scattered throughout the fields as were the holdings of John and George and William, "villeins," shown in the picture as A, B, C, etc. The church also had its land, the "glebe," and sometimes the "sexton's mead" or the "barber's furlong" represented special allotments.

A VILLEIN'S FARM

CHAUCER's pilgrims found the villagers in the fields busy with the spring's work. There were orders and degrees among them. A few freemen could be seen working on their separate plots aided by hired labor. They held their lands from the lords in return for a money rent or for military service. On the arable fields, busy with plowing, harrowing and sowing, were the villeins. The black strips in the diagram represent a rather prosperous villein's farm. The strips, usually about forty rods in length, varied up to an acre in size, and were separated by grassy balks. In payment for the use of this land the villein must work on the lord's *demesne* so many days each week with extra days at harvest time. In addition he must perform "any other of the forms of agricultural labor as local custom on each manor had established its burdens." The villein was neither a servant in husbandry nor a laborer for wages. He had cattle of his own and occupied land of various amounts as a partner in the village association. Below him was the cottager with little or no land besides his garden, who, when not working on the *demesne*, must eke out his substance by wages from freemen or from villeins. Of these last the lord evidently had none to good an opinion, for the word "villain" has gradually acquired a number of unpleasant meanings.

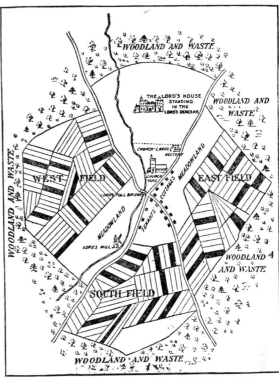

2   From Henry Allsopp, *An Introduction to English Industrial History*, London, 1912

3   From a copy, in the possession of Charles M. Andrews, of the original in Oriel College, Oxford University

MAP OF CHALFORD MANOR, 1743

EACH manor fitted in its own peculiar way into its surroundings and its laying out was the work of generations. As the village grew, a piece of land would here and there be added to the arable and cut up into strips to ensure an equal distribution of the good and poor soil. Of the three fields of the usual arable one would be planted to winter grain, rye or wheat, one sown to spring crops, oats, pease and barley, and one would lie fallow to recuperate. This crude crop rotation was called the "three field system." "On land which was inadequately manured and on which neither field-turnips nor clovers were known till centuries later, there could be no middle course between the exhaustion of continuous cropping and the rest-cure of barrenness." The land was cut into small strips so that the individual villein's holding might be distributed evenly among the arable fields, and also so that he might get his fair share of good and poor soil. The strips were usually but not always allotted afresh each season. But the strips themselves retained their boundaries of grass year after year. There are fields in twentieth-century England which have not yet smoothed out the unevenness born of the mediæval balks.

4   From William Henry Pyne, *Microcosm, or a Picturesque Delineation of the Arts,
Agriculture, Manufactures, etc. of Great Britain*, London, 1808

THE WHEELED PLOW OF THE MIDDLE AGES

WHEN the winter snow began to melt, the villagers brought forth their monster plow. Between the Feast of the Purification (February 2) and Easter, oats, beans and peas must be sown. "On St. Valentine's Day cast beans in clay. But on Good Chad sowe good or bad." Few scenes are more characteristic of the Middle

5   From Gervase Markham, *The English Husbandman*,
London, 1635, in the Library of Congress

Ages than plowing. Usually eight oxen drew the great plow; drivers on either side called to their animals in a sort of singsong and, every now and then, prodded a shirking beast; the plowman held the handle and sometimes carried a "clotting beetle" with which to break the lumps. Behind the crunching mouldboard lay the upturned furrow, smelling of the fresh earth, on which small birds and sea-gulls settled. Day after day the plow went slowly up and down the strips until the whole field was ready for planting.

ENGLISH PLOWS OF THE SEVENTEENTH CENTURY

BY the seventeenth century, when English peasants began to turn their faces to American forests beyond the seas, new plows might be seen at work on the fields enclosed by new hedges. The new tools were smaller and many were without the wheels which supported the heavy beam. Some had one and some two handles, varying with the farmer's fancy. These seventeenth-century plows were

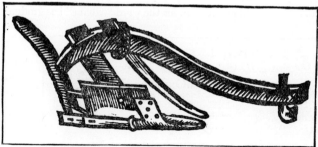

6   One Handle Plow, from Gervase Markham, *The English Husbandman*,
London, 1635

lighter and required fewer animals to drag them across the arable fields. But, in spite of innovation, the old, wheeled plow still remained in shire after shire the idol of the husbandmen. Many of them had seen the smaller new plows turning clean, black furrows in neighboring counties and then, in fall and spring, had dragged out the great heirloom of ancient days and gone about the season's work after the fashion of their forefathers. Custom has nowhere sturdier adherents than among those who wrest a hard-won living from the soil.

7   Two Handle Plow, from William Henry Pyne, *Microcosm*, etc., London, 1808

8   From William Henry Pyne, *Microcosm*, etc., London, 1808

THE HARROW

THE fallow was sometimes broken three times by the plow before it was ready for the harrow. For this purpose a hawthorn tree was sometimes cut from the lord's waste and weighted down with logs. Sometimes a home-made harrow built of ash and willow and shod with iron or wooden teeth was dragged over the soil. The harrower, as he walked long hours back and forth across the dusty fields, had need of the familiar bread of mixed rye and wheat flour called "maslin," much prized by laborers because it "abode longer in the stomach and was not so soon digested with their labour."

SEED TIME

THE sower followed the harrow, broadcasting the seed with a swinging motion of hand and arm. For a thousand years and more English husbandmen spread their seed-grain over the cultivated land in accord with immemorial custom. Two bushels of rye, the bread-grain, and four of barley, the drink-grain of the Middle Ages, were sown to the acre. When the growing straw had yellowed into ripeness, the wheat and rye seldom yielded more than ten, and oats and barley sixteen bushels for each acre sown. The farmer of the Middle Ages had not yet learned to use his land to full advantage. Because his crops were scanty winter was a season to be dreaded alike by his household and his cattle. Famine trod hard on the heels of feast-

9   From L. Jewitt, *Mediaeval Ballads*, in *Art Journal*, London, 1878

ing. "Even the most prudent housekeepers found it difficult always to remember the proverbial wisdom of eating within the tether, or sparing at the brink instead of the bottom."

10   From a miniature, early 14th century, in Queen Mary's Psalter, in the British Museum

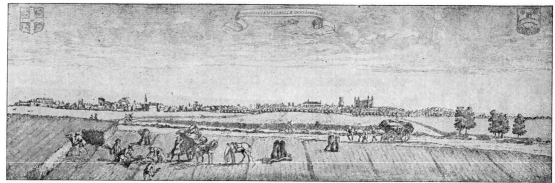

11   The Harvest at Cambridge Township, from F. W. Maitland, *Township and Borough*, Cambridge, 1898, after an engraving in *Cantabrigia Illustrata*, 1688, by David Loggan

HARVEST

IN spite of all the "payne and traveyle" that came with harvest days, it was the crowning season of the year. Then all the folk of the village labored as at no other time. Summer mornings found the reapers in the fields organized in "settes" of five, each set calculated to cut and bind two acres in a day. The lord had provided a cook, brewer, and baker who supplied dinner at nine and supper at five. The sickle, of long and honorable

12   From a miniature, early 14th century, in Queen Mary's Psalter, in the British Museum

history, still flashed and sheaves were bound by hand. Piled on clumsy carts the sheaves were hauled to the stacks in the village or in the lord's yard. With all this sweating labor, there was merry-making a-plenty: the harvest meant the end of the gaunt months and the return of plenty. The small pile of sheaves beside his cottage was the villein's wealth; from the grain which it contained he must live for a twelvemonth. Dread fears gnawed at his heart if a summer drought had ruined his crops.

THE MILL

THE harvest past, the grain was beaten out with flails and winnowed. The long rye straw was set aside for thatching and the rest was piled where it could be used to bed down a few animals in their winter stalls. Perhaps the busiest man in the autumn was the miller; from early morning until late at night the great,

clumsy stones slowly ground the lord's grain and that of the villagers. Between the Middle Ages and the time British husbandry was carried to America the mill had undergone not a little development.

This may be seen in the diagram published (with accompanying key) thirty-eight years after the landing of the Pilgrims. "*In a* Mill, 1. *a* stone, 2. *runneth upon a* stone, 3. *A* Wheel, 4. *turneth them about, and grindeth corn poured in by a* Hopper, 5. *and parteth the* Bran, 6. *falling into the* Trough, 7. *from the meal slipping through a* Bolter, 8. *Such a mill was first a* Hand-mill, 9. *then a* Horse-Mill, 10. *then a* Water-mill, 11. *and a* Ship-mill, 12. *and at last, a* Wind-mill, 13." — COMENIUS.

13   Redrawing from Johann Amos Comenius, *Orbis Sensualium Pictus*, 1658. 12th English edition, 1777

14   Drawn expressly for *The Pageant of America* by C. W. Jefferys

A MANORIAL ACCOUNTING

USUALLY in the autumn the lord, with the aid of his bailiff, had an accounting in the manor. The freemen and the villeins assembled at the great house, bringing the payments which were due. As a rule a villein paid for his holding in money, in labor, and in kind. In money he paid a small fixed rent known as the rent of assize. Besides this there were dues of various kinds, partly in lieu of services commuted into money payments, and partly for the privileges enjoyed by him on the waste of the manor. When he paid in kind, he brought honey, eggs, poultry, or perhaps a plowshare. These payments were in addition to the services in labor he rendered on the lord's *demesne*. The manor was, in reality, one great farm cultivated by the villagers. Over its destinies the lord presided. The peasants, but for occasional revolts and vagabondage, humbly accepted the station to which it pleased God to call them.

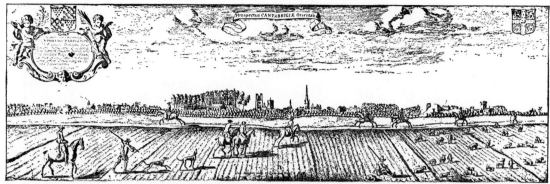

15 From F. W. Maitland, *Township and Borough*, Cambridge, 1898, after an engraving in *Cantabrigia Illustrata*, 1688, by David Loggan

THE VILLAGE SHEPHERD

A Shepeheards boye (no better doe him call)
When Winters wasteful spight was almost spent,
All in a sunneshine day, as did befall,
Led forth his flock, that had bene long ypent.
So faynt they wore, and feeble in the folde,
That now unnethes their feete could them uphold.— SPENSER

ENGLISH long wool always commanded a price and sheep raising went hand in hand with husbandry. In the morning the village shepherd could be seen driving the sheep from the fold on the wheat fallow to the common pasture. During the day he watched them to prevent straying over the crops or meadows. A lame man was prized because he could not drive the sheep too fast. At night he brought them back to the fold where he too slept with his dog. He must be a man of patience, steady and dependable, never absent without leave at "fairs, markets, wrestling-matches, wakes, or in the tavern." From time to time the fold was moved; sheep-folding was the chief mediæval method of fertilizing the soil. During the bleak months of winter each villager fed his own sheep and many times they fared ill indeed.

The shepherd was wont to be drawn from the poorest folk of the manor, the cotters. These held each a cottage, and an acre or an acre and a half in the fields. They were a grade below the villeins. The cotter's lot in life was hard indeed. In his rude habitation, sometimes built in the waste, he and his family lived on the very brink of disaster.

16 From facsimile edition, London, 1890, of Edmund Spenser, *The Shepheardes Calendar*, London, 1579

17 Redrawing from Johann Amos Comenius, *Orbis Sensualium Pictus*, 1658. 12th English edition, 1777

HONEY

"HE that hath sheep, swine, and bees, sleep he, wake he, he may thrive." Honey was the sugar of the Middle Ages. It was used in medicines and was an essential ingredient of mead and other liquors. The wax was made into candles for the gentry and for use in the churches and entered into the composition of salves and ointments. "*The* Bees *send out a* Swarm, 1. *and set over it a* Leader, 2. *That swarm being ready to fly away, is recalled by the* Tinkling *of a* brazen Vessel, 3. *and is put up into a new* Hive, 4. *They make little* Cells *with six corners*, 5. *and fill them with* Honeydew, *and make* Combs, 6. *out of which the* Honey *runneth*, 7. *The* Partitions *being melted with fire, turn into* Wax, 8."

SWINE

CATTLE and swine also roamed over the lands of the manor. The profitableness of the hog was summed up in the old Gloucestershire saying: "A swine doth sooner than a cowe bring an ox to the plough." The boar was a famous dish at feasts and ordinary animals were turned into the salt-pork and smoked bacon. But the system of common farming showed

18   From a miniature, early 14th century, in Queen Mary's Psalter, in the British Museum

at its worst in its stock. Where good animals and bad herded together on the common pasture, improvement was impossible and disease all too prevalent. "Murrain," the name given to all disorders, frequently ravaged widely among the mongrel herds and sadly diminished the salted meats that the housewife so much depended on for food supply.

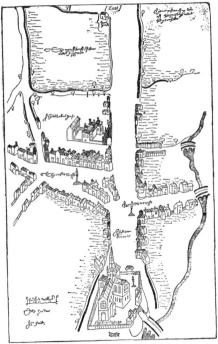

19   The Village of Ashborne, from George Laurence Gomme, *The Village Community*, London, 1890, after a Ms. in the Public Record Office, London

20   *The Return of the Warrener*, from the painting by George Morland (1763–1804) in the Corcoran Gallery of Art, Washington

VILLAGE LIFE

WHEN the day's work was done, the old-time villager went his way homeward to his cottage. Small enough and bare it was and close huddled to those of his neighbors. But the husbandman was satisfied; here was home. His father and his father's father had lived in such a house, if not in the very one where his own brood played upon the dirt floor. They too would grow up to live in similar cottages along the same street. Here his wife prepared the frugal evening meal. She was a drudge, untouched by refinement. For her life held little in store but endless years of labor in the house and on the fields and the rearing of many children. Village life kept the changeless tenor of its way. Even down to the time when English farmers began going to America, any notion of progress had scarcely entered into the peasant's thinking. He died in the same social class to which he was born and slept with his rude forefathers in that part of the graveyard set aside for those of his station. The man of God who sat beside the rough bedside of the dying peasant told him of that better land whither the faithful went. Here the heavy burdens of life would be lifted; here would be respite from labor, and rest.

21   A Village Street, Godshill, Isle of Wight, from a photograph in the possession of Charles M. Andrews

VILLAGE HOMES

HERE and there these relics of an older England have lingered with little change into the present. The cottages of the villagers were set snugly together along the village street where the women congregated to gossip and the men lounged after the day's work was done. Up and down the same street wandered from time to time the village animals, grunting swine, flocks of scrawny sheep followed by the shepherd, and herds of cattle. Home was not an idle place. The husbandman and his wife must make with their own hands most of the things that played a part in their lives. "In the long winter evenings, farmers, their sons, and their servants carved the wooden spoons, the platters, and the beechen bowls. They fitted and riveted the bottoms to the horn mugs, or closed, in coarse fashion, the leaks in the leathern jugs. They plaited the osiers and reeds into baskets and into 'weels' for catching fish; they fixed handles to the scythes, rakes and other tools; cut the flails from holly or thorn, and fashioned them with thongs to the staves; shaped the teeth for rakes and harrows from ash or willow, and hardened them in the fire; cut out the wooden shovels for casting the corn in the granary; fashioned ox-yokes and bows, forks,

22   A Reconstructed Cottage Interior (Scrooby), from the Chronicles of America
motion picture *The Pilgrims*

racks, and rack-staves; twisted willow into scythe-cradles, or into traces or other harness gear. . . . Meanwhile the women plaited straw or reeds for neck collars, stitched and stuffed sheepskin bags for cart-saddles, peeled rushes for wicks and made candles. Thread was often made from nettles. Spinning wheels, distaffs, and needles were never idle. Home-made cloth and linen supplied all wants. . . . The formation of words like *spinster, webster, lyster, shepster, maltster, brewster,* and *baxter* indicated that the occupations were feminine, and show that women spun, wove, dyed and cut out cloth, as well as malted the barley, brewed the ale, and baked the bread for the family."— Row-LAND E. PROTHERO, *English Farming Past and Present,* 1912.

23 Redrawing from Johann Amos Comenius, *Orbis Sensualium Pictus*, 1658.
12th English edition, 1777

SEVENTEENTH–CENTURY WELLS

THE many tasks of the housewife included the drawing of water. "*Where* Springs *are wanting,* Wells *are digged,* 1. *and they are compassed about with a* Brandrith, 2. *lest any should fall in, Thence is water drawn with* Buckets, 3. *hanging either at a* Pole, 4. *or a* Rope, 5. *or a* Chain, 6. *and that either by a* Swipe, 7. *or a* Windle, 8. *or a* Turn, 9. *with a* Handle *or a* Wheel, 10. *or to conclude, by a* Pump, 11."

WOMAN'S WORK

BUT the women-folk had also other tasks:

To tend the Dairy *and the* Poultry *rear,*
Bake, Brew, *and hive the* Bees *in seasons fair.*

Tess of the d'Urbervilles was a survival of the dairy-maid of earlier days. Because labor was scarce, women were pressed into the lighter tasks and their contribution to the sum of village life was great. Rearing a round dozen of children together with endless tasks within and without the cottage left little leisure for the finer things of life. Few peasants could read. Their thoughts were confined to the incidents and problems of the life of the manor. Affairs of politics were quite beyond their ken. The state of the crops, birth, marriage and death were the topics of conversation when the villagers assembled, while a fire or a robbery brought a brief period of excitement. The people of the manor beyond the fen were almost as strange to them as if they had lived in Scotland or in France.

The village folk of the Middle Ages lived in dampness and dirt. They suffered terrible diseases which they neither understood nor knew how to combat. Again and again the rumor of a pestilence came to the vill. Famine and pestilence were the terrors of these humble people and panic seized them when a plague appeared. There was little they could do to check its ravages; it must run its course. When it was over, often but a few wretched survivors remained beside the fresh graves of the dead. Perhaps the plague was a judgment of God; they knew of no other cause.

The picture shows not a village house but an iso-

24 From William Hogg, *The Farmer's Wife*, London, 1776(?)

lated farmstead. As changing conditions brought an end to the old manor, here and there appeared the farm set apart by itself. Some of the peasants who came to colonial America were familiar with such holdings. But they were not typical; most husbandmen still lived in villages.

25   The Godshill Church, Isle of Wight, from a photograph in the possession of Charles M. Andrews

THE SABBATH DAY AT THE MANOR

THE Sabbath was a day of rest. The herdsmen tended their animals in the pastures, but the plowing or sowing or harvesting on the arable fields ceased. At a given hour the villagers trooped into the parish church like that at Scrooby or, sometimes, to the chapel in the lord's castle. Here, in the Middle Ages, they listened to the service of the Church of Rome and knelt as the robed priest, so important a figure in the village, celebrated the mass. After the time of Henry VIII, except for a few years when Mary brought back the old order, the Church of England replaced that of Rome. Little difference to the peasants did it make when these changes occurred. Each Sunday they went to the same sanctuary and sat in the same pews where their families had sat for generations. With the humbler folk were the lord and his family, the bailiff, the freemen of the manor, the miller, all the figures that made up the variegated pattern of village life. The Sabbath congregation was an expression of the unity of the parish group. For an hour the solemn service lifted these humble folk out of their restricted sphere. They came into the presence of the Almighty. They gave thought to the life beyond the grave. Then, when the chants and responses had died away, they fell back into the humdrum of village life.

26   Chapel, Haddon Hall, from Joseph Nash, *Mansions of England in The Olden Time*, London, 1839-41

27   From Joseph Nash, *Mansions of England in The Olden Time*, London, 1839–41

THE YULE LOG AT CHRISTMAS

A man might then behold
At Christmas, in each hall,
Good fires to curb the cold,
And meat for great and small.
Old Song.

"THE English, from the great prevalence of rural habit throughout every class of society, have always been fond of those festivals and holidays which agreeably interrupt the stillness of country life; and they were, in former days, particularly observant of the religious and social rites of Christmas. . . . It brought the peasant and the peer together, and blended all ranks in one warm generous flow of joy and kindness. The old halls of castles and manor houses resounded with the harp and the Christmas carol, and their ample boards groaned under the weight of hospitality. Even the poorest cottage welcomed the festive season with green decorations of bay and holly — the cheerful fire glanced its rays through the lattice, inviting the passengers to raise the latch, and join the gossip knot huddled round the hearth, beguiling the long evening with legendary jokes, and oft-told Christmas tales." — WASHINGTON IRVING, *The Sketch Book.*

THE MAYPOLE DANCE

SPRING was the season of promise when the

rich leas
of wheat, rye, barley, vetches, oats, and peas
The Tempest, IV. 1. 60–1

foretold the abundance of autumn. But long before spring the winter's store had run low and often the good old rule was broken that "at Candlemas half the fodder and all the corn must be untouched." When the growing crops made the husbandman forget the winter's pinch, all England went a-maying. The villagers, off at dawn, brought back the Maypole, a young birch, and trimmed it with wreaths. All day and far into the night they danced and made merry about it. The modern drawing reproduces well the spirit of the May festival.

28   From Joseph Strutt, *The Sports and Pastimes of the People of England,* London, 1831

29   The Hall, Moat House, Kent, from Joseph Nash, *Mansions of England in The Olden Time*, London, 1839–41

THE MANOR HALL

The homeland which the Jamestown and Plymouth people left behind them was still essentially a farming nation. The aristocracy was as deeply rooted in the soil as the peasantry. Rural castles and manor houses were to be met with on every hand in the England from which America sprang. The folk of the lord's house lived, in the Middle Ages, from the produce of the *demesne* and from the butter, eggs, poultry and other dues that the villagers rendered. The food spread on the board in the great hall was often coarse and strangely seasoned, but it was always abundant beyond the imagination of men nowadays. By the time of Elizabeth and James I, however, money rents had replaced the old feudal obligations. Hardwicke Hall was not typical. In such a magnificent castle lived the nobleman whose income came from many manors. The usual manor hall was the less pretentious mansion of the country squire.

30   Hardwicke Hall, Derbyshire, from Joseph Nash, *Mansions of England in The Olden Time*, London, 1839–41

WOMEN AND CHILDREN OF THE CASTLE

IF the womenfolk of the cottage led busy lives, so also did those of the castle. "Joan, wife of the first Lord Berkeley, 'at no tyme of her 42 yeares mariage ever travelled ten miles from the mansion houses of her husband in the Countyes of Gloucester and Somersett, much lesse humered herselfe with the vaine delights of London and other Cities.' She spent

31   From Joseph Nash, *Mansions of England in The Olden Time*, London, 1839–41

much of her time in supervising her 'dairy affairs,' passing from farmhouse to farmhouse, taking account of the smallest details. The family tradition lingered long. The same housewifely courses were followed by the widowed Lady Berkeley, who administered the estates during her son's minority in the reigns of Henry VIII and Edward VI. At all her country houses she 'would betimes in Winter and Somer mornings make her walkes to visit her stable, barnes, dayhouse, pultry, swinetroughs, and the like.'" — ROWLAND E. PROTHERO, *English Farming Past and Present, 1912.*

SHEEP ENCLOSURES

A LITTLE before Columbus braved the terrors, real and imaginary, of the Atlantic, wool had grown dear and the producing of it unusually profitable. There were ruthless lords here and there who undertook, by fair means or foul, to turn their manors into great sheep-walks. The common, the meadows and even the arable fields became sheep pasture. "So greedy and covetous were some of these accumulators that they had as many as 24,000 sheep." The story of Stretton in Warwickshire is typical of the result. Eight hundred acres were there enclosed for pasturage "whereby twelve messuages [houses with adjacent buildings] and four cottages fell to ruins and eighty persons there inhabiting, being employed about tillage and husbandry, were constrained to depart thence and live miserably. By means whereof the church grew to such a ruin that it was of no other use than for the shelter of cattle." Despite the protests of the villagers whose whole way of life was thus violently altered, sheep farming had come to England to stay. So strong were the bonds, however, which held folk to their old homes that depopulation was relatively rare. This unsettling of the traditional routine of life in many villages was one of the factors driving a stolid peasantry to seek a new start in life in far-away America.

32   From William Henry Pyne, *Microcosm*, etc., London, 1808

AN ENGLISH COUNTRYSIDE, EARLY EIGHTEENTH CENTURY

SHEEP-FARMING did not long overturn the balance of English husbandry. Grain crops rose in value. In the days of the Stuart kings the traveler could see that the old husbandry of the feudal manor was passing away. The great open fields which the villeins had worked were broken up into plots. The grassy "balks" that had for centuries divided the strips had been effaced by the plow. About the fields of

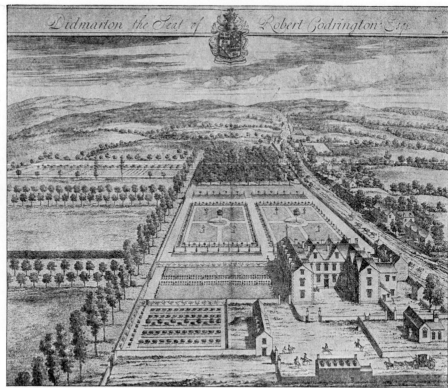

33   From Sir Robert Atkyns, Knt. *The Ancient and Present State of Gloucestershire*, 2nd edition, London, 1712.
Engraving by Jan Kip

the new day were neat hedges. The yeoman, descendant of the old villein, still lived in the village enriched by the memory of his fathers, but now he rented the enclosed fields from the lord. Usually he worked six of these. Three he used for grain; one he planted to wheat or rye, one to oats or barley and the third he left fallow. The other three provided for his animals, one for his sheep, another for his cattle, and the third served as a meadow where he cut his hay for the winter.

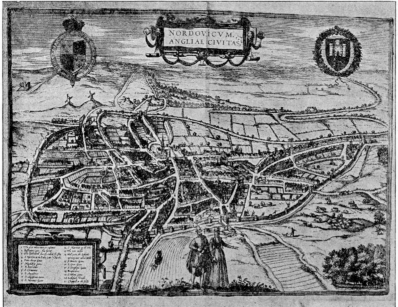

34   From Braun and Hogenberg, *Civitates Orbis Terrarum*, 1573(?)–1618. Courtesy of J. H. Innes,
Nyack, N. Y.

THE NEW COMMERCIAL TOWN

THE old engraving of a walled commercial town somewhat larger than a parish village depicts a situation common enough in the seventeenth century when English husbandmen were beginning to make their way to the American colonies. Outside the town gates lay, side by side, the old strips of the Middle Ages and the hedge-bordered fields of a new day. With just such a picture as this in their minds many English pioneers crossed the sea to Jamestown or Boston, to Philadelphia or the Carolinas.

CHAPTER II

A FOOTHOLD IN THE WILDERNESS

FOUR years before the *Mayflower* dropped anchor in Plymouth harbor, Shakespeare died, the greatest figure, to our eyes, of a great age. Of his generation were men like Bacon, Ben Jonson and Raleigh. He had felt an unwonted throb in English life; he had watched his countrymen shake off the shackles of their island boundaries and put out to sea bound for the far corners of a little known world. The quiet countryside which he knew so well had remained little changed save for the spread of sheep ranges, but in the cities he sensed the stir. A new commercialism brought to London shops articles from India and China, from Muscovy and the Levant. A new England was stirring with life.

The little band of humble folk who left the *Mayflower* and built their cabins on the slope overlooking the quiet New England harbor were also of this great Elizabethan England. Vaguely they had sensed the pulsing life of the new day. But destiny had first driven them out of their quiet village homes and had finally brought them to a vast wilderness where they must begin life anew. They felt that God had led them to America and would sustain them through the hard tasks that lay ahead. They prayed that good might come of their strange adventure across the vast ocean.

The first Jamestown folk had preceded the Pilgrims by thirteen years. Another thirteen saw a flood of people coming to the New World. Some came for trade; others to find a refuge from religious persecution. Perhaps land hunger, sharpened by the land-holding customs of feudalism, brought the greatest number. In America a man could shake off much of his dependence upon his superiors; he could strike out for himself; he could be independent. For all who came to stay the venture meant the starting of a new life where values and opportunities were different and where a man caught a new glimpse of life and its meaning. The continent was wild and conditions were hard and primitive. Men who had grown up in the static villages of the English countryside where passing years brought little change must adjust themselves quickly and accurately to the new environment. The penalty for failure was suffering and death.

The basic need of the pioneers was food and shelter. They might fish and hunt, but husbandry must be the foundation of the new communities. To the fields of America they brought the complicated methods that were the fruit of centuries of English agriculture growth. In the forests of the new country they met a race of men who had a simple agriculture suited to the needs of forest tribes. They borrowed from the red man. They adapted the knowledge and methods which they brought from England to the requirements of the new surroundings. They met the supreme test; they did not turn back; and they maintained life while cutting their farms out of the forest. Out of the great adventure came the establishment of an old civilization in a new world.

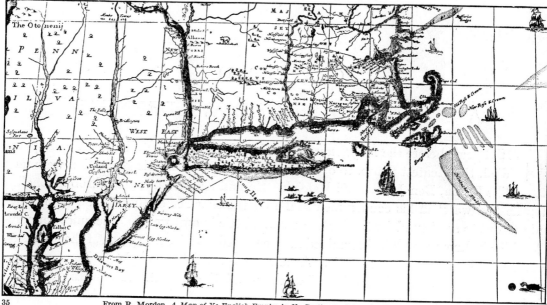

35   From R. Morden, *A Map of Ye English Empire in Ye Continent of America*, London, 1700(?)

THE COMING OF THE SETTLERS

HERE and there could be seen in the seventeenth century little ships from the Old World approaching the bays and the mouths of rivers along the wild coasts of America. The *Half Moon*, the *Sarah Constant* and the *Mayflower* and, as the seventeenth century progressed, many others in turn felt their way along uncharted shores and finally dropped anchor in sheltered waters. Debarking from these, Englishmen, many of them peasants, stretched their legs after a tedious voyage and looked with thankfulness and courage at the new land whither they had come to make their home.

SETTLEMENTS ABOUT BOSTON, ca. 1633

IN the first half of the seventeenth century tiny villages appeared here and there along the coast from New England to Virginia. The early map of the settlements of the Massachusetts Bay Colony about Boston shows small groups of houses scattered along the bays and rivers. Indians live just across the stream from Dorchester, and beside the Mystic. The forest is everywhere.

The rude sketch gives a vivid picture of the fundamental life conditions which the first settlers faced. A note in Governor Winthrop's hand describes the map: "A: an Iland cont[aining] 100: acres, where the Gouvenr hathe an orchard & a vineyarde. Tenhills: the Gouvenrs ferme [farm] house. Meadford: Mr. Cradock ferme [farm] house. C: the Wyndmill. D: the fforte. [Both at Boston.] E: the Weere.

36   Section of a sketch map, with notes by John Winthrop, in the British Museum

Drawn expressly for *The Pageant of America* by C. W. Jefferys

EQUIPMENT FOR LIFE IN THE WILDERNESS

THE men and women who forsook home and neighbors to risk their lives in America brought with them a knowledge of the handicrafts and the husbandry of Elizabethan England. They also brought the tools with which they were familiar; shovels, spades, irons for plows to be hewn out of the forest, sickles for cutting the grain, hoes, axes for the clearing of the land and adzes and saws for working up the lumber. Yet the little piles which the ships landed on the beach must sometimes have seemed pitifully inadequate for the great task which lay ahead.

THE AMERICAN WILD

NATURE presented no soft aspect to the first comers from the Old World; to the westward stretched the forest — rough hills, turbulent streams and noisome swamps. In this country they were uninvited guests.

If they would live, they must fight the forest and its wild life, fight the men whose moccasined feet moved noiselessly through its recesses. These European peasants must forget the homeland and adjust their lives to new conditions. They plunged into a primitive struggle for existence all too often ignorant of the full meaning of the high adventure laid upon them. Even today the eastern edge of that ancient wilderness can be traced by the line of graves that mark the first battlefield in the conquest of America.

38
© Gramstorff Brothers, Malden, Mass.

39   From a photograph by the United States Department of Agriculture

BARRIERS OF FORESTS AND SEAS

EXPLORERS and traders worked their way up the streams a little way into the interior. Woods were everywhere. The adventurers climbed to high places and looked out over the mantle of trees stretching endlessly westward. The leaders saw that if their settlements were to live and grow, this vast forest must be conquered, must be swept away. They returned with their tale to the little settlements set between the forest and the sea where the strange noises of the wilderness mingled with the ceaseless wash of the waves. There were many who, listening to the stories of wooded country without limit or boundary, despaired of ever overcoming the wild. Some wavered and went back to the quiet humdrum of the English villages. But, for the most part, the pioneers stayed. From their loins sprang the first of the race of Americans. In their adjustments to the wilderness may be found the beginnings of the civilization which occupies so great a part of North America.

40 From the painting *The Maine Coast*, by Winslow Homer (1836–1910), in the Metropolitan Museum of Art, New York

41   From an exhibit in the American Museum of Natural History, New York

WOLVES

THE forest was full of life. Beyond the edge of the clearing could be heard through the still night the calls of the wild cat and lynx. Many times the settler heard the soft footsteps of a bear as he made his way into the rough enclosure that sheltered the few animals which had been brought, with much labor and expense, across the Atlantic. The fox, the prying mink and the weasel brought destruction to the poultry. Crows and black-birds dug up the sprouting corn. But, worst of all, through the dark recesses of the forest roved the packs of wolves. The sheep or cow which strayed too far from the settlement seldom returned. The night howl of the wolves in the dead of winter, when hunger lent them an unwonted courage, sent a thrill of fear through the little family of the pioneer. It was a sound heard on every frontier until the last of the unoccupied spaces were gone.

42   From an exhibit in the American Museum of Natural History, New York

DEER

RELIGIOUS-MINDED pioneers sometimes felt that Providence caused a fruitful nature to bring forth an exuber-ance of hostile life that mortals might thus be punished for their sins. Yet not all the forest animals were enemies. Deer were everywhere. They sometimes damaged the settler's growing crops but, more often, they furnished him with much needed food. The white man soon learned to copy the Indian's methods of getting meat from the wilderness.

III—3

MOOSE

Moose roamed the northern woods, game the like of which English peasants had never imagined. Broad-antlered bulls moved swiftly through the undergrowth. The pioneer's clumsy matchlock was ill-adapted to the American forest but, for a time, it had to serve. Moreover, English peasants were not trained to the hunt, which was the prerogative of the gentry, and must learn woodcraft from bitter experience in the new land.

WILD FOWL

The salt marshes that bordered the ocean from Maine to the Gulf of Mexico at certain seasons of the year harbored thousands of wild fowl. Early travelers in the Chesapeake told tales of square miles of marshland and shallow water covered with stately swans, wild geese, and ducks. There were few enemies to check the

increase of these birds. For uncounted centuries they had winged their way northward and southward as the seasons changed and had looked down upon a monotonous expanse of forest whence only occasionally flew an Indian arrow. The smoke that now rose from the chimneys of the newly built cabins was a harbinger of a new era that was to bring extinction to many beautiful forms.

WILD TURKEYS

In the southern forest wild turkeys built their nests and were sometimes found by the whites in flocks of more than a hundred. Besides the game the pioneers found nuts and wild berries in profusion. Roger Williams saw in Rhode Island wild strawberries "as many as would fill a good ship within a few miles compasse."

46 From the wax group, *An Iroquois Council*, by Dwight Franklin (1888–),
in his possession

THE INDIAN

IN the forest the Indian watched the coming of the strange intruder. For many centuries his race had lived in the American forest. His culture was the outgrowth of long adjustment to the climate and the wooded areas. The traditions of his tribes, as far back as they could be remembered, were those of a forest people. The spirits of his dead lived in the streams and amid the trees; they hovered near his camp fires at night. From earliest childhood the Indian whom the English first met was trained a woodsman. He knew the artifices by which deer or wild fowl might be stalked or trapped. He knew where the fish ran in the streams. His culture was that of a hunting people with the beginnings of agriculture. But he had never achieved a full dependence upon cultivated crops or shaken off his dependence upon the forest.

AN INDIAN VILLAGE IN VIRGINIA
WITH ITS FIELDS

DURING the long evolution of his race in America the Indian had domesticated some wild plants. Had there been animals capable of domestication he would, doubtless, have tamed them. But there were none, and he remained dependent upon game for skins and meat. He had no source of power outside the human body with which to cultivate the soil. His villages were those of a primitive people.

The picture is a faithful copy of a drawing of a Virginian village by John White, 1585. In the background is a deer hunt. At the right are fields of corn in three stages of development. Beside the street is a patch of gourds, melons and squashes. At the end of the street and again at the left, just beside the sunflowers, are two fields of tobacco. One group before the huts is preparing a meal and another is eating. In the foreground with fire and ceremonial dance braves are worshiping the spirits of the dead chieftains whose bodies rest in the near-by hut.

47   From Theodore de Bry, *Grands Voyages*, Part I, 1590

48   Drawn expressly for *The Pageant of America* by C. W. Jefferys

INDIANS PLANTING CORN

Virginia squaws are planting corn in May. The April planting is already up and young redskins in rough shelters on scaffolds are keeping away the crows. The plot has been cleared after the time-honored method of girdling the trees and burning them down. The women with a sharpened stick or the shoulder blade of a deer are making holes four feet apart in each of which kernels of maize and two beans are placed with care to see that they do not touch. In the intervals between the holes are planted peas and pumpkin seeds. In June a third plot will be prepared. "The Corn grown up an hands length, they cut up the weeds, and loosen the Earth, about it. . . ."

49   Drawn expressly for *The Pageant of America* by C. W. Jefferys

A VIRGINIA HARVEST

The summer has come and gone and October finds the women harvesting their crop. They have been busy during the hot months keeping the plots free from weeds and, when the stalks were half grown, hilling them up. In August their families ate the April and in September the May planting, the ears plucked green and roasted in the ashes. But in October they lay by the stores for the winter. The corn is gathered in baskets. Haste is required for the men are anxious that the tribe shall get away for the hunting in the western country near the mountains, where the winter's meat will be gathered.

50   Drawn expressly for *The Pageant of America* by C. W. Jefferys

STORING THE CORN

THE ears, well dried, are brought to the lodge built for storage. The kernels are shelled off and the grain packed away in great baskets. Winter fare is ill fare without full granaries. As needed the corn is ground into meal with pestle and mortar and baked into cakes over an open fire.

INDIANS MAKING MAPLE SUGAR

IN the North in springtime when the warm sun of the lengthening days brought the sap up the maple trees, the Indians tapped the trunks. "The women busy themselves in receiving it (the sap) into vessels of bark, when it trickles from these trees; they boil it and obtain from it a fairly good sugar. The first which comes is the best."

The pioneers from Europe, for whom sugar had been a costly luxury and who, for the most part, had depended upon honey for their sweetening, soon learned the Indian custom. For a century and a half after the *Mayflower* anchored in Plymouth harbor, maple sugar and honey were the common sweetening of the farmers of the North.

The artist here, as in many of the early pictures of Indian life, has drawn somewhat upon his imagination and provided his Indians with utensils that have a European look. But the essentials are correct. In the background may be observed a planting scene the inspiration for which comes apparently from the engravings by Theodore de Bry, whose monumental work was published more than a hundred years earlier than Lafitau's. The whole picture well illustrates the busy life of the Indians at certain seasons of the year.

51   From Joseph F. Lafitau, *Mœurs des Sauvages Amériquains*, Paris, 1724

SQUANTO TEACHING THE PRINCIPLES OF CORN CULTURE

THE Indian husbandry was adjusted to the American environment. If the whites would live, they must use its plants and learn its methods. At Jamestown and at Plymouth the red men taught them how to raise the crops. Bradford wrote of the Pilgrims emerging from their first terrible winter: "Afterwards they (as many as were able) began to plant ther corne, in which servise Squanto stood them in great stead, showing them both the maner how to set it, and after how to dress and tend it. . . . Some English seed they sew, as wheat & pease, but it came not to good, eather by the badnes of the seed, or latenes of the season, or both, or some other defecte." Three centuries have passed since Squanto carried a knowledge of Indian husbandry to the Pilgrims and yet the basic principles of the red man's maize culture may still be found in the cornfields of America.

52   Drawn expressly for *The Pageant of America* by C. W. Jefferys

THE SELVAGE OF THE FOREST

IT was the fortune of some of the pioneers along the shore of the Atlantic to find open spaces in the edge of the forest where they could plant at once and build their habitations. Some were abandoned cornfields of the Indians where perhaps a village had been blotted out by pestilence. Some were due to the annual Indian practice of burning over the forest after the leaves had fallen. Others were tiny prairies, the result of natural causes. Where they were found they helped in the early days of settlement. Most of the settlers, however, faced the grim forest and the necessity for its destruction. Their tools were the awkward, straight-handled ax and the grubbing hook to dig up the stumps.

53   From the painting by J. Francis Murphy (1853–), courtesy of the Howard Young Galleries

54   Drawn expressly for *The Pageant of America* by C. W. Jefferys

BURNING UP THE LOGS

THE forest was an enemy. From the Indians the early settler learned to burn over the woodland where the trees had already been killed by girdling. This swept away the underbrush and many of the branches. Amid the blackened ghosts of a former splendor the pioneer "stubbed in" his European seeds and the corn he obtained from the redskins. At certain seasons the men of the village were called out to burn over the village lands. Later they felled the charred stubs and rolled the logs together into great piles for destruction.

55   The Stump Lot, from a photograph by the United States Department of Agriculture

Smoking heaps of ashes marked the extension of the clearing. The settler needed capital to make permanent his enterprise, a shelter for his family and cleared land. Such capital was the fruit of long and hard labor continued through many years.

CLEARING AWAY THE STUMPS

HEAVY toil followed the burning of the logs. A multitude of tasks called the men who, each morning, left the rough log shanties of their frontier village for the work of the day. In the spring they scratched the surface of the soil and sowed their seed in the midst of stumps and stones. In the fall they harvested the meager crop that must carry them and their animals through the winter. At other times there was hunting and fishing to be done. Trees must be girdled and the woods burned to increase the village fields. And finally, when time permitted, the stumps and knotty roots must be dug out. The pioneer had no labor-saving devices with which to drag his stumps from the ground; he must do the work by hand.

56   A Modern Pioneer, from a photograph by Clifton Johnson

57   From a photograph by the United States Department of Agriculture

THE STONY HILLSIDES OF NEW ENGLAND

WHEN the trees were cleared away and the stumps uprooted, the boulder *débris* which had been left ages ago by the glaciers remained — a depressing prospect for the husbandman.

THE STONE WALL

As the seventeenth century wore on and the severity of frontier life relaxed, the last task of preparing the soil was undertaken. With ox team and sledge the pioneer farmer and his brood of sturdy sons picked up the cobblestones and dragged the larger boulders from their sockets. Countless loads were hauled to the great stone pile in the corner of the lot or to the line marked for the fence. Then, for the first time, the plow could turn a straight and unbroken furrow across the field. "If there are ever sermons in stones," once remarked Burroughs, "it is when they are built into a stone wall, — turning your hindrances into helps, shielding your crops behind the obstacles to your husbandry, making the enemies of the plow stand guard over its products." The walls were laid without mortar. Large and small stones were fitted nicely into a structure of great stability. Winter frost heaved the stones and woodchucks dug their burrows beneath them. Repairs were constantly necessary. Many times the wall enclosed soil too poor for profitable husbandry. The traveler of today may find them running through thick New England woods, melancholy relics of futile labor.

58   From a photograph by the United States Department of Agriculture

59   © Detroit Publishing Company

THE STUMP FENCE

THE forest also furnished materials for fencing. The stumps themselves uprooted and trimmed to lie flat on the ground made enclosures as secure as the hedges that the colonists had left behind in England. Particularly in the regions where the white pine flourished stump fences were common, guarding the fields of grain from wandering hogs and cattle and symbolizing in their ragged uncouthness the victory of the husbandman over the wilderness. But fences, because their making required much labor, were limited to the smallest possible number in the earliest settlements.

60   A Farm Fence in New England. © Keystone

THE RAIL FENCE

THE rail fence likewise was the product of the forest. On frosty winter mornings before the snow lay too deep in the woods could be heard the heavy pounding of the pioneer's great wooden maul driving the wedges into the tough logs of pine, oak or chestnut.

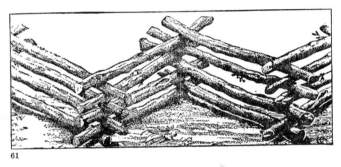

61

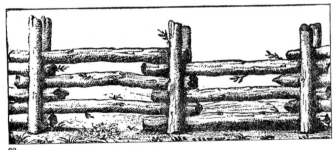

62

With the same process the frontier farmer cleared his land and enclosed his fields. The rail splitter was a common figure on each successive frontier until the forest gave way to the broad stretches of the open prairie. Many of these relics of the days when the forest covered great stretches of America have lingered into modern times.

"Worm" fences were built of rails alone laid in a zig-zag line about the field. Others were combinations of posts and rails which, though not so easy to build, had the advantage of using both less timber and less ground. The combination of rails with a stone wall made the most effective enclosure.

63   From L. Castiglioni, *Viaggio negli Stati Uniti dell' America Settentrionale*, Milano, 1790

64   Drawn expressly for *The Pageant of America* by C. W. Jefferys

SEVENTEENTH–CENTURY PLOWING IN NEW ENGLAND

WHEN the trees and stumps were largely cleared away, the great plow appeared in the fields. The heavy beam was shaped from a seasoned log. Of wood also was the handle and the moldboard on which the farmer or the village smith fastened some crude strips of iron. The smith also made the coulter that cut the sod ahead of the point. Not every settler owned a plow. The owner, sometimes paid a bounty by the community, made plowing his business during the season; it went from field to field as, for centuries, it had done in England. The calls of the driver to the laboring oxen that had come down with the language out of antiquity now echoed from the hillsides of America.

65   From *Picturesque America*, New York, 1872, wood engraving after drawing by
        J. Douglas Woodward (1847–1924)

THE OX CART

BACK and forth over the lanes that led from the village to the fields jolted the two-wheeled cart of the manor with little loads of produce. Often the clumsy wheels were but the cross-section of a hardwood log. The man who could not afford a cart used a rough sled or sledge. The hardy ox that could be used both for meat and power was a mainstay of pioneer husbandry. Perhaps, if it were the haying season, an ill-shaped scythe and an awkward wooden fork or two clattered aboard the cart on the way to the meadow. Such tools as the pioneer possessed were crude and ill-adjusted to his needs. Looking back at these early husbandmen from the vantage point of an age of cunningly devised machines one feels the immensity of the task which faced them and the greatness of their achievement.

THE COWHERD

66   Drawn expressly for *The Pageant of America* by C. W. Jefferys

FROM England the pioneer brought the old customs of the manor for caring for the village animals. The swineherd, the shepherd and the cowherd appeared in America. Before the arable fields were fully fenced the animals must be tended during the growing season. The agreement in 1661 of Ipswich, Massachusetts, with its cowherd, follows:

"Daniel Bosworth is to keep the herd of cows on the north side of the river, from the 1st of May to the 20th of October. He is to go out with them half an hour after sunrise and to bring them home a little before sun-set, at 13s. a week. . . . 'Agreed with Henry Osborn to join Bosworth to keep the cows on the same terms. One of them to take the cows to Scott's Lane and to blow a horn at the meeting-house green in the morning.'"

MARKING THE ANIMALS

67   Ear Marks, Long Island, 1752, courtesy of E. P. Buffet, Stony Brook, Long Island

68   Courtesy of E. P. Buffet

THE cattle which Bosworth tended could readily be distinguished from one another. Sheep could not be easily identified nor the droves of swine rooting in the woods. The ancient custom of marking ears enabled the owner to prove his property. A notch, a curve, or a "swallow tail" was cut at a certain place in the right ear or the left and a formal record made of the mark in the books of the township. So James Abbet knew, when the flock was brought back to the village, which ewes were his and could claim the unmarked lambs which followed them. In the southern colonies the pioneers lived less in village groups. The animals of the settlers roamed at large through the woods and often became practically wild. As their number increased, some communities began the practice each year of "rounding up" these wild cattle and horses. Cowpens in South Carolina, where, during General Greene's southern campaign in the Revolution, Morgan defeated the brilliant Colonel Tarleton, retained its name from the days when the wandering, untamed animals of the Carolina back-country were rounded up and driven into the enclosures built at that place. In the South, particularly the western areas near the mountains, appeared, during colonial times, the first American cowboy. Perhaps he was not so picturesque as his later counterpart, but his functions were essentially the same.

Towne Marks agreed by yᵉ General Coᵗte for Horses, cx, x · x x x x, ordered to be set upoⁿ one of yᵉ nere qᵗrᵗ x x.

Charlestowne,	Braintree,	Hingham,
Cambridge,	Roxberry,	Hampton,
Concord,	Rowley,	Haverell,
Salem,	redding,	Sloster,
Salsberry,	Watᵗtowne,	Meadford,
Sudberry,	Meymoth,	Manchestᵗ
Strawberrybanke,	Woburne,	Andiver,
Dorchester,	Northam,	bull,
dedham,	Linn,	Springfeild,
Dover,	Ipswich,	x ashaway,
Boston,	Nuberry,	Exiter.

69   Massachusetts Pitch Marks, from *Records of the Governor and Company of the Massachusetts Bay in New England 1628–86*, Boston, 1853–54

PIONEER LIVE STOCK

70 American Razor-backs, from *The Cultivator*, Albany, N. Y., January, 1840

When the sheep were left untended, a bell was sometimes fastened to the neck of the leader of the flock, who became the "bell wether." Poor and stunted, when measured by modern standards, were the animals brought to America from English fields. The summer grazing in the rich forests fattened the cattle and the swine, but in winter the shivering stock, unsheltered from the biting cold, hovered disconsolately about the farmstead eating ravenously the little fodder that the pioneer threw out to them. The hard months of winter weeded out the weak. Natural selection brought into being the tough and hardy but ragged and undersized "native" cattle. Scrawny cows, "rat-tailed" sheep and "razor-backed" swine lived about the settlements. Even had better breeds been available, it would have been impossible to hold the improved strain in the common flocks and herds of early times.

71 Cowbell and Sheep Bell, from the collections of the Pocumtuck Valley Memorial Association, Deerfield, Mass.

72   From the painting *The Birth of Springfield*, by J. J. LaValley (1858–) in the City Hall, Springfield, Mass.

PIONEER HOMES

The habitation of the pioneer told vividly the story of his initial hardships. In the earliest days of New England, New York and Pennsylvania dugouts were common. "They burrow themselves in the Earth for their first shelter under some Hill side, casting the Earth aloft upon Timber; they make a smoaky fire against the Earth at its highest side." So wrote Edward Johnson of Massachusetts. There followed cottages of wattle, with or without a daubing of clay, reminiscent of the cottages of the manorial vill. Wistfully the settler tried to reproduce the old home.

73   Standish House, Duxbury, Mass., built 1666. © Halliday Historic Photograph Company

SEVENTEENTH–CENTURY FARMHOUSES

CABINS of timber soon rose but in the earliest of these the logs were placed vertically after the manner of the palisade. The typical American log cabin was a later development. As the years passed and the pioneer's fields grew in size and number, the wattle cottages with their thatched roofs and the timber cabins gave place to larger houses. The farmer, aided by the local carpenter, built the structure while neighbors gathered to help in setting up the heavy frame. The sills and plates and corner posts were rugged timbers hewn from the forest. The sides were encased in clapboards and the roof covered with shingles that perhaps the husbandman himself had shaved. Here and there one of these early homes still stands as sound and true as the day the last wooden peg was driven into the frame. The new house signified that the day of tensest struggle had passed. The simple lines of these early houses have aroused the admiration of a later and wealthier generation. Perhaps it is not without point to remember that most of them were built by farmer-carpenters to house the families of farmers.

74   John Cook House, Hadley, Mass., built about 1700. © Halliday Historic Photograph Company

75   The Meeker House at Lyons Farms, N. J., demolished in 1913, from a drawing by E. J. Meeker, 1886

A NEW JERSEY FARMHOUSE BUILT IN 1676

SIMPLE enough was the husbandry of the pioneer. While he had been busy clearing his lands, his animals had made shift to live in the woods. When the trees were gone, his fields gave him Indian corn and wheat for food and flax for the manufacture of cloth. His cattle and sheep provided leather and wool and, together with the swine, furnished the meat which the housewife salted down for winter use. Balancing an animal and

a crop husbandry, the early farmer established his farm as a self-sufficient unit. He required practically nothing from beyond his own boundaries. With the passing years his acres increased. As his crops became larger and his animals more numerous he grew in substance and independence.

76   Reconstructed Colonial Interior. © Topsfield (Mass.) Historical Society

77 Weaving, from a photograph by Rudolf Eickemeyer.
© Campbell Prints, Inc., New York

HOME INTERIORS, SEVENTEENTH CENTURY

BUT home was more than a shelter against storm and cold. It was a busy factory where the settler mended and improvised the rough tools that he used and where his wife wove the cloth and made the garments that the family wore. The home economy of the mediæval manor was set down in the edge of the American forest. The skill derived from generations of hand manufacturing in England now stood the pioneer in good stead. Like the husbandry of the Indians, the handicrafts of the Middle Ages contributed to the founding of permanent settlements in the New World.

A VILLAGE SETTLEMENT, FAIRFIELD, CONNECTICUT, 1648–57

In early New England the village group was the most important social and economic unit. Here were reproduced many of the aspects of the manorial vill. Each villager was allotted a house plot on the village street. The arable fields, the meadow and the common pasture lay outside the cluster of cabins. Beyond all was the forest.

COMMON AND UNDIVIDED FIELDS, HARTFORD, CONN.

From the village, lanes radiated to the fields. As in the old home across the sea, there was an ox pasture and

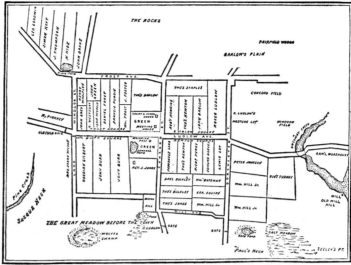

78   From Elizabeth Hubbell Schenk, *History of Fairfield*, New York, 1889

a cow pasture and the meadow lay beside the banks of the stream. But there were elements that no English village knew — the lane to the Indian land and the wolf pound. Englishmen started their settlements in America with the knowledge and customs they had. Adjustments to the new conditions began the long process of the making of the American.

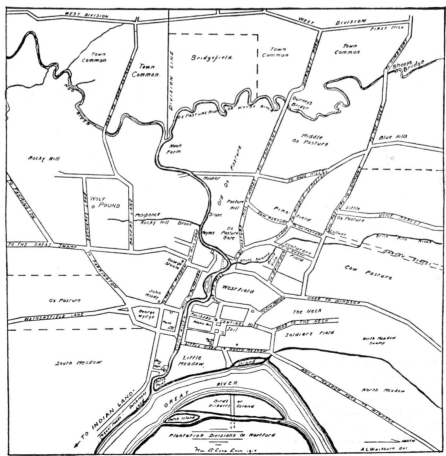

79   From William De Loss Love, *The Colonial History of Hartford*, 1914

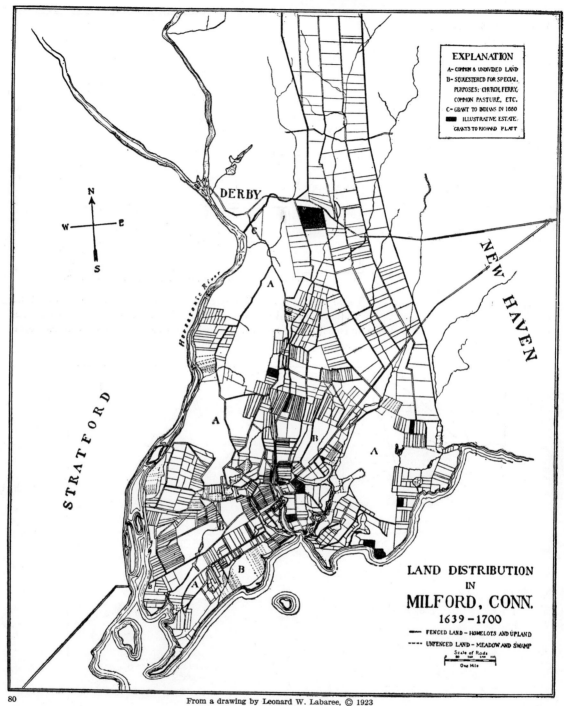

EXPLANATION
A- COMMON & UNDIVIDED LAND
B- SEQUESTERED FOR SPECIAL
   PURPOSES: CHURCH, FERRY,
   COMMON PASTURE, ETC.
C- GRANT TO INDIANS IN 1680
   ▪ ILLUSTRATIVE ESTATE.
   GRANTS TO RICHARD PLATT

LAND DISTRIBUTION
IN
MILFORD, CONN.
1639 – 1700

FENCED LAND – HOMELOTS AND UPLAND
UNFENCED LAND – MEADOW AND SWAMP

Scale of Rods
One Mile

From a drawing by Leonard W. Labaree, © 1923

As a community the little New England village group acquired its land. There was no lord to order the doings of the commoners. The "farms" of the villagers were not the compact units of a later day but, as in the mediæval manor, were made up of fields scattered here and there over the community lands. The shaded plots in the map show one man's holdings. The community lands were divided not at once, but at various times over a period of years, as the villagers became able to utilize their holdings. Men received plots in the new divisions. The system of scattered holdings for an individual made more equitable the distribution of good and poor soil.

GROWTH OF SETTLEMENT

ALMOST universally, the center of the New England village was the church, where on the Sabbath the villagers came to worship. As the community grew, perhaps a rich bottom a few miles away would attract a group of adventurous persons and a little cluster of cabins would appear in the new place like Bryan's Farms (4) or Northrup's Farms (3) outside of Milford. On Sundays these outlying husbandmen brought their families over the rough woods roads to the home church. When the winter snow lay deep among the trees, the journey was hard. No wonder the new community sought a church of its own. When it grew to the point where it could support a minister, it broke away from the mother settlement and, like Woodbridge or Orange, became a separate township. So farther and farther from the coast the first New England settlements pushed back into the interior.

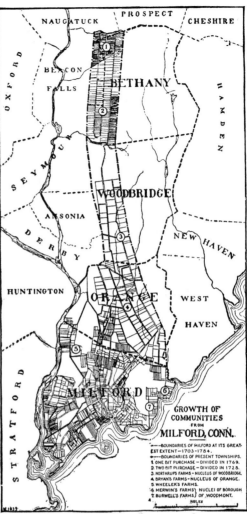

81   From a drawing by Leonard W. Labaree, © 1923

82   Hingham (Mass.) Meeting-House, from a drawing after a photograph

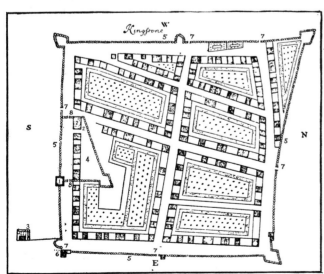

83   From Reverend John Miller, *A Description of the Province and City of New York*, London, 1695

A DUTCH VILLAGE, WILTTVICK (NOW KINGSTON, N. Y.) 1695

ALMOST all the first village settlements were surrounded by palisades. As the number of towns increased, the Indian danger lessened. But the settlements of the interior had still to maintain the old precautions. The diagram is a contemporary drawing of a Dutch stockaded settlement on the Hudson with extra protection for the church. The legend reads: 1, the blockhouse; 2, the church and burying place; 3, the minister's house; 4, the part separated and fortified; 5, the stockade; 6, the house where the governor is entertained; 7, the town gates; 8, the gates of the separate fortified part. The dots perhaps represent orchards.

84   From an engraving after a drawing by F. O. C. Darley (1822–88)

THE INDIAN MENACE

THE Indian menace could never be forgotten. As the whites encroached upon the lands of the redskins, war after war flamed up. Again and again a line of smoking ruins showed where the frontier had been driven back. Always the pioneer was farmer, hunter, and artisan. But there were times of crisis when all other occupations gave way and he became a warrior. He must be skilled in the use of his weapons and in the Indian method of fighting. If he were deficient, not only his own life but those of his family might pay the price.

85   Van Rensselaer Manor House of 1666, from *Albany Chronicles*, 1906

86 Patroon Kiliaen van Rensselaer, 1595–1644, from *Albany Chronicles*, 1906, after the portrait owned by Howard van Rennselaer, Albany, N. Y.

FEUDAL MANORS UNDER THE DUTCH

To the west of New England in the valley of the Hudson occasional feudal manors took the place of the village settlements. The Dutch in New Netherland with their system of patroons started the development. To the man who would bring out to America and settle fifty colonists above fifteen years of age the Dutch West India Company offered sixteen miles of frontage along a navigable river and also gave extensive powers. The settler became the tenant of the patroon, owing him a money rent and certain services. Kiliaen van Rensselaer, though he never came to America, founded in the rich country adjacent to Fort Orange the most famous of the patroonships.

Simplified from E. B. O'Callaghan, *The Documentary History of The State of New York*, Albany, 1850, after a survey by John R. Bleecker

RENSSELAERSWYCK MANOR IN 1767

IN Rensselaerswyck (the present Albany, Columbia and Rensselaer counties) the tenant must assist in keeping up the roads and repairing the buildings, must give the patroon each year three days' service with horse and wagon and must cut, split and bring to the waterside two fathoms of firewood. Rensselaerswyck, by original grant and later purchase, became a vast estate founded on the principles of European feudalism. It was galling to be a tenant bound to the land and subject to the law of the manor court when all about him were freemen working out their own destinies. The estate lay on both banks of the Hudson with Albany near its center. In the early days of settlement van Rensselaer had ordered that no settlers should establish themselves far from the village church for fear of Indian attack upon isolated cabins. As the years passed and the Indian menace lessened, the tenants scattered widely to exploit the best lands. The cottages were thickest along the river but were found as far as the mountains on the east and west. Such an arrangement of population is in sharp contrast to the closely-knit villages of New England.

From E. B. O'Callaghan, *The Documentary History of the State of New York*, Albany, 1850, after the survey signed by John Beatty, 1714

MAP OF THE LIVINGSTON MANOR, 1714

WHEN New Amsterdam became New York, the policy of granting large tracts of land grew in favor until the forests of the region about the Hudson and the Mohawk were a checkerboard of great estates, all too frequently the fruit of official favoritism or chicane. Half way between Rensselaerswyck and New York was the Livingston manor, granted by Governor Dongan to Robert Livingston in 1685. It lay east of the river and covered many thousands of acres. Very like the old patroonships of the Dutch, its manor house, mill, and "King's hieway" were reminiscent of the Middle Ages. But independent freeholders like those of Long Island and Staten Island steadily laid out farms also in the Hudson valley. It was they rather than the landed aristocracy who made New York the princely province it became.

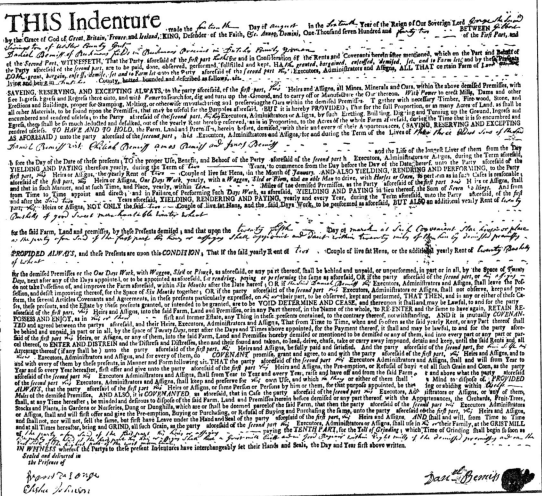

AN EXTRACT FROM AN INDENTURE ON THE LIVINGSTON MANOR

THIS indenture is that of a tenant on the Livingston Manor, and is dated Aug. 14, 1742. Daniel Bemiss contracts for the use of a property which is described as "being part of a Lot known by the name of Lot No. 3 in Beekmans precinct."

The landlord reserves to himself

"all Mines, Minerals and Oars within the above demised Premises, with free Ingress, Egress and Regress there unto, and with Power to search for, dig and turn up the ground, and to carry off or Manufacture the Oar thereon."

The tenant and his heirs are to hold the land "during the Term of the Lives of the three eldest sons of the said Daniel Bemiss viz: — Chileab Bemiss, Amos Bemiss, and Jonas Bemiss."

He is to pay for two years

"the yearly Rent of two Couple of live fat Hens in the Month of January. And also Yielding, Rendering and Performing to the Party of the first part . . . one days Work yearly with a Waggon, Sled or Plow, and an able Man to drive, with Horses or Oxen, to perform as in such Cases is reasonable . . . and in Failure of Performing such Days Work, as aforesaid, Yielding and Paying in lieu thereof the Sum of Seven Shillings."

At the end of the two years he is to pay

"Not only the said two couple of live fat Hens, and the said Days Work to be performed as aforesaid but also an additional Rent of twenty Bushells of Good Sweet merchantable winter wheat."

The tenant moreover

"shall and will from Time to Time and at all Times hereafter, bring and Grind, all such Grains as . . . [he] shall use or his family at the Grist Mill" of the landlord "paying the Tenth Part for the Toll of Grinding; which Time of Grinding shall begin so soon as [the landlord] shall have a Grist mill built and in Good Repair within Eight miles of the demissed premisses and on the east side of the highest part of the west mountain."

90   Feudal Estates along the St. Lawrence; from an original color sketch in the Dépôt des Cartes et Plans de la Marine, Paris

THE FEUDAL SYSTEM IN FRENCH CANADA

NORTHWARDS of the English colonies the French along the St. Lawrence had founded their agricultural communities on the feudal system. The seigneur was the lord who had title to a considerable tract of land. The habitant was the small husbandman who held his land from the seigneur and who must grind his corn in the lord's mill after the time-honored custom. The chart of Three Rivers and the view of the St. Lawrence about Quebec (No. 90) both show the river banks lined with seigniories which are broken up into the small farms of the habitants.

Feudalism, which gradually died out among the English who came to America, proved a marked success among the French, perhaps because the burdens it put upon the common people were very light. Small profit did the seigneurs derive from their tenants. Yet they were respected and even honored. Feudalism united New France, small in population and faced with dangerous Indians and the aggressive English. The seigneurs were the natural leaders of the people and the habitants who worked their estates in time of peace followed them in four successive wars against their southern neighbors. In the region of the St. Lawrence it lasted well into the nine-

teenth century. Occasionally in the twentieth may be found a suggestion of the ancient order.

91   The Region around Three Rivers, 1709, insert on a map by Jean Baptiste Decoüagne, in the Dépôt des Cartes et Plans de la Marine, Paris

CHAPTER III

THE AMERICAN SIR ROGER DE COVERLEY

THE first encounter with the untamed wilderness of America was the fiercest. With little to guide them the earliest pioneers set themselves to the task of establishing permanent settlements and of discovering by hard experience how life must be lived in the New World. Maize was adopted from the red men and throughout the northern and many of the southern colonies the Indian corn became the most important food grain. In Virginia tobacco was found profitable and speedily became the chief reliance of the province. Farther south, in the Carolinas, after many experiments rice established itself as the most important crop. Before the seventeenth century was over certain tested ways of life had emerged on the frontier, and a body of experienced men had gathered which made less arduous the task of later adventurers who crossed the waters to try a hazard of new fortunes.

But the long thin line of settlement from Maine to the Carolinas crossed many differing environments. New England differed from Virginia and the adjustments of the first comers were not the same in each. The differences grew as colonial life unfolded. Jamestown was much more like Plymouth than eighteenth-century Virginia was like eighteenth-century Massachusetts. Two quite distinct ideals among the husbandmen of America had emerged.

In the English homeland agriculture had supported an aristocracy. The lord had owned the land and the common people had rented from him. The feeling of class was deep; the peasant could not aspire to the nobility. In America there was land enough for all and an invitation to every able-bodied man, whatever his initial disabilities, to become a freeholder. In the boundless forests the aristocratic ideals of the English landed gentry seemed cramped and stuffy. But tobacco and rice could best be grown on the plantation system, and the planter in the Carolinas and Virginia quickly assumed the position of the English squire. Since there was no supply of renting farmers, the American gentry cultivated their broad estates by means of white indentured servants whose services they purchased for a period of years, and of negro slaves whom they owned outright. Different outwardly and in detail, the ideal of landed aristocracy was the same in the Old World and the New.

92   The Sedan-Chair, detail from the painting *Maryland in 1750*, by
F. B. Mayer (1827–99), in the Maryland Historical Society, Baltimore

49

93 Detail from Theodore de Bry, *Grands Voyages*, Part II, Florida, 1591

INDIAN USES OF TOBACCO

ALONG the banks of the James sprang up in the
early seventeenth century the settlements of the
Virginia colony. Five years after the landing of
the *Sarah Constant* tobacco was first grown by the
Jamestown people. Tobacco gave life and prosperity to Virginia. Its cultivation led to the first
English development of the plantation system on
the continent of North America.

The first Virginians exploring the country about
their settlement found the Indians paying particular attention to tobacco. It was the plant
with a spirit in it, the special gift of a benign deity.
It was used in the sacrifice to propitiate angry
ghosts. If a drouth parched the ground or a storm
blackened the distant sky, the dust of powdered
tobacco was cast into the air. When the fish began
coming in from the sea, tobacco was sprinkled along
the weirs. Should a stranger visit the village, he
smoked, together with the principal men, the cere-
monial pipe. Tobacco was medicine, useful in driving the evil spirit from the sick. It grew in every Virginian
Indian's garden, small plants of inferior quality.

"TABACO" BROUGHT TO SPAIN

FROM the West Indies tobacco was first introduced into Spain in
1558 by a physician whom Philip II had sent out to New Spain to
investigate the products of Mexico. But its use was largely for medici-
nal purposes.

95   From an etching attributed to Barry (1741–1806)

94 From Nicholás Monardes, *Joyfull Nevves out
of the newe founde worlde.* Englished by John
Frampton, London, 1577

RALEIGH INTRODUCES
SMOKING INTO ENGLAND

TOBACCO and the implements for
smoking seem to have been first
brought to England by Sir Francis
Drake and Ralph Lane, governor of
Raleigh's first colony. Raleigh himself set the fashion and soon the
practice of smoking was common among the courtiers of Elizabeth. The picture is a fanciful representation
of the old story that Raleigh's servant, on first catching sight of his master at the new trick of "drinking
tobacco," dashed water in his face to put out the fire.

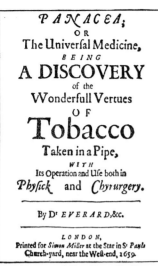

PANACEA;
OR
The Univerfal Medicine,
BEING
A DISCOVERY
of the
Wonderfull Vertues
OF
Tobacco
Taken in a Pipe,
WITH
Its Operation and Ufe both in
Phyfick and *Chyrurgery.*

By Dr *EVERARD,*&c.

LONDON,
Printed for *Simon Miller* at the Star in St *Pauls*
Church-yard, near the Weft-end, 1659.

96 Title-page of Dr. Everard's *Panacea,*
London, 1659, in the Library of Congress

CONTROVERSY OVER TOBACCO

THROUGHOUT the seventeenth century the use of tobacco spread rapidly over Europe. Importation into Great Britain grew steadily in volume, yet there were many who opposed "taking tobacco," among them none other than James I, writing in 1604: "And now good Countrey men let us (I pray you) consider, what honour or policie can moove us to imitate the barbarous and beastly maners of the wilde, godlesse, and slavish *Indians*, especially in so vile and stinking a custome?"

ROLFE'S TOBACCO SHED

KING JAMES'S avowed hostility to the "stinking custome" of "taking tobacco" did not prevent John Rolfe from experimenting with the weed in Virginia. Rolfe was himself a smoker and apparently soon tired of the inferior leaf he got from the Indians. The merit of Rolfe's work lay in his attempt to improve the Indian plant under different methods of cultivation. In this he succeeded. Tobacco became a common crop, the staple upon which the province depended. With its advent the days of uncertainty ended and the permanence of the Virginia settlement became assured.

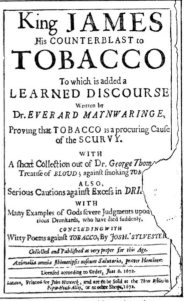

King JAMES
HIS COUNTERBLAST to
TOBACCO
To which is added a
LEARNED DISCOURSE
Written by
Dr. *EVERARD MAYNWARINGE,*
Proving that TOBACCO is a procuring Caufe
of the SCURVY.
WITH
A fhort Collection out of Dr. *George Thom*
Treatife of *BLOUD;* againft fmoking TOB
ALSO,
Serious Cautions againft Excefs in *DRI*
WITH
Many Examples of Gods fevere Judgments upon
rious Drunkards, who have died fuddenly,
CONCLUDING WITH
Witty Poems againft *TOBACCO,* By *JOSH.' SYLVESTER*

Collected and Publifhed as very proper for this Age.
Animalia omnia fibimetipfis nofcunt Salutaria, præter Hominem.
Licenfed according to Order, *Juſſ* 6. 1672.
London, Printed for *John Hancock,* and are to be Sold at the *Three Bibles* in
Popes-Head-Alley, or at other Shops, 1672.

97 Title-page of pamphlet written by
Everard Maynwaringe, London, 1672

98   From the Chronicles of America motion picture *Jamestown*

THE FIRST LANDING OF SLAVES IN VIRGINIA

TOBACCO brought an opportunity for profit to the early Virginians. Not many years after Rolfe's demonstration, tobacco raising had become universal among the colonists. The new crop emphasized the need for labor which every American frontier has felt. Indentured servants were imported by some of the more prosperous planters. There was mingled curiosity and satisfaction among the Virginians when, in 1619, a Dutch ship left a load of African negroes. In later years negroes came in increasing numbers. They hoed the tobacco fields and did the heavy work. They became, ultimately, the foundation upon which the plantation system rested.

99   After the painting by Howard Pyle (1853-1911) for
Woodrow Wilson, *A History of the American
People,* 1901. © Harper & Bros.

BROAD PLANTATIONS IN EARLY VIRGINIA

AFTER the first critical years Virginia grew steadily in population. Habitations appeared along the banks of countless creeks and rivers flowing into the Chesapeake. Unlike New England these were seldom grouped into tiny, close-set villages. As the seventeenth century drew to a close, broad plantations appeared among Virginia farms. A few outstanding men arose who amassed great holdings and became the leaders of an incipient planter aristocracy. Colonel William Byrd, Sr., acquired by in-

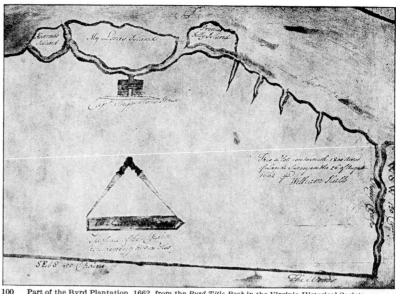

100   Part of the Byrd Plantation, 1662, from the *Byrd Title Book* in the Virginia Historical Society, Richmond

heritance the Captain Stegge stone house at the falls of the James where Richmond was one day to stand. Before his death he had become the owner of more than twenty-six thousand acres. Yet Byrd was by no means the largest landholder in Virginia.

VIRGINIA AND ITS PLANTATIONS, 1673

EARLY Virginians lived in the "tide-water" country. The estuaries of the York, the Rappahannock, and the James cut deep into the mainland and offered safe anchorage for ocean-going ships. Along the banks of these

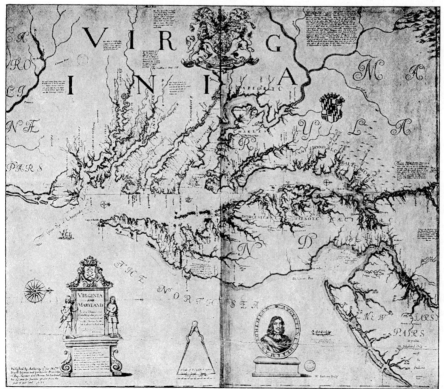

rivers plantations began to add acre to acre before the seventeenth century had run its course, and beside them the small farms continued to exist and increase in number. Much of the plantation was woodland; new fields were cleared as old ones became exhausted and were allowed to grow up to underbrush. Early Virginia was almost literally a colony that grew up at the water's edge. There were few towns like those in New England. The population was scattered and the houses of the people separated often by considerable distances from one another.

101   From the Augustine Herrmann map, 1673, engraved by W. Faithorne, in the Dépôt des Cartes et Plans de la Marine, Paris

THE WHARF OF A VIRGINIA PLANTATION

THE sturdy little ships that plied the trade across the Atlantic between England and the colonies tacked up the Virginia estuaries, and touched at the plantations. Sometimes the planter had his own rough wharf where his tobacco casks were piled high. Usually the ship dropped anchor in midstream, for the water shoaled near the banks. The ship once in, there was business to be done. Arrangements must be made with the captain; the merchandise which the planter's London agent had purchased upon his requisition must be checked off; the great tobacco casks must be put on board. Mingling with the shouts and curses of the sailors were the grunts of the negro slaves often only a few months from the jungles of Africa.

102 After the painting by Howard Pyle for Woodrow Wilson, *A History of the American People*, 1901. © Harper & Bros.

103 From *Graham's Magazine*, Aug., 1844, engraving by James Smillie, after a drawing by John G. Chapman (1808–89)

THE ROAD AT YORKTOWN

THE eighteenth century saw the desirable river frontage taken up. Plantations were laid out farther and farther from the water's edge. When the crop had been gathered and cured, these inland planters set their faces to the rivers. Rude carts jolting back from the dock brought loads of goods from London to the folk of the mansion house, dresses for the ladies and clothing for the men, things for the house and such luxuries as the income or credit of the planter could command.

"ROLLING" TOBACCO

ONE of the chief problems of the inland planter was to get his leaf to the river warehouse. The great casks in which the tobacco was packed for shipment to England were too heavy for the clumsy plantation carts to haul over the rough, ill-kept roads of the colony. At first they were rolled by hand over the highways by gangs of servants or negroes. Later the indispensable slave drew them, sometimes with strangely assorted teams, to the docks. This was "rolling" tobacco. Throughout most of the seventeenth century the indentured white servant had been the most important element among the laborers but, as the century drew to a close, the slave rapidly took his place. The soft voices of the negroes gave new inflections to the ancient calls to the laboring beasts. When the long road ended at the river, the negro would have his hour of pleasure with the grinning slaves from other plantations brought by tasks like his to the warehouse.

104 From *Harper's Weekly*, Dec. 11, 1869, after a drawing by W. L. Sheppard (1833–1912)

105   From William Faden, *The North American Atlas*, London, 1777, inset on map of Virginia by
                               Joshua Fry and Peter Jefferson

THE TOBACCO WAREHOUSE

AT the inspection warehouse established by the colony centered much of the economic life of old Virginia.
Here the leaf, hauled in from far and near, was graded and the rejected product destroyed.   Receipts were
given for the planter's crop and these served as currency in the colony.   Again and again Virginia production
outran the demand.   The colonial government made rigid requirements as to the quality of the product for
export and at times attempted to restrict the output.   But Maryland and North Carolina were also tobacco-
raising settlements and there could be little restriction without agreement among the three.   Mutual rivalries
and jealousies made this difficult to obtain.

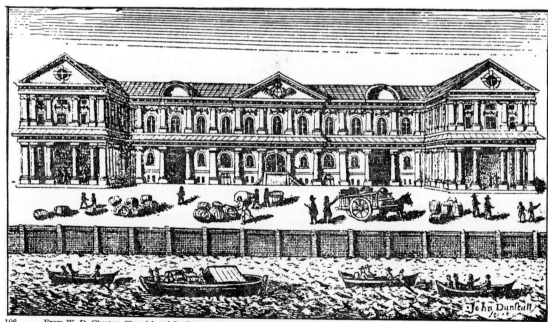

106   From W. D. Chester, *Chronicles of the Customs Department*, London, 1885, after an old engraving by John Dunstall (1644?-75)

THE CUSTOMS HOUSE, LONDON

THROUGH the London Customs House passed the Virginia leaf and paid the revenue duties that gave to the
Crown a lively interest in the colonial crop.   Here the merchant agents for the planters received the lots
consigned to them and reckoned their value at the current price.   They credited the total against the worth
of the goods they had sent out to meet the requisitions of the colonial gentry.   There was opportunity for
knavery in so loose a system in an age when communication was slow.   Yet the planters had no option; it
was the only way by which their crop could be disposed of.

RICE IN SOUTH CAROLINA

WHAT tobacco did for Virginia rice did for South Carolina. David Ramsay in his *History of South Carolina*, 1809, published the accompanying plan of Charleston which is based upon a plan at the side of Herman Moll's *Map of the Dominions of the King of Great Britain in America*, 1715. Ramsay added to the Moll map the rice patch (W), in the rear of Governor Landgrave Smith's house, which is noted as the "first" rice field in Carolina. On January 13, 1672, a barrel of rice was among the articles "Shipped by the Grace of God in Good Order & well condicioned

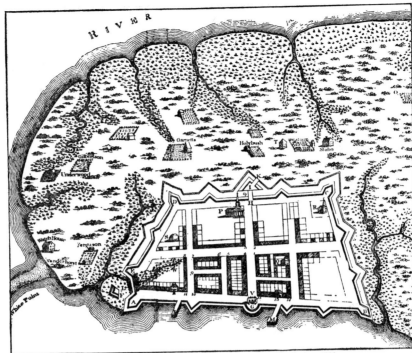

107   From David Ramsay, *History of South Carolina*, Charleston, 1809

by me Richd Kingdon, for the prop. acct. of the Lords Proprs. of Carolina, in & upon the good ship called the William & Ralph, whereof is master under God for that present voyage William Jeffereys, & now riding at anchor in the River of Thames, & by God's grace bound for Charles Towne in Ashley River." In 1699, one of the Carolina proprietors wrote the Commissioners for Trade and Plantations: "I have herewith sent you a sample of our Carolina rice . . . a staple the Province of Carolina may be capable of furnishing Europe withall. The Grocers do assure me its better than any Foreign Rice by at least 8s. the hundred weight, & wee can have it brought home for less than 4s. pr. tonn. wch. is not dear."—A. S. SALLEY, JR., *The Introduction of Rice Culture into South Carolina*, Columbia, S. C., 1919.

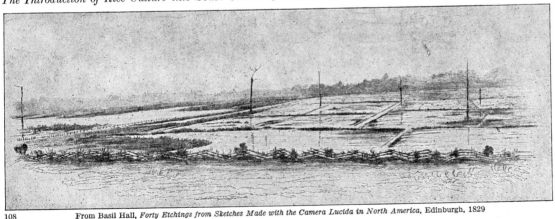

108   From Basil Hall, *Forty Etchings from Sketches Made with the Camera Lucida in North America*, Edinburgh, 1829

THE RICE LANDS OF SOUTH CAROLINA

AMERICA offered no better place for rice culture than South Carolina, where the low, flat coastal plain slopes so gradually into the sea that a fringe of marshes divides the interior from the sandy beach. At first rice was grown in dry soil but the advantage of flooding the fields was quickly discovered. So plantations appeared along the sluggish streams whose waters were just about to mingle with the ocean. White men could not labor in these hot, sultry lowlands. Negro slavery was inevitable. As rice culture increased, more and more ships left batches of savage blacks from the Gold Coast of Africa.

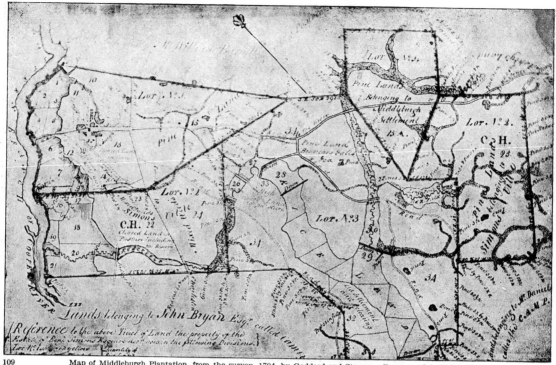

109 Map of Middleburgh Plantation, from the survey, 1794, by Goddard and Sturges. Courtesy of A. S. Salley, Jr., Secretary of the Historical Commission of South Carolina, Columbia, S. C.

RICE LANDS ON COOPER RIVER

In time, rice plantations in South Carolina, like tobacco in Virginia, grew in size and number. One of the larger plantations with rice lands was that of Benjamin Simons, Esquire, known as Middleburgh, having two thousand five hundred ninety-nine acres. The owner of such an estate, living in provincial elegance in the mansion house, was an aristocrat, a colonial lordling feeling something of the emotions of the British nobility who sat in the House of Lords. The rice lands are the shaded areas along the streams.

110 From *Harper's Weekly* Jan. 5, 1867, after a drawing by A. R. Waud
A. MAIN FLOOD GATES. B. DITCHING. C. FLOOD GATE.

PREPARING FOR THE RICE CROP

The eighteenth century developed a style of rice culture that persisted into the nineteenth. The pictures of the later day portray the earlier practice. In the spring the first labor was to repair old ditches and run new ones to facilitate the flooding of the fields. The main flood gates that held back the water in the big reservoir were inspected, and the lesser flood gates in the canals put in order. The work must be done early for there would be scant opportunity during the growing season.

LABOR OF THE GROWING SEASON

THE ditching done, gangs of negro men and women moved up and down the fields cultivating the soil, using in the eighteenth century a hoe, but, in the nineteenth, on the more progressive plantations following the more efficient plow. The upturned soil was trenched for planting and negroes trotted up and down the rows dropping in the seed. Then the "sprout water" was let in and allowed to stand for eight or nine days. When it was drawn off the rice was left dry until it put out leaf. Again the

111 Hoeing Rice, from *Harper's Weekly*, Jan. 5, 1867, after a drawing by A. R. Waud

flood gates were opened and the "stretch water" covered the fields, drawing the young plant up until the desired height was reached. The "stretch water" was then drawn off slowly to prevent the falling of the stalks which it had helped to support. In a week or so the ground was dry enough for the first hoeing which was immediately followed by the second. Then, intermittently, the fields were flooded and drained until the "harvest water" was let in which stood upon the fields until the grain had matured. Then, for the last time the water was drawn off. Rice culture was thus a complicated process requiring considerable judgment on the part of the manager who supervised the raising of the crop. A rice field represented a considerable investment of capital in ditches, dykes, and water gates. The plantation system with its large areas and its supply of labor was better adapted than the small farm to the raising of this grain.

112 Rice Fields Flooded, from *Harper's Weekly*, Jan. 5, 1867, after a drawing by A. R. Waud

THE RICE HARVEST

THE negroes were hurried into the fields as soon as the ground had dried after the draining off of the "harvest water." The ripe grain must be cut and threshed at once. Fortunate the planter who had his crop out of the fields before the sky was darkened by flocks of bobolinks, "rice birds," flying southward to escape the northern winter. Into the primitive rice mill went the sheaves where the kernels were whipped from the straw.

113

From *Harper's Weekly*, Jan. 5, 1867, after a drawing by A. R. Waud
A. REAPING   B. THRESHING MILL

A SOUTH CAROLINA RICE MILL, 1802

RICE threshing was as primitive as its cultivation. Ordinarily, during colonial times, the straw was pounded with flails leaving the grain still encased in heavy husks which were rubbed off in great mortars. Then the chaff was winnowed out by hand. The illustration shows a more complicated machine in use at the end of the eighteenth century. It was a tide mill

114   From J. Drayton, *A View of South Carolina*, Charleston, 1802, after a sketch by B. H. Latrobe

and was operated by an undershot wheel when the tide was low. In this mill the grain in husk fell from the loft above whence it passed to a mill stone which stripped off the outer covering. Below the stone was a fanning mill which winnowed the grain and beyond that a bin for holding the cleaned product. On the left were mortars where the rice was beaten before being put into barrels.

Anno vicesimo primo

Georgii II. Regis.

An Act for encouraging the making of Indico in the *British* Plantations in *America*.

Whereas the making of Indico in the British Plantations in America would be advantageous to the Trade of this Nation, as great Quantities are used in dying the Manufactures of this Kingdom; which at present being furnished from Foreign Parts, the Supply of that necessary Commodity is become at all Times uncertain, and the Price frequently exorbitant: And whereas the Culture thereof has been found to succeed so well in the Provinces of South and North Carolina, that there is Reason to hope, by a proper Encouragement, the same may be encreased and improved to such a Degree, as not only to answer all the Demands of His Majesty's British Subjects, but furnish considerable Quantities to Foreign Markets; be it therefore enacted by the King's most Excellent Majesty, by and with the Advice and Consent of the Lords Spiritual and Temporal, and Commons, in this present Parliament assembled, and by the Authority of the same, That from and after the Twenty fifth Day of March, One thousand seven hundred and forty nine, all and every Person or Persons who shall import, or cause to be imported into this Kingdom, directly from any of the British Colonies or Plantations in America, in any Ship or Vessel, Ships or Vessels, that may lawfully trade to His Majesty's Plantations, manned as by Law is required, any good and merchantable Indico, free from any false Mixtures, and fit for Dyers Use, being the Growth or Product of the Colony or Plantation from whence the same is imported, shall have, and be intitled to, a Reward or Præmium for such Importation, after the Rate of Six Pence for every Pound Weight of such Indico so imported as aforesaid, under such Regulations as are herein after-mentioned, to be paid upon Demand to the Importer of such Indico, by the Collector of the Port where the same shall be imported, out of the Customs;

6d. per Pound Præmium, allowed on the Importation of Indico, of the Growth of the British Plantations

(P.)   and

ROYAL ENCOURAGEMENT TO INDIGO PLANTING

IN the middle of the eighteenth century indigo became a crop second only to rice in importance in the life of colonial South Carolina. The British government, anxious to shake off dependence on foreign supply for this indispensable dye product, urged indigo culture in the southern colonies. Upon the offering of a bounty the crop became established.

THE INDIGO PLANT

INDIGO is a shrub that grows three or four feet high, with bluish green leaves. It bears small pods which contain much of the coloring matter. In these latter days of cheap production of dyes from coal tar indigo is no longer the indispensable plant that it was in early times. In its time, however, this shrub contributed greatly to the prosperity of the Carolinians. The traveler found it growing on numberless farms and plantations.

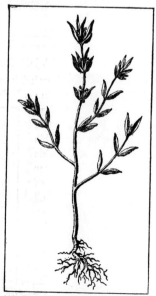

116   From *Proceedings* of the Académie Royale des Sciences, Vol. XXIII, Paris, 1770

MANUFACTURE OF INDIGO
IN SOUTH CAROLINA, 1770

A GENERAL perspective of the indigo machine appears in Fig. 1; the well for water in Fig. 2 and the drying shed in Fig. 3. Figure 4 shows the machine as seen from above and Fig. 5 a cross section. The machine is divided into three main parts, the rotting vat, A; the beating vat, B; and the drying room, C. "After the indigo is cut it is put into a vat (A) to be soaked. This vat is then filled with water. At the end of twelve or sixteen hours the indigo begins to ferment and rise. The rising is stopped by means of cross bars placed over the vat (GG HH). After the fermentation has reached its maximum, a stop-cock (E) is opened, and the water flows into the battoir or beating vat (B). The weed from the first vat is

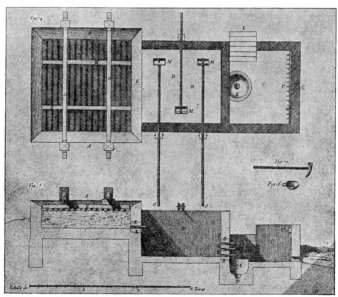

117   From *Proceedings* of the Académie Royale des Sciences, Paris, Vol. XXIII, 1770, articles on *L'Art de l'Indigotter*

used as fertilizer. In the battoir the indigo juice is beaten with ladles (M) until it becomes foamy and rises above the level of the container. To stop the violence of the fermentation oil is poured over the water. After about thirty or thirty-five minutes of heating, crystals form. [The liquid is tested by scooping out a little with the tip of a horn (Fig. 7) and examining it in a silver cup (Fig. 6).] The liquid is then drained through the stop-cocks (XXX) and the sediment settles in the vat (KP). The sediment is then put into bags to dry, which are hung on pegs (U)." — WILLIAM BURCK (translation from a paper presented by him before the Académie Royale des Sciences, Paris).

118   Lower Brandon, built 1730, © Detroit Photographic Company

A SOUTHERN PLANTER'S RESIDENCE, 1730

INDIGO and rice in the Carolinas and tobacco in Virginia and Maryland were foundations on which a new American aristocracy reared itself. The customs and ideals of the gentry of old England found congenial environment on the warm, rich coast plain between the southern Appalachians and the sea. Lower Brandon built on the James River in 1730 typifies the surroundings of the rising planter-aristocrats.

WASHINGTON'S HOME AT MOUNT VERNON

GREATEST among Virginians was Washington, whose home overlooked the quiet Potomac. Like many of his planter friends, he traced his origin to an English family of rank. Like them, also, he had many acres, many indentured servants and many slaves. But, unlike a large number of his neighbors, he was not satisfied merely to use the first richness of the newly cleared field and, when it was cropped out, to let it grow up again to underbrush. One of the deepest interests of the soldier-statesman lay in the improvement of his farming. He managed his estate with meticulous care; he corresponded with men in England and America who were in the van of agricultural progress; he experimented for himself. Had his countrymen not demanded so much of him, he would have been one of the greatest of the little band of pioneers who at the end of the eighteenth century laid in America the foundation of agricultural science.

119   From Isaac Weld, *Travels Through the States of North America,*
London, 1799

Washington like the other planters prided himself on his hospitality. Travelers were frequent visitors at the estates of these wealthy landowners. Isaac Weld, who visited Mount Vernon in 1795, while Washington was held at the national capital by his presidential duties, says of his reception there: "As almost every stranger going through the country makes a point of visiting Mount Vernon, a person is kept at the house during General Washington's absence whose sole business it is to attend to strangers. Immediately on our arrival every care was taken of our horses, beds were prepared, and an excellent supper provided for us, with claret and other wine."

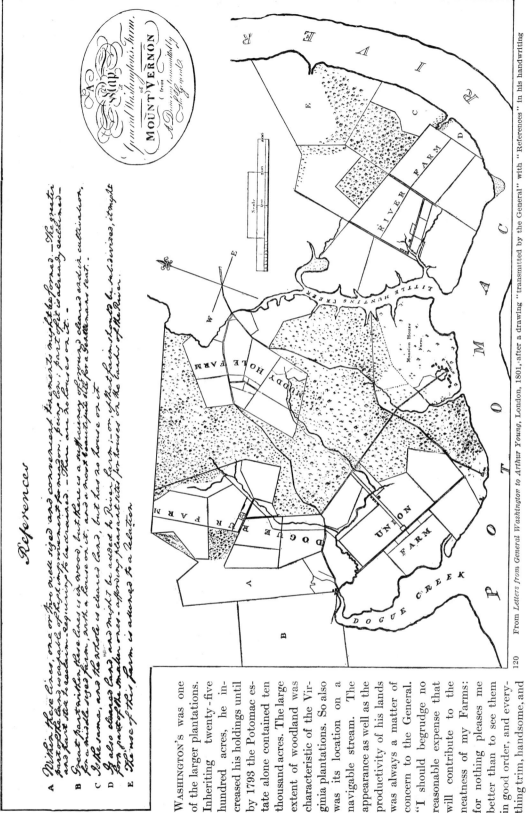

THE WASHINGTON PLANTATION

From *Letters from General Washington to Arthur Young*, London, 1801, after a drawing "transmitted by the General" with "References" in his handwriting

WASHINGTON'S was one of the larger plantations. Inheriting twenty-five hundred acres, he increased his holdings until by 1793 the Potomac estate alone contained ten thousand acres. The large extent of woodland was characteristic of the Virginia plantations. So also was its location on a navigable stream. The appearance as well as the productivity of his lands was always a matter of concern to the General. "I should begrudge no reasonable expense that will contribute to the neatness of my Farms; for nothing pleases me better than to see them in good order, and everything trim, handsome, and thriving about them."

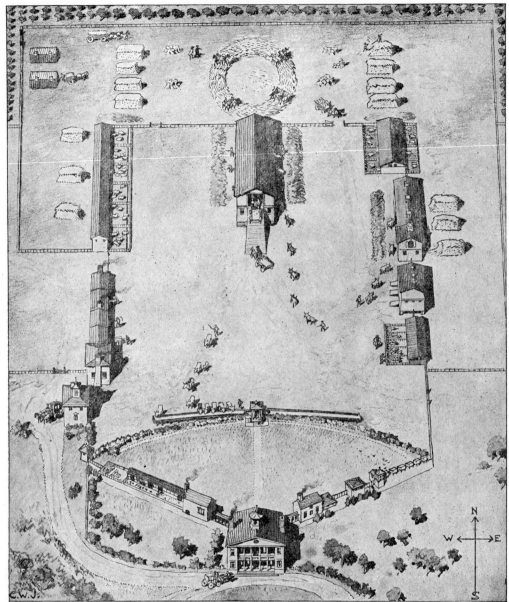

121   A reconstruction by C. W. Jefferys, after a diagram in J. B. Bordley, *Essays and Notes on Husbandry and Rural Affairs*,
                                                    Philadelphia, 1799

BIRD'S-EYE VIEW OF IDEAL PLANTATION BUILDINGS

JOHN BORDLEY, planter and one of the prominent writers on agriculture at the end of the eighteenth century, laid out an ideal scheme for a Maryland plantation on which tobacco was not the sole crop. In the foreground stands the mansion. To the left are the kitchen, poultry house and wood yard; to the right the smokehouse, milk house, ice house, pigeon house and bee hives. Back of the hives stand, in order, the house and pens for brood sows, the granary, the stable for the draught animals and the cow house and the pig pens. The barn, with an elevated approach, is directly behind the mansion. Beyond it are straw ricks and a threshing floor. In the corner of the orchard to the left are root cellars. Near them are the sheep house and yard, with three hay ricks beside it. Between the sheep house and the mansion grounds stand, in order, the herdsman's hovel, the work shop, the tool house and the carriage house all under one roof. The chaise house and stables for the riding and driving horses are beside the lane that leads to the mansion door. By the hedge in the rear of the mansion house are the pump and the watering trough for the stock.

THOMAS, THE SIXTH LORD FAIRFAX

NEXT the Washington pew in the parish church was that of the Fairfax family. Lord Fairfax, after spending his early life in the brilliant society of London, had come out to Virginia and lived, a lonely old man, at Greenway Court in the Shenandoah Valley. His title passed to the succeeding generations during the colonial period. The Fairfax family was one of the many links between the aristocracy of the Old World and the New.

122 Lord Fairfax, from the copyright portrait in the possession of Alexandria-Washington Lodge, No. 22, A. F. & A. M., Alexandria, Va.

"KING" CARTER

123 Robert Carter, from the portrait by Sir Joshua Reynolds (1723–92) in the possession of Mrs. R. Carter Wellford, Sabine Hall, Warsaw, Va., courtesy of the Frick Art Reference Library

ROBERT CARTER, known over Virginia as "King" Carter, was in his day probably the richest man in the province. "Councilman Carter owned, we are told, some sixty thousand acres situated in nearly every county in Virginia, six hundred negroes, lands in the neighborhood of Williamsburg, an 'elegant and spacious' house in the same city, stock in the Baltimore Iron Works, and several farms in Maryland. It was not at all uncommon for men in one county or colony to own land in another, for even in New England the owners of town lands were not always residents of the town in which the lands were situated." — CHARLES M. ANDREWS, *Colonial Folkways*, The Chronicles of America Series, New Haven, 1920.

"AFTER–CHURCH GOSSIP"

THERE was a charm about the plantation life of old Virginia that seldom failed to impress travelers. The planters, like the folk of all thinly settled rural communities, were hospitable to a fault and the latch strings of the "great houses" were always out for the stranger, who could stay as long as he pleased. Writing of Virginia about 1700, Robert Beverly said: "A stranger has no more to do but to enquire upon the road where any gentleman or good housekeeper lives and there he may depend upon being received with hospitality. This good nature is so general among these people that the gentry when they go abroad order their principal servant to entertain all visitors with everything the plantation offers. And the poor planters who have but one bed will very often sit up or lie upon a form or couch all night to make room for the weary traveler to repose himself after his journey." The guest recompensed his host by the news he brought. On Sabbath days, when church was over, the gossip of the neighborhood was exchanged; the London tobacco market surveyed, and the politics of the colony discussed.

124 From the painting by Thure de Thulstrup (1848–) in possession of James Barnes, Princeton, N. J., by permission of the successors of Goupil & Co., Paris

VIRGINIA IN THE OLDEN TIME

It could be gay, too, in old Virginia. At any time friends from afar might drive up to the door in a coach and four or six, following close upon the gentlemen who had ridden ahead. What with children and young people, the coachman and footmen, and the maids for the ladies, the arrival of guests, nearly always unannounced and unexpected, presented problems which the hostess must be prepared to meet. Yet such arrivals were the commonplaces of life. Perhaps the company would stay a day, perhaps a week.

125   From the painting by Alfred Wordsworth Thompson (1840–96) in the possession of J. McAlpin Pyle, Morristown, N. J.

A bountiful table would be spread; there would be much drinking and many toasts by the gentlemen; and, in the evenings, the negro fiddlers would call the dances. There were jigs and reels. Old and young swung their partners in the picturesque country dances and quadrilles. But the favorite was the immensely popular "Sir Roger de Coverley," in later years known as the Virginia Reel.

THE COURTSHIP OF WASHINGTON

Virginia customs of courtship were reminiscent of the etiquette of the English gentry. If a young cavalier desired to pay court to the maiden of his choice, he first informed his father who promptly wrote the lady's parent. If the alliance was acceptable, the elder gentlemen agreed as to the amounts they would settle upon the couple if the young gentleman succeeded in his wooing. He was then free to put his hand and heart

to the hazard. Much simpler were the formalities of paying court to a widow, for she was the disposer of her own hand. Young George Washington met a succession of damsels by whose "sparkling eyes" he was "undone." But he seemed unlucky in love. Finally, in the French and Indian War, after he had become a military hero, he met at Williamsburg, where so many of the planters had their town houses, the young Martha Custis, wealthy and recently widowed. They became acquainted in March and were engaged before the month ran out. In the following January Martha Custis became the mistress of Mount Vernon.

126   From the painting by J. L. G. Ferris (1863–) in Independence Hall, Philadelphia

127   From the painting by J. L. G. Ferris in Independence Hall, Philadelphia

THE MARRIAGE CONTRACT

In Virginia, as in England, the banns of matrimony were thrice published but it became the habit among the young folks of the plantations to avoid the publication by obtaining a special license. The wedding was a time of festivity. The establishment of a new fireside was the symbol of the prosperity of the colony. The bride, after listening with many blushes to a marriage sermon preached in honor of her wedding, assumed the dignity of the mistress of a household. She took charge of the servants and directed the entertainment of her many guests. She supervised the cooking and baking, the making of butter and the putting down of preserves. She watched over the weaving and the making of clothing for the slaves and for the persons of the family. She must be nurse and doctor to the sick in the great house and in the negro cabins. The badge of her au-

thority was the basket of keys that she carried on her wrist. These opened the closets where the linen and clothing were kept, the cellar where the provisions were set to cool, and the smokehouse from whose cross-beams hung the hams and bacon that graced her table.

CHILDREN'S EDUCATION

When the children came, they were cared for by the negro mammy or the white indentured servants. As they grew older, they recited their lessons to a tutor who lived with the family and who was also frequently an indentured servant. The boys sometimes went to college at William and Mary, and often crossed the sea to England for their education. The children were taught to dance by masters (often indentured servants) who went from plantation to plantation. The little girls were trained in sewing and other accomplishments necessary for the mistress of a great house. Little Martha Carter Fitzhugh was but seven years old when she laid aside this sampler and slipped into another world.

128   A Cross-stitch Sampler, from the collections of the Essex Institute, Salem, Mass.

129 From the painting by Alfred Wordsworth Thompson (1840–96) in the Metropolitan Museum of Art, New York

OLD BRUTON CHURCH, WILLIAMSBURG, TIME OF LORD DUNMORE

WILLIAMSBURG was the political and social capital of colonial Virginia and at one time or another in the pews of Old Bruton Church sat the *élite* of the province. The coaches that brought the planters' families to worship were drawn by pairs and often by spans of four or six horses. Sometimes, however, the lady rode behind her husband seated on a pillion, and often she had her own mount. There were also chariots and chairs. At Williamsburg and Bruton Church the planter aristocracy of Virginia appeared to be one great family.

130 From the painting by Thure de Thulstrup in the possession of James Barnes, Princeton, N. J., by permission of the successors of Goupil & Co., Paris

"WHEN QUALITY GOES TO TOWN"

ONE of the attractions which drew the planter to Williamsburg was the meeting of the House of Burgesses. To the occupants of the estates scattered along tidewater, sessions of the House offered an opportunity to meet and discuss the latest political gossip. They rode into town to attend to their political duties and incidentally the social functions of the capital. The cumbersome coaches driven by postillions were occupied by the ladies, their escorts riding alongside.

131   From the painting by Thure de Thulstrup in the possession of James Barnes, Princeton, N. J.;
by permission of the successors of Goupil & Co., Paris

"AFTER THE LADIES LEFT THE TABLE"

THE Virginia aristocracy of the eighteenth century aped the vices as well as the virtues of the contemporary nobility of England. But they were not effete as the lords at New Spain became — the American aristocracy was too near its vigorous origin for that. The picture shows a scene typical of European as well as American social life of the period. A party at Westover have just finished their repast. The ladies have retired and the men remain about the table to smoke and drink punch, while they talk politics or enjoy a good story. The host, Colonel Byrd, is seated at the right exchanging banter with a young guest. The Reverend John Dunbar — "Sporting parson" and boon companion of the colonel — is enjoying the dialogue.

A VIRGINIA PLANTER, 1740

CARDS and gambling were favorite pastimes. At taverns or "ordinaries" as they were commonly called, or at the home of a friend, the young bloods would play through the night losing perhaps prodigious sums of money. The eighteenth century was a drinking age, and wines, cider, beer, flips and a host of other concoctions played an important rôle in the social life of the colonies. Cock-fighting and horse racing were popular sports among the planters, who were very proud of their fighting birds and their horses.

132   After the painting by Howard Pyle, for Woodrow Wilson,
A History of the American People, 1901.   © Harper & Bros.

133   From the painting *Washington's Silver Wedding*, by J. L. G. Ferris in Independence Hall, Philadelphia

THE VIRGINIA ARISTOCRACY

THE Virginia aristocracy contributed heavily to that small group of able men who fought the Revolution and established the new nation. With all the faults of the planters there was a quality in their heritage and a fineness of texture in their society which produced men of large mind and broad sympathies. Yet from first to last they were men of the soil, despising commercial pursuits and the wrangling of the marts of trade.

At the end of the century one of their number, John Bordley of Maryland, wrote: "Commerce feeds the passions; agriculture calms them."

WILLIAM BYRD, 2ND, OF WESTOVER, 1674–1744

NOR were the planters devoid of literary culture. On the bookshelves of the great house the best literature of the day might be met with. Daniel Parke Custis, the first husband of Mrs. Washington, left a library including the works of Fuller, Smollett, Defoe, Dryden, Bacon, Pope, Swift, Johnson, Shakespeare and Milton. Works in Latin and Greek were abundant. William Byrd, 2nd, was an author as well as a

134 From the portrait attributed to Sir Godfrey Kneller (1646–1723) at Shirley, Va.

planter and man of affairs. His *History of the Dividing Line, A Journey to the Land of Eden* and *A Progress to the Mines* present lively pictures of the Virginia in which he was so important a figure.

A BACK–COUNTRY CABIN

IN the back-country between the broad plantations and the mountains lived the poor folk of the frontier. By hunting and a little farming on their half cleared acres they supplied the needs of a restricted life. About these primitive cabins played a swarm of children. Amid such surroundings Thomas Lincoln and Nancy Hanks were born and reared.

135   From C. C. Coffin: *Old Times in the Colonies*, New York, 1880, drawing by H. M. Snyder

CHAPTER IV

PLAIN FOLK OF THE SOIL

IN the country south of the Potomac agricultural conditions brought forth an aristocracy, but to the north the small farmer of humble origin and simple aspirations predominated. If not so gay and brilliant, the life of these common folk was as significant as that of the planters. By a curious destiny the most sympathetic record of these eighteenth-century tillers of the soil has been left to posterity by a gentleman who lived with them and became one of them. Hector St. John de Crèvecœur, a young French aristocrat and seeker of adventure, found his way to America during the French and Indian War. After the conflict was over he lived with his American bride on a farm in the rich province of New York. Farming and writing were his chief pleasures, and just before and during the early part of the Revolution he wrote with singular perception and rare beauty of the life of the people with whom he had cast his lot. His *Letters from an American Farmer* were a success in his own day and have become classic. But the published book says little of the real life of his neighbors. It is in the unpublished essays that for nearly a century and a half have gathered dust in the libraries of his descendants that the old American farmer stands forth in all his simplicity and uncouthness, in all his vigor and rugged strength.

Life was not easy on the northern farms. The years brought a round of unremitting toil. On the small farms of a hundred or two hundred acres the husbandman produced practically all the things that the family needed — heavy work for both the farmer and his wife. But the Americans of the day were equal to the task. They supported themselves in independence. Their tables were heavy with the plain fare that their farms produced. They had their "frolicks" and their round of social pleasures. With all its hardships and labor and in spite of the curse of heavy drinking which characterized the age, life was sound and wholesome. On the farms and in the homes of the eighteenth-century husbandmen were laid securely the foundations of a great nation.

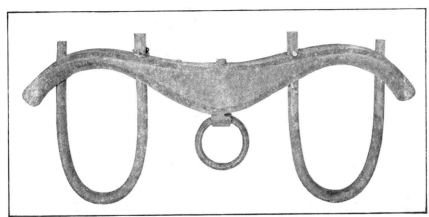

136   An Old Ox-Yoke, from the collection of the Worcester (Mass.) Historical Society

69

MIDDLETOWN — A NEW ENGLAND VILLAGE

In the northern colonies, as the frontier pushed westwards, life in the little villages of the seventeenth century settled into well worn grooves. Some men became more prosperous than their neighbors. The equality of the old frontier days was modified. Yet, after all, there was little difference between the extremes of wealth. In

137   From J. W. Barber, *Connecticut Historical Collections*, New Haven, 1836

the Hudson valley were a few rich planters like those of Virginia, but the folk of the New England villages were nearly all small farmers or artisans for whom life was a round of hard and unremitting toil. The carpenters and blacksmiths and even the ministers and doctors eked out a living by farming. Middletown lay on the bank of the Connecticut, in touch, through the sailing craft of the river, with the stirring world of trade. Commerce brought a vigor and stir to the river town unknown to the inland village a score or more of miles away. In such old towns, whose records often ran back for a century and more, life was quiet, almost static, reminiscent of the sleepy vills of the English manors.

BETHLEHEM, A MORAVIAN SETTLEMENT IN PENNSYLVANIA

Not all these towns were English. To the Dutch and Swedes of the seventeenth century were added the Germans and Scotch-Irish of the eighteenth. The newcomers passed through the older settlements and built their villages on the frontier. They brought with them the traditional knowledge of their homelands. But, in its essentials, agriculture varied little among the peoples of western Europe, and the husbandry of the German villages in New York and Pennsylvania and throughout the back-country of Virginia and the Carolinas did not differ greatly from that of the small farmers of English stock in the northern colonies.

138   From Isaac Weld, *Travels Through the States of North America*, London, 1799

139   From the painting *Light Triumphant*, by George Inness (1825–94), courtesy of Scott and Fowles, New York

THE FARMSTEAD

In the eighteenth century a change came over the countryside of the northern colonies. The pioneers generally had lived in small villages about which lay their fields. Now more and more the farmer built his house in the midst of his acres, perhaps a mile, perhaps two or three, from the center. The compact village community, which had been brought from Europe, was modified and, in adjustment to the conditions of the New World, along the country roads appeared the farmsteads characteristic of later America. More than ever the family group stood out as the most important economic and social unit in the life of the people. In a peculiar sense the home was the institution on which the nation was built. The typical northern farm contained from one hundred to two hundred acres. There was no possibility and no pretext of cultivating this area intensively. Extensive husbandry and self-sufficiency were the outstanding characteristics of the farmsteads north of the Potomac.

140   From a photograph by Clifton Johnson

LEACHING ASHES

In the spring the farmer's household turned its thoughts to the work ahead. The ash barrel by the kitchen door came again into use. The custom of leaching ashes long clung to the frontier. The drippings from the well-soaked ashes contained lye which, after boiling in great iron kettles, the farmer's wife used in the manufacture of soap.

141   From the *New York Gazette or Weekly Post Boy,*
March 17, 1768

FARM FOR SALE, 1768

SPRING was a time for vendues, at which farms and household goods were put up at auction. Perhaps a farmer had died. Perhaps the family was leaving the community to try its fortune elsewhere. Concealed behind the formal little notices in the colonial papers are the stories, often tragic enough, of those who for one reason or another found their lives out of adjustment with their surroundings. To the able-bodied family who had failed in the old home the frontier always offered an opportunity to start afresh.

SHEEP SHEARING

THE sheep which had been folded in little sheds during the long winter or had been left to shift for themselves in the open were brought together for the shearing. During the cold months the farmer had given them each day a little hay or rough fodder from his threshed grain. When this had given out, he had fed them on pine boughs from the woods. A thin and scrawny flock survived the winter season, reduced by exposure and

the depredations of the wolves. But the cold had given the sheep a thick fleece which, in the spring, was sheared off and turned over to the housewife for manufacture into the woolens that the family needed. In due time the wool was transformed into the blue and white checked shirt and the deep blue stockings that the farmer wore in winter or the heavy shawl and coat of his wife.

142   From the *Farmer's Almanac,* about 1820, after a woodcut by
Alexander Anderson (1775–1870)

CATTLE IN PASTURE, CONNECTICUT

WHEN the snow was off the ground and the busy season approached, the dry cattle and young stock were driven off to the mountains or some common pasture like Hempstead Plain or Montauk Point to graze during the summer. Thither, once a week, many a farmer went to salt them, which kept them used to human kind and prevented their becoming utterly wild. In the autumn they were brought back, some to be slaughtered and their meat smoked or put down in brine.

143   From a print in the possession of the publishers

THE PLOW

When the frost had left the ground and the buds were swelling, the farmer got out his awkward plow, rusted from the inaction of the winter, and turned his attention to the fields. Sometimes the plow was all of wood, but more often the point and mold-board were shod with strips of iron. The custom of the early days, when the great plows were rela-tively rare, was passing, and more and more farmers

144   Plow of Nathanial Harrington (1742–1831) in the Worcester (Mass.) Historical Society

owned the indispensable tool. The two-handled plow was heavy and served to break up rooty and stony land. Two horses and two oxen pulled it back and forth across the field, a boy riding one of the horses and another driving the oxen. A farmer of New York wrote, a little before the Revolution: "The one-handled plough is the most common in all level soyls; it is drawn by either two or three horses abreast. . . . Three horses abreast is the most expeditious as well as the Strongest Team we know of for common land. We cross Plough with Two Horses, commonly 1½ acres a day." Plowing at best was heavy work with the clumsy tools of the eighteenth century. Very often the land was little more than scratched. As the fields grew old with cropping, the shallow and unlevel furrows gave less and less promise of a bountiful autumn harvest.

145   Minute Man Plow, 1775, in the Essex Institute, Salem, Mass.

146   Plow entirely of wood in the Lexington (Mass.) Historical Society

HARROWING

Farming has often been called the most conservative of occupations. Here and there on the fields of the twentieth century can be seen the husbandry of the eighteenth. Harrows, square and triangular, some with wooden and others with iron teeth, were dragged back and forth across the plowed land, pulverizing the clods. It was slow and tedious business.

147   From a photograph by Rudolf Eickemeyer

148 From the *Farmer's Almanac*, about 1820, after a woodcut by
Alexander Anderson

THE SOWER

OUT of antiquity has come the sower with his bag or bucket, walking in straight lines back and forth across the fields and swinging his arm in time with his stride. Out of antiquity also has come the most beautiful appreciation of the meaning of his labor. "And as he sowed, some seed fell on the road and was trampled down, and the wild birds ate it up; some other seed dropped on the rock, but it withered away when it sprang up because it had no moisture; some other seed fell among thorns, and the thorns sprang up along with it and choked it; some other seed fell on sound soil, and springing up bore a crop, a hundredfold."

FARM PESTS

SPRING brought a promise to the independent farmer of America. He need not fear that his growing crops would be trampled and ruined by a fox-hunt of the nobility. But nature, as yet untamed, was full of dangers. There were foxes, muskrats, skunks and weasels to prey upon his poultry. Wolves, not yet wholly withdrawn from the settlements, threatened his sheep. Bears sometimes visited his calf-pens or climbed his apple trees when the fruit was large, breaking the limbs by their weight. Crows and blackbirds flocked to his fields of young corn. As it ripened, black and grey squirrels came out of the woodlands to gather the kernels. Life for the farmer was a struggle, not only in preparing the soil and keeping down the hostile weeds, but in protecting his crops and stock from the depredations of wild life. Often the individual farmer was unable to cope with the animal and bird enemies of his environment. Parties were organized to go into the woods to exterminate the squirrels. Bounties were placed on the heads of wolves. Out of this conflict came an independence and a self-reliance that began to set off the American husbandman from the European peasant.

149 From William Faden, *The North American Atlas*, London, 1777

150   From the painting, 1870, by Samuel P. Scott, in the Mattatuck Historical Society, Waterbury, Conn.

SUMMER — BEFORE THE HAYING

WHEN the planting season was over and the growing crops were well out of the ground, the eighteenth-century farmer had a lull before "haying" began. He usually went hunting or fishing in the streams. Crèvecœur spent a week alone in the woods in search of bee trees and brought home many pounds of exquisitely flavored wild honey which his wife used in making the liquors which he offered his guests. Then as the hot weeks of early June slipped by, the farmer-essayist took down his scythes and rakes from the pegs where they hung and struck into the meadows.

151   From a photograph by the United States Department of Agriculture

TIMOTHY

THE seventeenth-century farmer had used for his fodder the vigorous but not nutritious native grasses. In the first half of the eighteenth century Timothy Hanson, of New Hampshire, took to New York, Maryland and Virginia an Old World grass that had first been used as a hay plant by a man named Herd living near Portsmouth, New Hampshire. Timothy, as the grass came to be called, spread rapidly over the farms of the colonies. Clover, another imported grass, also grew on many meadows. The spread of these two cultivated grasses meant larger haystacks beside the farmer's barns and more winter fodder for his ill-kept sheep and cows.

152   From the painting by Winslow Homer, courtesy of
Frederic Fairchild Sherman, New York

HAYMAKING

On a June morning the mowers let down the bars in the weather-beaten fence and entered the field of waving grass. "Haying" had begun. Hour after hour the scythes swung steadily in long, full sweep. The scythe blade was in most cases the work of the local blacksmith; its awkward handle was contrived by the husbandman himself on a winter's evening. From time to time rang out the sound of the whetstone on the blade. In echelon the mowers made the circuit of the field. The good workman kept his selvage straight and his corners sharp. Mowing was an art, and like the artisans whose craft traditions ran back to the Middle Ages, the mowers were proud of their workmanship. Yet many eighteenth-century farmers were slovenly workmen, tillers of ill-kept farms. The vast task which confronted them and the meager labor supply gave them little leisure for the niceties of their vocation. Haying was a time of exhilaration, the beginning of the fulfillment of spring promise.

DRAWING HAY

In the late morning, when the dew was off the grass, the farmer drew his hay. He piled it on the ox cart or the four-wheeled wagon which was found on almost every farm. His plodding teams made such haste as they could from field to farmyard where the hay was piled in stacks. Scudding thunder showers meant serious injury to the winter's forage. Along the New England shore "salt mash," the tough grass of the salt meadows, was cut for winter use.

153   After the painting *The Berkshire Hills*, by George Inness, formerly in the collection of George A. Hearn

154

AN OX TEAM IN THE HAYFIELD

HERE and there in agricultural America may be seen in the twentieth century the oxen and the hand rakes of the eighteenth. Slowly and laboriously the hay is gathered as it has been for generations. Slowly and laboriously also it is pitched by hand off the load into the waiting mow.

FARMER AND HIRED MEN NOONING

LABORERS were hired at high wages for the busy haying season. Help was scarce in eighteenth-century America. Side by side with his negro and his hired man labored the farmer. All drank of the jug of beer or cider that his wife sent out to the hayfield. The day's work done, the slaves went to their quarters, while the husbandman invited his laborers to sit at his own table. Thus early was the spirit of equality born. Should the farmer spread a separate board, he might lose his help. Travelers from Europe observed the custom and commented adversely upon the democratic ways of Americans.

155   From the painting *The Farmers' Nooning*, by W. S. Mount (1807–68) in the possession of Frederick Sturges, Jr., New York

TO Be fold, — a likely Negro Wench, about 37 Years of Age, fit for all forts of Houfe Work, and is a tolerable good Cook; fhe can be well recommended,   mII

TO BE SOLD,

A LIKELY young fturdy Negro Wench, about 19 years of Age, fit for Town or Country; She is a trufty Wench, and, with a little Inftruction, being young, may be of great fervice to any Family in Town. Enquire of Weyman, in Broad-Street.

TO BE SOLD,

A Likely negro Man, his Wife and Child; the negro Man capable of doing all forts of Plantation Work, and a good Miller: The Woman exceeding fit for a Farmer, being capable of doing any Work, belonging to a Houfe in the Country, at reafonable Rates, inquire of the Printer hereof.

156   From the *New York Gazette*, March 10, 1765   157   From *The Pennsylvania Journal*, Feb. 8, 1743

SLAVERY AND INDENTURED SERVANTS

THE problem of labor was insistent. Both negro slaves and indentured servants were to be found in every northern colony. Notices of a "very likely negro wench" for sale, and of some "artful fellow" who has run away, were of common occurrence in the newspapers of the northern colonies. The same problem, scarcity of help for work, brought slavery to both the northern and southern provinces.

HOEING THE CROP

ONE of the hardest summer labors of the farm was the hoeing necessary in the corn and in the small crops of the garden. There were no horse-drawn machines to expedite the work. The husbandman must combat the persistent weeds with only a simple hand tool. Before haying and again between haying and harvest, hoeing must be done. The farmer had need of many hands to meet the varied labors of the summer. Anderson's crude cut suggests not only the task of hand cultivation but the bird pests of the countryside.

158   From a woodcut by Alexander Anderson

A NEW ENGLAND PASTURE

THROUGH the still summer days the milch cows grazed in the meadows or stood for hours in the cool water of a quiet stream. At night they were driven home where the housewife milked them. She made her own butter and cheese. The skim milk after the cream had been taken went to feed the calf or the pet lamb that the children were raising. Pests there were even here. The uncleared woodland, the swamps that had not been reclaimed, and the salt meadows that bordered the coast bred mosquitos. Crèvecœur wrote to his friends in England that he had seen cattle milked in the evening inside a circle of smoking fires. Weary from the heavy work of haying, the farmer, in the days before screens were placed at doors and windows, came home to spend the evening in a room thick with smoke from a smudge built in the fireplace, and to fight the tiny insect scourge through the hot hours of a summer night.

159   From an engraving, 1872, by R. Hinshelwood after the painting *On the Housatonic*, by James M. Hart (1828–1901)

SHEEP

On the fields and in the lanes grazed the sheep, a scrawny, mongrel lot. They cropped the grass so close that the knolls and hillocks changed from green to brown. As the summer wore on, the spring lambs grew to maturity, some destined to furnish mutton and wool, and others to join next year's flock on the hills.

160   From a retouched woodcut by Alexander Anderson

161   The Sickle, from the *Farmer's Almanac*, about 1820, after a woodcut
by Alexander Anderson

THE HARVEST

CLOSE on the heels of haying came the harvest. In the early pioneering days the reaper had cut the yellow fields of wheat and rye and oats with a sickle little different from that used in Boaz' field where Ruth had gleaned. But, by the eighteenth century, the cradle, still used on out-of-the-way farms, shortened the task of cutting the grain. With a long, sure sweep the cradler cut and laid the straw in gavels for binding. With a wisp of straw the binder deftly secured his sheaves, which were piled into orderly shocks. Harvest, like haying, was a season of heavy manual labor hurried by the danger of rains that might spoil the crop before it could be gotten under shelter.

162   Cradling Grain, from a photograph by Rudolf Eickemeyer

163 From Henry R. Stiles, *The History of Ancient Wethersfield, Connecticut*, New York, 1904, after a drawing by Samuel Broadbent

BRINGING IN THE HARVEST

PILED high on wagons which on Sunday, after a change of body, took the farmer's family to church, the harvest jolted to the farmyard. Wheat was cut in July, but usually September was waning before oats were in. The crops were generally poor. Shallow plowing and unintelligent cropping soon exhausted the fertility of the richest mould. The farmer seeking speedily to win from his acres satisfaction for almost all his family's needs had little time for experiment or the reading of learned discourses. So, with something of the same conservatism that had held the English peasant to the ways of his ancestors, he went on from year to year following the methods that had been hit on in the first years of settlement.

FALL PLOWING

IN August and September the fallow was plowed and winter wheat was sown.

A lonely task it is to plow!
All day the black and shining soil
Rolls like a ribbon from the mould-board's
Glistening curve. All day the horses toil
And battle with the flies, and strain
Their creeking harnesses. All day
The crickets jeer from the wind-blown shocks of grain.
—HAMLIN GARLAND, *Prairie Songs*, 1893

Before winter laid its blanket of snow over the fields, some were green with the crop of another year.

164 From a woodcut by Alexander Anderson

THRESHING

THRESHING followed the harvest and the crisp November days heard the rhythmic beating of the flails, or the steady tread of the animals on the threshing floor. After the threshing the straw was tossed aside and the grain scooped into the great winnowing baskets. As the kernels spilled over the edge of the baskets the wind blew the chaff away.

Into the bins in the granary was piled the winnowed rye, wheat and oats. The oats were for the animals. Much of the wheat was shipped to the southern colonies or to the West Indies. Rye and corn were the bread grains of the north and "rye and injun" a dish on every farmer's table.

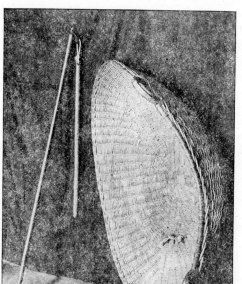

165 A Flail and Winnowing Basket, from the collection of the Lexington (Mass.) Historical Society

166 Beating Grain with Flails, from the *Farmer's Almanac*, after a woodcut by Alexander Anderson

A FARMYARD AFTER THE HARVEST

In the complex life of the twentieth century, where each one has his own small special task in a highly organized society, there are few to appreciate the feelings of the eighteenth-century husbandman in the fall of the year when his crops had been gathered. He was independent. His farm produced what his family required. No man was his master. Around him were his herds and flocks. He knew each individual ani-

167   From *Harper's Weekly*, Jan. 6, 1877, after a drawing by Granville Perkins

mal and had names for many of them. His home was the center of his life.

About him were his family, his wife and children, aiding him and depending upon him. Perhaps beside his own were adopted children or boys and girls, whose parents could not support them, "bound out" to him until they became of age. "Do not blame us for living well," wrote one of them, "upon my word, we richly earn it." Yet there were many homes heavily burdened with debt and the annual interest took from the farmer much of the hard-earned products of his labor.

THE HUSKING BEE

The work of the autumn harvest brought into play the co-operation that characterized the farm life of the eighteenth century. Where labor was scarce it was necessary for folk of separate farms to come together to assist in the performance of certain tasks. None better than Crèvecœur can describe the spirit of the "bee," whether for husking corn, raising a barn, or plowing a sick neighbor's acres. In every case the abundant food and genial fellowship furnished the attraction:

"Poor as we are, if we have not the gorgeous balls, the harmonious concerts, the shrill horn of Europe, yet we dilate our hearts as well with the simple negro fiddle, and with our rum and water, as you do with your delicious wines. In the summer it often happens that either through sickness or accident some families are not able to do all they must do. Are we afraid, for instance, that we shall not be able to break up our summer fallow? In due time we invite a dozen neighbours, who will come with their teams and finish it all in one day. At dinner we give them the best victuals our farm affords; these are feasts the goodness of which greatly depends on the knowledge and ability of our wives. Pies, puddings, fowls, roasted and boiled, — nothing is spared that can evince our gratitude. In the evening the same care is repeated, after which young girls and lads generally come from all parts to unite themselves to the assembly. As they have done no work, they generally come after supper and partake of the general dance." — St. John de Crèvecœur, *Sketches of Eighteenth-Century America*, Yale University Press, 1925.

168   From the painting *Corn Husking at Nantucket*, by Eastman Johnson (1824–1906) in the Metropolitan Museum of Art, New York

169   From *Harper's Weekly*, Nov. 26, 1859, after a drawing by Winslow Homer

THE APPLE BEE

CRÈVECŒUR also describes the apple bees which, as the picture shows, persisted into a later day. "In the fall of the year we dry great quantities, and this is one of those rural occupations which most amply reward us. . . . The neighbouring women are invited to spend the evening at our house. A basket of apples is given to each of them, which they peel, quarter, and core. These peelings and cores are put into another basket and when the intended quantity is thus done, tea, a good supper, and the best things we have are served up. Convivial merriment, cheerfulness, and song never fail to enliven these evenings, and though our bowls contain neither the delicate punch of the West Indies, nor the rich wines of Europe, nevertheless our cider affords us that simpler degree of exhilaration with which we are satisfied."

THE OLD–TIME GRIST MILL

WITH his grain threshed and winnowed the farmer made his way over the dirt roads to the mill. Almost every small stream had a mill somewhere on its course. The rough dam and the great wheel over which the water fell were a source of never-ending interest to the small boy who came with his father to the mill. The miller, usually a farmer as well, took his toll from the "grist" and piled into the sturdy wagon flour for

170 Old Mill, near Salisbury, Conn., from *Picturesque America*, 1874, after a drawing by J. D. Woodward

the family and feed for the animals. With the passing years the old dams have been partly washed away and the mills have tumbled in, but here and there in New England and elsewhere may be found a pile of stones beside a stream and a broken half-rotted wheel, relics of a civilization that has forever passed. In flat country near the sea, where streams were sluggish, appeared the windmills of Europe. The top of the mill turned as the wind shifted and presented the vast sails to the slightest breeze.

171 Grist Windmill at Easthampton, L. I., from *Picturesque America*, 1872, after a drawing by Harry Fenn

GOING TO MARKET — BALTIMORE

His first grain threshed and ground, the farmer set off to market with such produce as he had for sale. Stretching along the coast and sending re-entrant angles inland along the navigable rivers lay a zone in which the farmers found a market for the surplus of their acres. Within this area was progress. The husbandman had a little money with which to buy equipment for his farm, furnishings for his house or pretty things for his wife and daughters. Some clearly foresaw the time when the farm would no longer pro-

172 From John Pinkerton, *A General Collection of the Best and most Interesting Voyages*, London, 1812, after an engraving by G. Cooke

vide the farmer with all the things he needed and when a money crop, as in the South, would enable him to supply his wants from the stores.

173 From William Birch, *Views of Philadelphia*, 1799

THE PORT OF PHILADELPHIA, 1799

At the ports wheat and other produce were loaded on board the square-rigged sailing ships that followed the West Indian trade or touched at the Carolinas. Thousands of barrels were sometimes exported in a year from Philadelphia and New York. But, important as the shipments sometimes seemed, they comprised but a small part of the fruits of the farmer's labor. Most of his crops were still consumed at home or in the little towns and cities that bordered the coast.

174   From *Artists of America*, 1878, after the painting *The Drover's Halt*, by F. O. C. Darley (1822–88)

DRIVING ANIMALS TO MARKET FROM THE BACK–COUNTRY

BEYOND reach of the market lay the broad interior where the farmer had no choice but to depend upon his farm for such as he must wear and eat. The distance to the commercial centers was too great and the roads led through miles of forest and over bridgeless streams. "Were we not to consume all those articles which our farms produce," remarked a farmer, "were they not converted into wholesome pleasant food, they would be Lost. What would we do with our fruit, our fowls, our eggs; there is no market for these articles but in the Neighborhood of great Towns." The settler's surplus sheep and cattle could be added to the herd that the picturesque drover took overland to the distant market. With the money that the stock brought the farmer could buy salt and a few other necessary articles that he could neither raise nor contrive. But they were not many. Within this zone husbandry was often bad and isolation stifled progress. Its people must wait for improved transportation, the turnpikes and the canals.

175   From the painting *The Old Homestead, Connecticut*, by Willard L. Metcalf (1858–) in the City Art Museum, St. Louis

AN EIGHTEENTH–CENTURY FARMHOUSE

DILIGENCE and careful management brought the farmer who could reach the market a meager prosperity. His early cabin was changed for a substantial house whose framework of hewn timbers has given more than one of these buildings a life of over two centuries. It should never be forgotten that the simple grace of the structure, the doorways and staircases so often in exquisite taste, were, in the main, the work of farmer-carpenters for the use of tillers of the soil. In these old colonial houses may be seen the flowering in America of the handicrafts whose traditions reached back to the Middle Ages.

176   From a lithograph by Currier & Ives, 1864, after the painting *The Old Homestead in Winter*, by
G. H. Durrie (1820–63)

THE FARM IN WINTER

IN December the snow brought new problems to the farmer. The stock were driven in from distant mountain pastures or the common land to be cared for in sheds and barn. When blizzards came the outlying farm was sometimes shut in for weeks. But, in general, winter was not a time of isolation. With the rush of summer passed and little more than chores to do, with the roads hard and sleighing good, the farmer's family turned the winter into a time of merrymaking.

THE MILL IN WINTER

IT was now easier to take the grist to mill, for there were no longer mud holes or deep worn ruts in the roads. The heavy sleighs with their iron runners were hauled from the tool sheds. The frozen streams could be crossed on the ice. The mill was a busy place on cold mid-winter days. Lounging about the hoppers were men from all over the surrounding countryside exchanging gossip. The miller, who each day came in contact with a different group, was the dominant figure. Here in the decade before the Revolution the taxes imposed upon the colonials by the British government were heatedly discussed, and the news of American resistance exchanged. Here, later on, were lived over again the fights at Lexington and Concord and Bunker Hill.

177   From a lithograph by Currier & Ives, 1864, after the painting *The Old Grist Mill*, by G. H. Durrie

178   From the painting *Sleighing*, by Edward W. Redfield (1868–) in the possession of C. C. Glover, Jr.,
Washington

ON THE WAY TO THE STORE

AFTER the roads were frozen the people who lived far out from the village center could be seen bringing loads of produce to exchange at the store for a few necessaries. They had but little to sell, perhaps a few pounds of butter or flax or two or three yards of tow cloth. It might be that the family had been using their milk to make a great cheese of many pounds which the village merchant would purchase for cash and merchandise. There would be a few hours of bargaining and buying and then the sleigh would start homewards with its little parcels of salt, ginger and, perhaps, alum and molasses. There might be an iron pot or skillet, perhaps an earthen basin and a small piece or two of cloth. Yet, when the sleigh drove up to the farmhouse, an excited family looked over the purchases from the store. Happy the boy who was old enough to share in the adventure of the trip.

THE BREAKDOWN OF THE CHRISTMAS COACH

RETURNING from the village the farmer might meet the overland coach traveling across country from one important town to another. It would leave a little mail and some old newspapers at store or tavern and then push on toward its destination. For many localities it was the one bond between the settlement and the outer world. The unimproved roads were rough and full of holes and a breakdown was common enough. But there were many villages to which no coach ever came and where the mounted postman left his sheaf of letters and the news that he had gathered. Eagerly such isolated communities listened to tidings of the outside world.

179   From the painting by Stanley M. Arthurs (1872–) in possession of Walter S. Carpenter, Jr.,
Wilmington, Del.

THE HOME — THE TRAVELING SHOEMAKER

In the home and its interests centered the farmer's life. Yet the husbandman was more than a farmer. If once a year a traveling shoemaker or traveling tinker visited his farmstead to make the footgear for the family or repair the kitchen utensils, they were the exceptional artisans. For the most part he was dependent upon himself. Chancellor Livingston of New York said of him: "He can mend his plough, erect his walls, thrash his corn, handle his axe, his hoe, his sithe, his saw, break a colt, or drive a team, with equal address; being habituated from early life to rely on himself he acquires a skill in every branch of his profession, which is unknown in countries where labor is more subdivided."

SPINNING

In the summer the women had taken their wool spinning to the broad barn floor where the breeze blew through the great open doors and where there was space enough

180   From *The Ladies' Home Journal*, Dec. 1900; painting by W. L. Taylor (1854–).
© Curtis Publishing Company

to make long threads.   In the winter they spun the flax beside the fire.   Cooking, baking, making wine and beer in the spring and brandy in the fall, drying apples, brewing special beer from apple skins and cores

from which they got their yeast, spinning, weaving and making clothing, extracting dyes from roots and bark with perhaps a little alum and imported indigo, dying yarn and cloth, tending the poultry and sometimes helping in the fields, even these varied activities did not complete the full round of life for the farmer's wife. From before sunrise until evening the woman of the house was busy with the tasks that pressed upon her. Happy the man who was blessed in his wife. "Small is his chance of prosperity if he draws a blank in that Lottery."

181   From a photograph by Rudolf Eickemeyer

182   From a photograph by Rudolf Eickemeyer

THE FARMER'S WIFE

ALONG with all the work came the children — not one or two but ten and twelve and very often more. Governor Dongan of New York found "a Woman yet alive from whose loins there are upwards of three hundred and sixty persons now living." Usually there was no doctor to assist the babe into the world. Handy neighbor women helped out at such times. But if a crisis arose, there was no one who really knew what to do and many an agonized woman died in childbirth. As the years passed the older children grew up to be helpful, but very often, before that time came, the tired mother had gone to her last, long rest. A curious eighteenth-century traveler counted the graves of ten married women in a little New England cemetery. Eight of these had passed away before their thirtieth year. This was a part of the price that the farmer's family paid for independence.

THE COUNTRY DOCTOR

THERE were but few educated doctors in America and the smaller country towns were usually without them. Fortunate was the farm family who, when trouble came, could get prompt medical assistance. In New England disease was still looked upon as a chastisement from God to be cured as much by abandoning sin as by taking medicine. The doctors knew little or nothing of the science that forms the foundation of modern medical practice. They were physicians, surgeons, pharmacists and dentists all in one. But for the most part the more isolated farm folk doctored themselves. Their medicines were drawn from a strange blend of folk knowledge, superstition and Indian practices. They used amulets and charms and swallowed strange and sometimes repulsive concoctions. Bleeding was a common remedy for many different disorders. Diseases like yellow fever that have since been stamped out or brought under control often raged as epidemics. Death took a heavy toll among the people.

183   From the painting by Thomas W. Wood (1823–1903) in the Wood
                Art Gallery, Montpelier, Vt.

CHOPPING WOOD

WHILE the women were busied with their multitude of domestic labors, the yawning fireplace spoke to the farmer of its needs. Some farmers burned as many as seventy cords of wood in a year. The cutting and preparing of the household wood was a heavy labor that must be got out of the way before the spring rush began.

THE VILLAGE IN WINTER

BUT there was joy as well as sorrow among the country people. The eighteenth-century winter was a time for visiting. As in Virginia, families

184   From the painting *Wood Choppers*, by Horatio Walker (1858–) courtesy of the Howard Young Galleries, New York

arrived unannounced to spend the day with their neighbors. The evenings were gay with dances and assemblies. Crèvecœur was impressed with the opportunity these gatherings gave for studying the American. He wrote to an English friend: "I could have wished when you were with me that I could have carried you to such an assembly. There you would have seen better what the American farmers are than by seeing them singly in their homes. The cheerful glass, the warmth of their country politics, the ruddy faces of their daughters, the goodness of their horses would give you a more lively idea of their happiness as men, of their native pride as freeholders than anything I could tell you. At these assemblies they forget all their cares, all their labours. They bring their governors and assemblymen to a severe account; they boldly blame them or censure them for such measures as they dislike. Here you might see the American freeman in all the latitude of his political felicity, a felicity—alas!—of which they are not so sensible as they ought to be." — ST. JOHN DE CRÈVECŒUR, *Sketches of Eighteenth-Century America*, New Haven, 1925.

185   From the painting *Through Hills and Valley*, by Gardner Symons (1863–)

CHAPTER V

AN AGRARIAN AWAKENING

WHEN the British army of General Clinton, which had held New York during the Revolution, sailed for the last time down the harbor and out to sea, Americans turned their thoughts to re-establishing in their communities the old quiet and stability that seven years of war had sadly interrupted. Among the farmers of the northern states the readjustment was often peculiarly severe. The war had given them an unwonted market. The British commissary officers had bought cattle and produce for gold and, sometimes, Washington's army had been able to pay for its supplies in hard coin, though more often its foraging parties had forced the Continental scrip upon the husbandmen. With the signing of the peace treaty the armies sailed away or melted into the populace. The farmers must adjust themselves as best they could to new conditions.

Then it was that the results of the rude colonial husbandry became manifest. Behind the older settlements of New England and New York lay almost a century and a half of continuous cultivation. Pennsylvania and New Jersey were not far behind. Taught in the school of the frontier and isolated wholly or in part from a market, the farmers of the seventeenth and eighteenth centuries had misused the soil. Fields had been cropped year after year with only the rest which came from lying occasionally for a twelve-month in fallow, after the old custom in England. When the war was over, the complaint was heard from every hand that the soil was worn out. Discontent appeared throughout the countryside.

The rich lands of the frontier always beckoned. After the Revolution discharged soldiers and an ever-growing number of farmers turned hopeful faces westward and joined the caravans that began to fill the roads. In New York the settlers left behind them the Mohawk and Susquehanna Rivers and pressed into the country of the Iroquois, defeated in the late war. Farther south the pioneers crossed the Appalachian mountains to find new homes in Kentucky or Ohio. But, though it sometimes seemed that the whole country was moving westward, a majority of the eastern farmers remained in their old homes. The back-country folk were held by an immovable burden of debt. Among these debtor farmers, driven finally to desperation, rebellion once raised its head.

A few of the public-spirited Americans who set about the task of welding the revolted colonies into a nation also saw clearly that, much as the American people needed a new constitution and an efficient central government, they needed likewise a better husbandry. Across the Atlantic, England had for nearly half a century been undergoing a great agrarian awakening. New crops, better methods and improved breeds of animals had appeared in the older nation. Thoughtful Americans, anxious to serve their country's needs, turned their attention to the fields of the late enemy and read the writings of the British leaders of agricultural thought. The result of the labors of these American pioneers was the laying of the foundations of that science of American agriculture which has influenced so profoundly the welfare of the nation.

A FARMHOUSE IN THE BACK SETTLEMENTS

It is hard for people accustomed to the ways of a later crowded age to realize the full significance of the isolation of the interior farms of America. Far back from busy seaports and pressing against the primeval forest that stretched westward, the settlers of the back-country lived lonely and apart. Perhaps a little group of squalid cabins would be huddled together

186   From Robert Sutcliff, *Travels in Some Parts of North America, in the Years 1804, 1805 and 1806*, York, England, 1815

in a rich river bottom. Often a single cabin would be found beside a forest trail. Rough clad children would eye the chance traveler with unconcealed curiosity and the settler and his wife who shared with him their simple fare would ask him eagerly for news of the civilization that lay to the east. So had come, sometimes after many months, the tidings of Bunker Hill to the people of the frontier.

187   From a photograph by the United States Department of Agriculture

IN THE MOUNTAINS OF VIRGINIA

The frontiersmen, always pushing westward, chopped out their clearings in the mountain valleys of Pennsylvania, Virginia and the Carolinas. There, in the southern Appalachians, live the great-great-grandchildren of the first pioneers. The isolation of the eighteenth century still clings to this rugged region where, for a century and a half, the fences, fields and cabins have changed but little. Here the traveler may still get a glimpse of a life that elsewhere has passed away.

OUR "CONTEMPORARY ANCESTORS"

THE ways and even the language of old America still live among the people of the southern mountains. The farmer still goes afield with the clumsy tools of his forefathers. By dint of hard labor he and his wife wrest from his scanty acres the necessities of a meager life. Of a civilization beyond the mountains there reaches him but a vague rumor. He and his fellows of the mountain settlements are the product of stagnation resulting from lack of contact with the life-giving centers of thought and trade.

188   From a photograph by the United States Department of Agriculture

AN "AMERICAN NEW CLEARED FARM"

As the eighteenth century closed, the frontier pushed on across Kentucky, Tennessee and Ohio. A British traveler, on a tour through the interior in 1791 and 1792, published a diagram of a newly cleared farm. His legend reads as follows: "1, a birch canoe poled by an Indian; 2, a birch canoe paddled by squaws; 3, a papoose or Indian child; 4, a log fence; 5, worm fences; 6, post and rail fence; 7, Virginia rail fence; 8, dwelling house and wings; 9, barracks or Dutch barn; 10, barns roofed with shingles; 11, shed for cattle to lie in winter; 12, shed for storing Indian corn; 13, fold for confining cattle at night and in which they are milked; 14, a dwelling log house covered with bark; 15, an Indian dog."

189   From Patrick Campbell, *Travels in the interior inhabited parts of North America*, Edinburgh, 1793

A FRONTIER CABIN

THE curse of the back-country was poverty. Crèvecœur, traveling just before the Revolution in Pennsylvania, wrote of a settlement he found deep in the hills. "These people raised what they pleased: oats, peas, wheat, corn, with two days' labour in the week. At their doors they had a fair river, on their backs high mountains full of game. Yet with all these advantages, placed as they were on these shores of Eden, they lived as poor as the poorest wretches of Europe who

190   From V. Collot, *Voyage dans L'Amerique Septentrionale*, Paris, 1826

have nothing. Their houses were miserable hovels. Their stalks of grain rotted in their fields. They were almost starved, not for want of victuals but of spirit and activity to cook them. They were almost naked.

191 From a print after the painting *Too Near the Warpath*, by George H. Boughton (1836–1905)

This may appear to you a strange problem. . . . This people had not nor could they have, situated as they were, any place where they might convey their produce. . . . This . . . rendered them careless, slothful, and inactive. This constituted their poverty, though in the midst of the greatest plenty." — ST. JOHN DE CRÈVE-CŒUR, *Sketches of Eighteenth-Century America*, Yale University Press, 1925.

THE INDIAN

THE Indians east of the mountains had been subdued, but on the new frontier the menace still stalked in the forest. The redskins had become aroused to the danger of the advancing whites. No one knew when a band of Cherokees might leave a trail of blood and ashes across the settlements. The folk of the mountains and of Kentucky and Ohio lived in constant dread of the redskins. During the Revolution many a lonely settlement leaped from uneasy slumber at the sound of the war-whoop and all who did not escape into the forest were hacked down by the savages. When the storm had passed, the wretched survivors returned to the smoking ruins of their cabins to bury their dead and begin afresh their hard adventure. Moreover the farmer faced a hostile nature. The lynx and wild cat made depredations; the clumsy, heavy-pawed bear disturbed his stock; and packs of wolves never let him forget that he had built his home on the edge of the wilderness.

192   From *Harper's Weekly*, Dec. 7, 1867, after a drawing by A. W. Thompson

DISTILLING WHISKEY

DESPERATE poverty found desperate remedies. Animals were raised and driven with infinite labor to the eastern markets. In western Pennsylvania and the mountains to the south the latter half of the eighteenth century saw the growth of whiskey distilling. The farmer's grain was thus transformed into a product of small bulk and high value. Whiskey and livestock first brought hard money into the back-country and with it the power to command a scant supply of goods from the distant store.

THE COUNTRY TAVERN

IT was inevitable that the dark shadow of excess should fall across the stagnant settlements of the interior. Inns and taverns and, in places, the whiskey still, afforded a release from the utter monotony of life. Heavy drinking, loud talking and rough fighting were but the natural expression of the poverty, the shiftlessness, and the coarseness of back-country life.

In such an environment many of the boys of Revolutionary America grew to manhood.

193   The Muzzey Tavern, Hampstead, N. H., from a photograph by the
Halliday Historic Photograph Company

194   From a copy dated June 15, 1787, in the
Boston Public Library

SHAYS' REBELLION — HANCOCK'S PROCLAMATION

WHEN the excitement of the Revolution passed and the thirteen independent states sought to adjust themselves to the responsibilities of the new freedom, the misery and despair of the back-country reached its height. Through all the interior there was scarcely a farm but had its mortgage. By the end of the century the soil which had once been rich was impoverished by ruthless and slothful cropping. The future offered little to the debtor farmer, the creditor and the tax gatherer were at his door. Rebellion, born of desperation, broke out in western Massachusetts in 1786. Daniel Shays led the farmers in an armed assault upon the courts as the source of the husbandman's misery. But militia scattered the revolters and the uprising came to naught.

195   A Frontiersman, from a woodcut by Alexander Anderson

AGRARIAN LEGISLATION

Shays' Rebellion marked the "debtor farmer's" political failure in Massachusetts but in state after state they won control of the legislature. If, by legislation, the men from the backwoods cabins could stay the hand of the creditor, money to pay off their mortgages might slowly accumulate. Farmer-controlled legislatures passed "stay laws" which prevented the collection of debts between certain dates. Moreover, these agrarian legislators flooded the country with paper currency which depreciated while it fell from the press. This cheapened the debts they owed and inflated the prices of their produce. But the day of the "debtor farmer" was short. In 1787, the new Constitution was framed by a convention in which sat not a single representative from the interior settlements. The document contained provisions which outlawed the two methods of relief offered by the agrarian politicians. Not by such means could the ills of the farmer be permanently remedied. Improved communication that would put the isolated back-country in touch with the life-giving market was the only sound solution.

196   The home of a "Debtor Farmer," from a print in the possession of the publishers

197   From the Chronicles of America motion picture *Alexander Hamilton*

THE WHISKEY REBELLION, 1794

THE new government under the Constitution needed revenue, and Hamilton, Washington's great Secretary of the Treasury, secured the passage of an excise tax. For many people in western Pennsylvania and the mountains to the south this tax on whiskey struck a heavy blow at the one means of selling the products of their acres. Deep indignation flamed up. They defied the government and the excisemen were driven from the frontier communities. Hamilton assembled an army larger than any that had met the forces of England during the Revolution, and marched into western Pennsylvania. Again the farmers of the interior went down in defeat.

THOMAS JEFFERSON, 1743–1826, POLITICAL LEADER OF THE FARMERS

WHEN Peter Jefferson, Thomas Jefferson's father, laid out his Virginia farm, it was not far distant from the frontier. His son became a planter, wealthy and aristocratic. Yet in his heart was a genuine sympathy for the plain people who had been his father's neighbors. In the last decade of the eighteenth century he organized them into the Democratic-Republican party and challenged the policies of the aristocratic Federalists, of whom John Adams and Alexander Hamilton were the leaders.

In 1800, when Jefferson won the presidency, the party of the plain farmers came into power. Many of its most conspicuous figures were Virginia planters,

198   From the portrait, 1805, by Rembrandt Peale (1778–1860)
              in the New York Historical Society

Jefferson himself, Madison, Monroe and Randolph. For a time the farmer seemed to have come into his own, yet it was not through politics that the most difficult problems of American agriculture were to be solved. During the years when the Democratic-Republican party was forming, a small group of Americans were giving thoughtful attention to the need for bettering the methods of husbandry.

199

Retouched from the print in *Albany Chronicles*, 1906

THE VAN RENSSELAER MANOR HOUSE, EIGHTEENTH CENTURY

IN sharp contrast with the rough simplicity of the back-country were the great estates of the coast region. Few were as magnificent as the van Rensselaer manor on the Hudson yet there were many by no means unimposing. The tradition of a landed aristocracy, passing from England to America, had in the South produced the planters. In the northern colonies men who achieved professional or commercial success frequently set about establishing an estate. This aristocracy watched with growing apprehension the political activities of the debtor farmers.

THE HOME AND FARM OF ST. JOHN DE CRÈVECŒUR

ONE of the most interesting of this agrarian group was St. John de Crèvecœur of the province of New York. He was not a man of wealth or even the owner of a great farm, but was, as he loved to think of himself, a simple farmer who wrote letters to his friends in England. Written from a background of eighteenth-century culture they portray with a delicate refinement and an almost poetic idealism the simple story of American husbandry. Crèvecœur caught the spirit of independence and self-reliance that contact with the wilderness had bred in the American husbandman. He stands, above all other writers, as the friend and interpreter of the common folk of the small farms of the North on the eve of the great struggle for national freedom.

200   From the original painting in the possession of Countess Marie de Crèvecœur, Paris

ARTHUR YOUNG, 1741–1820

THE English friends who read Crèvecœur's letters saw going on about them in their own country a great agricultural awakening. In the early years of the eighteenth century Tull had introduced his "horse-hoeing husbandry," Townshend had experimented with turnips, and Bakewell had been establishing his breed of Shorthorn cattle. Now, in the decade following the American Revolution, Arthur Young had become the leader of a widespread movement for agricultural improvement. Echoes of the changes in England were heard on the western side of the Atlantic and helped to bring about an agrarian awakening in the new nation.

JARED ELIOT, 1685–1763,
A PIONEER OF THE AGRARIAN AWAKENING

JARED ELIOT, a Connecticut clergyman, was not the first to observe the defects of the American husbandman. Again and again European travelers had called attention to "their gross mistakes and carelessness for futurity." The reader of *American Husbandry*, by "An American," published in London in 1775, sees again and again the

201 From the chalk portrait of Arthur Young by George Dance (1741–1825), in the National Portrait Gallery, London

same picture: "most of the farmers in this country are, in whatever concerns cattle, the most negligent ignorant set of men in the world . . . worse ploughing is no where to be seen . . . and of this bad tillage the farmers are very sparing, rarely giving two ploughings if they think the crop will do with one; the consequence of which is their products seldom being near so great as they would be under a different management." Poor tillage was, in part, the result of virgin land which yielded crops with little cultivation. By the latter half of the eighteenth century, however, the older settlements were feeling the pinch of a depleted fertility. Jared Eliot was a John the Baptist among the stony hillsides of New England, calling upon his generation to mend its ways.

202   From the portrait of Jared Eliot in the possession of George E. Eliot, Clinton, Conn.

ELIOT ON FIELD-HUSBANDRY

ELIOT's little book was the first extended American treatise upon farming methods. But the development which he helped to initiate was checked by the War of the Revolution. Not until the marching of armies had ceased could Americans again turn their thoughts to the improvement of their husbandry. The eighteenth century was almost spent before the new effort began to be justified by its fruits.

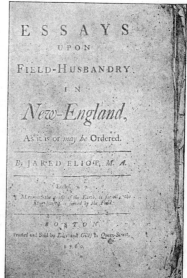

203   Title-page of the issue, Boston, 1760

JOHN BEALE BORDLEY OF MARYLAND, 1727–1804

ONE of the most striking figures in the American agrarian renaissance was John Beale Bordley, lawyer and planter of Maryland. Only through the landed aristocracy, of which Bordley was a member, could improvement come. The small farmer who held his own plow to the furrow was so busied with his work that he had no time for study or experimentation. Moreover, although life in the New World had not been without effect upon him, the conservatism of the peasant was still strong in him. The infant states just broken loose from the British Empire could do as yet but little for the improvement of husbandry. That task then devolved upon the aristocracy, among whom were men of ability who had time for reading and for correspondence with English leaders and who had capital to carry on experiments. Of the source of his interest in improved husbandry Bordley wrote: "The writings of the respectable Mr. Tull, first excited the author's attention to agriculture: but also to Mr. Young he is mostly indebted for his knowledge of its present state and the modes of practice in Europe."

204 From the portrait attributed to John Hesselius (1728–78), in the Maryland Historical Society, Baltimore

205   Drawn expressly for *The Pageant of America* by C. W. Jefferys

BORDLEY'S THRESHING FLOOR

ON his own farm at Wye, Bordley had one of the best threshing floors in America. The sheaves of grain with bands cut were laid in careful order on the hard earth that encircled the small barn. Over them the teams were driven at a trot by negroes under the direction of the overseer. When the kernels had been beaten out, the straw was pitched off and the grain was ready for winnowing. For the benefit of his contemporaries Bordley wrote in his *Essays* a detailed account of his floor and the methods that he used. With this device he could in a few days thresh more grain than could be done in many weeks with the flail.

ESSAYS AND NOTES

ON

HUSBANDRY

AND

RURAL AFFAIRS.

By J. B. BORDLEY.

Still let me COUNTRY CULTURE scan:
My FARM's my Home: " My Brother, MAN :
" And GOD is every where."

THE SECOND EDITION WITH ADDITIONS.

PHILADELPHIA:
PRINTED BY BUDD AND BARTRAM,
FOR THOMAS DOBSON, AT THE STONE HOUSE,
N° 41, SOUTH SECOND STREET.

1801.
[*Copy-Right Secured according to Law.*]

206   Title-page of the issue, Philadelphia, 1801

BORDLEY CRITICIZES AMERICAN FARMING METHODS

BORDLEY's interests were almost as wide as agriculture itself. One cannot turn the yellowed pages of his *Essays and Notes,* first published in 1799, without being struck by the clearness with which he grasped the problem and by the sanity of the remedies proposed. In straightforward phrase he condemned the farmer's usual three year rotation of "maize, wheat or rye, and spontaneous rubbish pasture." He wanted to abandon the fallow that had been brought from England and plant it to clover. "The man who manures the whole of his arable fields" and who does not shy at clover on account of the cost of the seed or the labor of raising it "will accomplish a great object, tending highly to his domestic comfort, his reputation, and his independency of creditors."

AMERICAN SOCIETIES FOR PROMOTING AGRICULTURE

MEN with a vision of better husbandry on the farms of America banded themselves together into societies. The earliest was that at Philadelphia, founded in 1785. Other organizations were established at New York, Charleston and Boston. These pioneer societies, looking toward a new day, were the outgrowth of the ideal expressed in the later motto of the Philadelphia organization: "Let us cultivate the ground, that the poor, as well as the rich, may be filled; and peace and happiness established throughout our borders."

AN
ADDRESS,
FROM
THE PHILADELPHIA SOCIETY
FOR PROMOTING AGRICULTURE,
WITH
A SUMMARY OF ITS LAWS,
AND
PREMIUMS OFFERED.

He who can make two ears of corn grow where only one grew before, ranks as a benefactor to society before all the heroes that ever existed.
SWIFT.

M.DCC.LXXXV,

207   Title-page of a pamphlet issued by the Philadelphia Society for Promoting Agriculture, Philadelphia, 1785

RICHARD PETERS, 1744–1828, A FOUNDER OF THE PHILADELPHIA SOCIETY

IN the time of Washington and Adams, when the young country was struggling through the period of foundation laying, there were some men of broad vision who chose to serve their fellow countrymen rather through improving husbandry than through political life. Agriculture was the dominant national industry supporting the homes of the great majority of the American people. To improve agriculture was to make more firm the country's foundation. Richard Peters, leader of the Philadelphia bar, Revolutionary soldier, an important figure in the Protestant Episcopal Church, long the intimate friend of Washington, together with his other activities was for thirty years president of the Philadelphia Society for Promoting Agriculture. His correspondence was voluminous; his researches covered the whole field of agriculture. A hundred essays in the pages of the Society's *Memoirs* represent but a small part of his great contribution.

208   From the portrait by Rembrandt Peale in the possession of Richard Peters, Jr., Philadelphia

THE AGRICULTURAL SOCIETY will meet on Bufinefs, at PATRICK BYRNES's in *Front-ftreet*, on TUESDAY the *Firft* of March. Your Company is defired by *feven* o'Clock, P. M.

To Richard Peters Efqr.

A MEETING OF THE PHILADELPHIA SOCIETY

THE Philadelphia Society, like its contemporaries, was made up almost entirely of men of wealth and influence. In its list of members appeared the names of Zachariah Paulsen, publisher and owner of the first American daily newspaper; John Dorsey, in his day the country's leading physician; and Joshua Humphries, shipbuilder, in whose yards were built the famous warships, *Constitution, Chesapeake, Congress* and *Constellation*. The small farmers of the countryside who drove their own oxen and pitched their own hay were not included. Yet the organization was for their benefit.

From the portrait by Charles Willson Peale (1741–1827), in the Pennsylvania Academy of Fine Arts, Philadelphia
210

GEORGE CLYMER, 1739–1813, VICE–PRESIDENT OF THE SOCIETY

ON January 21, 1794, Richard Peters, George Clymer, signer of the Declaration of Independence and one of the organizers of the Philadelphia Society, Timothy Pickering, Secretary of State under Washington and Adams, and John Beale Bordley, presented an unsuccessful petition to the legislature of Pennsylvania for the establishment of a state agricultural society for the promotion of agricultural education. It was men of this sort who believed with Bordley that the health and comfort of nations are founded upon a spirited and flourishing husbandry.

THE MEDAL OF THE PHILADELPHIA SOCIETY

THE Philadelphia Society, like its contemporaries, offered prizes and medals in the hope of stimulating agricultural experimentation and the adoption of improved methods. "For the best essay, the result of experience, on the breeding, feeding, and management of cattle;" "For the best experiment of a five years course of crops;" "For the best cheese made on one farm in the United States — to be not less than 500 pounds;" these are but a few of the premiums offered. The Society described the significance of the medal as follows: "On one side is a plough and oxen at rest — one pawing, impatient under idleness, the other looking for the arrival of the ploughman. This emblem is preferred to the plough with horses to show emphatically the Society's desire to encourage the use of oxen and the breeding of cattle. On the reverse are agricultural implements; honorable badges of husbandmen, more estimable and generally useful than armorial bearings. A space is reserved for engraving the cause and occasion inducing the mark of approbation bestowed." A prime object of the Massachusetts society was "to obtain and publish an account of the improvements of other countries, and to procure models of the machines in which they excel."

211   From *Memoirs of the Philadelphia Society for Promoting Agriculture*, 1814

212 From the portrait of Ezra L'Hommedieu by Ralph Earle (1751–
1801), in the New York Historical Society

ROBERT R. LIVINGSTON, 1746–1813, A GREAT AMERICAN PATRON OF AGRICULTURE

GREATEST of all this eighteenth-century group who laid the foundations of an American science of agriculture was Robert Livingston of New York, who as minister to France negotiated the purchase of Louisiana. He was long the president of the New York Society. For years he carried forward a variety of experiments on his great estate at Clermont, Columbia County. He was in correspondence with Arthur Young and other leaders of the English agricultural awakening. An astounding number of essays and letters came from his pen. He hoped that posterity would remember him as the man who had established *lucerne* (alfalfa) on the fields of America.

ESSAY
ON

SHEEP;

THEIR VARIETIES—ACCOUNT OF THE
MERINOES OF SPAIN, FRANCE, &c.

REFLECTIONS ON THE BEST METHOD OF TREATING THEM,
AND RAISING A FLOCK IN THE UNITED STATES;

TOGETHER WITH

MISCELLANEOUS REMARKS
OF

SHEEP AND WOOLLEN MANUFACTURES.

BY ROBERT R. LIVINGSTON, LL. D.

President of the Society for the Promotion of Useful Arts, Member of the
American Philosophical Society, President of the American Society
of Fine Arts, Corresponding Member of the Agricultural
Society of the Seine, Honorary Member of the
Agricultural Society of Dutchess County.

Printed by Order of the Legislature of the State of New-York.

NEW-YORK:
PRINTED BY T. AND J. SWORDS,
No. 160 Pearl-Street.
1809.

214   Title-page of the issue,
New York, 1809

EZRA L'HOMMEDIEU, 1734–1811, VICE–PRESIDENT OF THE NEW YORK AGRICULTURAL SOCIETY

THE group of men in New York supporting agricultural improvement was as significant as that in Philadelphia. Ezra L'Hommedieu, lawyer, member of the Continental Congress and of the State Senate, was for years vice-president of the New York Society. His papers and addresses made an important contribution to the agricultural knowledge of the time.

213 From the portrait of Robert R. Livingston by John Vanderlyn
(1776–1852), in the New York Historical Society

LIVINGSTON'S *ESSAY ON SHEEP*

ONE of the famous contributions to the early literature of American agriculture is Livingston's *Essay on Sheep*. Barbary Mountain sheep had been introduced into the United States as a result of President Jefferson's war with the Barbary pirates of the Mediterranean. Merinos had come from Spain when the Napoleonic wars broke up some of the great sheep farms and nullified the law which had prevented the export of the famous breed. Robert Livingston had a fine flock of pure-bred Merinos. For the benefit of American sheep raisers he published the results of his experience and observation in his *Essay*.

215 From *Miscellaneous Works of David Humphreys*, New York, 1804

DAVID HUMPHREYS' MEDAL FOR INTRODUCING MERINOS

COLONEL David Humphreys, minister to Portugal in the days when the embargo of Merinos was broken, served his country well by providing his countrymen with some of the sheep. His flock of one hundred on his Connecticut farm has become historic. The day of the inferior "rat-tailed" colonial sheep had passed.

DON PEDRO — THE FIRST AMERICAN MERINO

Don Pedro, imported in 1801, is believed to be the first pure-blood Merino ram to come to North America. His fleece weighed eight and one-half pounds, contrasting with the three and four pound fleeces of the native animals. Within a dozen years after the Merinos crossed the Atlantic they had revolutionized the sheep industry of the United States. In the War of 1812 to wear American-made cloth from American-grown wool was to be a patriot.

SPECULATION IN MERINOS

THE newly introduced Merino fell upon fortunate times. From Jefferson's Embargo of 1807 until the end of the War of 1812 Americans were practically cut off from English factories. America must raise her own wool and weave her own cloth, or go without. Sheep culture spread rapidly over the farms of the North. In his preface the anonymous writer of the pamphlet, *Merino-Mania*, says: "We have heard it stated that $500, $1,000 and even $1,500 have been paid for a Merino ram and that cloth from the Merino wool has been sold at $14 and $15 per yard. The present publication will evince if these riches are not beyond all limits of propriety and whether the business thus carried on is not likely to degenerate into a mere system of speculation which, whilst it benefits a few, will bring ruin to thousands." When the end of the war brought again British competition, sheep culture was established on a sounder basis. The improvement in American sheep had come to stay.

216 From *The Cultivator*, Albany, 1834, after a copper plate in the *Archives of Useful Knowledge*, Philadelphia, 1810

ANTIDOTE
TO THE
MERINO-MANIA
NOW PROGRESSING THROUGH THE
UNITED STATES;
OR,
THE VALUE OF
THE MERINO BREED,
PLACED BY OBSERVATION AND EXPERIENCE, UPON A PROPER BASIS.

LOOK BEFORE YOU LEAP

PRINTED AND SOLD BY J. & A. Y. HUMPHREYS, CHANGE-WALK, Corner of Second and Walnut-streets. PHILADELPHIA. 1810.

217 Title-page of a pamphlet in the New York Historical Society

ELKANAH WATSON, 1758–1842

ELKANAH WATSON was not among the founders of the eighteenth-century school of agricultural experimenters and writers, but he was its most distinguished pupil. As a business man he had traveled along the Atlantic seaboard and in Europe. Then he came under the influence of Livingston and gained the friendship of Humphreys. In 1807 he gave up commerce and took up farming at Pittsfield, Mass. During the next four years he made his great contribution to the development of American agriculture. By 1811 he had completed the organization of the Berkshire Agricultural Society.

218 From the portrait of Elkanah Watson by J. S. Copley (1737–1815), in the possession of Mrs. John I. Kane, Ossining, N. Y.

WATSON'S FIRST EXHIBITION

WATSON wrote in 1820: "In the Fall of 1807 I procured the first pair of Merino sheep that had appeared in Berkshire. . . . I was induced to notify an exhibition under the great elm tree in the public square in Pittsfield [Mass.] of these two sheep on a certain day. Many farmers and even women were excited by curiosity to attend my humble exhibition. . . . The farmers present responded to my remarks with approbation. We became acquainted, and from that day to the present, agricultural societies, cattle

219   From Elkanah Watson, *History of Agricultural Societies on the Modern Berkshire System*, Albany, 1820

shows, and all in connexion therewith have predominated in my mind."

SEAL OF THE BERKSHIRE AGRICULTURAL SOCIETY

THE Berkshire Agricultural Society was founded in 1811. The principles on which it was based proved popular. Slowly at first, then more and more rapidly, the Berkshire System spread until it reached west into the new states of Indiana and Illinois and even penetrated the southern cotton kingdom. Unlike its predecessors, the agricultural societies of Philadelphia and New York, it was an organization of the common farmer. In its time it served his interests well.

221   From Elkanah Watson, *History of Agricultural Societies on the Modern Berkshire System*, Albany, 1820

220   From a Berkshire Agricultural Society pamphlet, 1817

THE BERKSHIRE SYSTEM — CERTIFICATE OF HONORABLE TESTIMONY

WATSON was a student of human nature. The purpose of the organization was to hold each year an exhibition of the best handiwork and the best products of the farmers of the locality. Prizes were awarded for pre-eminence in farm animals and crops, and in butter, cheese and cloth made in the home. At the end of the exhibition came the general assembly in the largest village church. Here amid impressive ceremonies, the honors were distributed, each prize accompanied by a certificate of distinction which, handsomely framed, held a place of honor on the wall of the farmer's parlor.

222   From Elkanah Watson, *History of Agricultural Societies on the Modern Berkshire System*, Albany, 1820

AN INVITATION TO A PASTORAL BALL

Watson's greatest problem was to arouse the active interest of the ladies in these exhibitions. The diplomatic shifts to which he and others resorted in order to win over the country women, unaccustomed to activities outside their own homes and fearful of arousing comment by appearing in a public competition, were finally

everywhere triumphant. At the end of the general assembly came the "pastoral ball." The whole plan was a skillful blend of competition, social intercourse and dignified formality. The general assemblies were usually graced by one or more political celebrities, and a great many by Watson himself.

THE EMBLEM OF THE BERKSHIRE SOCIETY

"At our first fair," wrote Watson in 1820, "a procession was formed, the society carrying appropriate ensigns, and each member carrying a badge of wheat in his hat." The heyday of the Berkshire societies was from 1820 to 1825 when farm prices were declining and the need for bettering the farmer's condition was widely felt. They collapsed with the withdrawal of state aid in the late 'twenties and 'thirties. Yet in little more than a decade county societies were again forming. The Berkshire Society is the first of that succession of organizations which include the Grange and the Farm Bureau that have done much for the betterment of American agriculture.

223   Sketch of Elkanah Watson with the Wheat Cockade, from *The Cultivator*, Albany, 1848

224   From a drawing on stone made in 1886 by Louis Maurer

THE "COUNTY FAIR"

THE direct descendant of Watson's Berkshire System is the "county fair." Unlike the ancient fairs of Europe or those of early colonial days its central purpose is not to facilitate exchange and sale but to exhibit the best products and handiwork of the locality and to stimulate improvement by offering prizes. Horse races and a host of other attractions have added to its interest and excitement. From one day it has grown to three and four. Country folk drive in from miles around to look at the stock in their sheds and the produce on exhibition in the fair house and to watch the demonstration of the improved machinery. The merry-go-round plays its strident tunes, the Ferris wheel swings round its lofty circuit, the barkers for the side-shows bawl of the mysteries or the amusements within their tents. Yards of the inevitable taffy are consumed as acquaintances from distant corners of the county meet and gossip and separate in the ever changing crowds that move over the grounds. It has become the farmer's carnival — far removed indeed from that first

225   New York State Fair, 1844.   From *New York State Agricultural Society Transactions*, 1844

exhibition when Watson displayed his two Merino sheep under the elm tree. In the twentieth century the automobile has again brought changes. Farmers come from distant counties and with them crowds of city people. The fair is no longer merely a farmer's institution.

THE "STATE FAIR"

THE idea of the county exhibition extended to the state. "State fairs" further stimulated the enterprise and broadened the horizon of the farmer and his family. In the 'thirties and 'forties the states again began to grant aid for agricultural surveys and the improvement of husbandry.

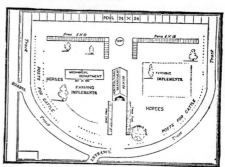

226   Ground Plan of the New York State Fair, 1824. From *The Cultivator*, Nov., 1842

227   Shorthorn Bull *Duke of Wellington*, imported 1840.   From the *New York State Agricultural Society Transactions*, 1843

228   Jersey Cow *Faith*, imported 1854.   From *The Cultivator*, July, 1858

229   Jersey Bull *Commodore*, imported 1854.   From *The Cultivator*, March, 1858

230   Hereford Bull *Dallimore*, imported 1839.   From *The Cultivator*, 1840

THE IMPROVEMENT OF CATTLE

In the cattle pens of the rural exhibitions of the early nineteenth century the farmers sometimes saw animals that contrasted strangely with the small, ill-formed stock that had come down from colonial times. These were foreign breeds that had been imported by farmers of wealth. Shorthorns, developed in northeastern England from native cattle, began to come to the United States in the year that the Revolution closed. Herefords from England were not definitely established in America until 1840. Jerseys from the small island whose name they bear were brought over in 1850. For generations the Jersey islanders had worked at the development of a breed that would yield rich milk plentifully and had kept all other cattle from their shores. In the 'fifties the farmer at the fair looked curiously at these new, bronze cattle. His sons have made it one of the most popular American breeds.

III—8

231 Holstein Bull *Van Tromp* of the original Chenery herd. From *The Country Gentleman*, March 19, 1868

232 Holstein Cow *Lady Midwould*. From *The Country Gentleman*, March 5, 1868

THE COMING OF THE HOLSTEIN

"HOLSTEINS" and Jerseys are the two most common milk-producing breeds in the United States. Tacitus wrote of the Friesians who lived in the low country which is now Holland: "They owned cattle, not excelling in beauty, but in number." The people of North Holland and Friesland are descended from this ancient German tribe, and the black and white cattle that graze in their pastures are the descendants of the cattle mentioned by the Roman historian. Winthrop W. Chenery of Massachusetts was the first to import and maintain a pure-bred herd of what were then known as "Dutch" cattle. Most of his importations were made in the 'fifties. By some mischance the name of the province of Holstein rather than that of Friesland became attached in America to the stock from the Netherlands and the error has persisted.

But the coming of the Holstein-Friesian cattle had its darker aspect. Mr. Chenery's importation of 1859 brought to America pleuro-pneumonia. The distemper broke out in his stables. This disease made its way over the country and became a scourge of American cattle. The story of its conquest belongs to the history of the development of the United States Department of Agriculture and its battle against the natural enemies of the farmer.

233   Stables of Winthrop W. Chenery at Belmont, Massachusetts. From *Harper's Weekly*, July 21, 1860, after a drawing by T. Marsden

234   An Improved Essex.   From *Eighty Years' Progress of the United States*, Hartford, 1869

235 A Berkshire Hog.   From *Eighty Years' Progress of the United States*, Hartford, 1869

IMPROVED SWINE

In 1832 a contributor to the *New England Farmer* wrote of swine: "Formerly New England was over-run with a raw-boned lank-sided race of animals, which devoured the substance of the farmer, and like Pharaoh's *lean kine* 'were still ill-favored and lean as before,' and whose chief return to the owner, was skin, bone, and bristles. But we think that we may now congratulate the Society on the almost entire extinction of this race, whose very existence was a waste, and whose disgustful and uncouth appearance was a mere nuisance. We now generally find a small-boned, well-proportioned breed of Swine, whose handsome appearance and good qualities, abundantly compensate for the change." Most of the improved breeds of hogs in America were brought from England and many are named for the counties in which they were originated. The improvement of American pigs preceded that of cattle by a quarter of a century. The new animals increased the farmer's supply of lard and bacon. In the fall of the year he would load a pig or two into his farm wagon to take to market. They would buy shoes and warm clothing for the children starting in the winter term at school.

236   Percheron Horse *Diligence*.   From *The American Agriculturist*, 1844

THE FIRST PERCHERON

New machinery appeared on the farms of nineteenth-century America and the day of the ox waned. From France, where since antiquity improved horses had been bred for war, transportation and husbandry, Edward Harris of New Jersey in 1839 imported *Diligence*, one of the first Percherons in the United States. In mid-century further importations stamped the qualities of the new breed on American draft horses.

237   Clydesdale Horse *Champion*.   From *The Country Gentleman*, July 15, 1858

AN EARLY CLYDESDALE

From the banks of the Clyde in the Scottish lowlands Clydesdales were imported into Canada in the 'forties and 'fifties. *Champion* was one of the offspring of these importations to find his way across the Niagara River into the United States. The chief development of the breed in America, however, did not occur until the last quarter of the century.

Facsimile page of the first number of *The Plough Boy*, Albany, N. Y., June 5, 1819

THE BIRTH OF THE FARM PAPER

LEADERS like Bordley, Livingston and Peters had laid at the end of the eighteenth century the foundations of an agricultural science but had failed to spread their ideas among the conservative small farmers. The leaven of Watson's Berkshire System in the first quarter of the nineteenth had brought to the country communities a spirit of progress. In 1819, the agricultural press was born. In the newspapers before this date articles of interest to husbandmen had appeared from time to time but in this year two papers were launched in the belief that the interest of the farmer in the improvement of his husbandry was sufficient to make them profitable. Said the editor of *The Plough Boy* in his first announcement: "Political and domestic economy, and not party politics, then, are to form the basis upon which this paper is to be conducted. . . . But if it be insisted that he [the editor] take his stand with some party or other, he will chuse for himself, and adhere to the HOMESPUN PARTY — the party of the PLOUGH BOYS — theirs it is that must be the true republican party; for theirs is the party whose first leaders were the patriarchs of the human race; since the just and eternal God not only created man equal, but gave him the earth for his inheritance, and the cultivation of it for his natural and most noble employment."

NEW ENGLAND FARMER.

Published every Saturday, by THOMAS W. SHEPARD, Rogers' Building, Congress Street, Boston: at $2,50 per ann. in advance, or $3,00 at the close of the year

VOL. I.   BOSTON, SATURDAY, AUGUST 3, 1822.   No. 1.

PROSPECTUS
OF THE
NEW ENGLAND FARMER.

AGRICULTURE, within a few years, has been improved with a rapidity without precedent in the annals of art; and new discoveries and processes, in its various branches, are still in a train of successful developement. These improvements are of paramount importance, not only to the practical farmer, but to the whole community. Every human being has an interest in that art which is the foundation of all other arts, and the basis of all civilization.

Skill as well as industry is at least as requisite in agriculture, as in any of the finer but less useful arts. The head must direct the hand of husbandry; and in cultivating the earth, the most incessant toil, without the guidance of knowledge, and the superintendance of intellect, is of little avail. The science of agriculture is in a great degree founded on experience. It is therefore of consequence that every farmer should know what has been done, and what is doing by others engaged in the same occupation, and that he should impart to others the fruits of his own experiments and observations. Knowledge of this description can in no way be so cheaply, beneficially and generally diffused

that no more than one fourth part of his paper shall, in any case, be filled with advertisements; and in general a still smaller portion of it will be occupied by advertising customers. Party politics, and polemical divinity shall be likewise absolutely excluded from the columns of the New England Farmer.

Massachusetts Agricultural Repository and Journal.

We know of a publication so well deserving of liberal patronage and general diffusion among an agricultural community, as the above named. We have turned over the leaves of many works of a similar nature issued on either side of the Atlantic, but have seen none, which we think contains, in proportion to its quantity of matter, so much to be remembered and practised upon as the subject of this notice. Some foreign journals which we have seen, contain articles more elaborately written, but at the same time they are generally more speculative, and less useful. Good Sense, Science and Agricultural Experience are exhibited in every number of the Massachusetts Journal, and by their union give results, which cannot fail to benefit that portion

agriculture, our Journal during the last thirty years has contained a great number of opposite and irreconcileable opinions. But this ought not to diminish the public confidence, since it is avowed to be conducted on the principles of free enquiry, and since it is not more liable to this objection than all similar works, published in this or in the European world. Men of science are found to differ on most essential points. How many theories have been published, have prevailed for a time, and have gone into oblivion in the important science of medicine! How materially has chemical science changed, not only since the time of Priestly and Black, but since it was supposed to be irrevocably fixed by Lavoisier and the French chemists of his school! How great are the divisions of theoretical opinion among the Geologists, the Wernerians and Huttonians!"

We give the preceding with a view in part to solicit the indulgence of the reader, should our Journal, (as it doubtless will,) exhibit opposite theories and clashing opinions. Light is often elicited by the collision of opaque bodies, and the publication of erroneous theories, will sometimes lead to their refutation and the consequent developement of important prin-

239   Facsimile of the first number of the *New England Farmer*, Boston, August 3, 1822

THE CONTRIBUTION OF THE AGRICULTURAL PRESS

THE farm press opened its first attack upon the stifling conservatism of the men who tilled the soil. The new papers provided vehicles for the spread of agricultural thought and for the interchange of farm experience. They gave to the man who toiled on his own land "useful facts, adapted to the comprehension of uneducated common sense." Their contribution to the farm life of the nation can never be measured. Within a little more than a quarter century after the founding of the first farm paper, there was established the first of those colleges of agriculture which have revolutionized the husbandry of America.

NEW-YORK FARMER,
AND
Horticultural Repository.

VOL. I.]   NEW-YORK, JANUARY, 1828.   [NO. 1.

INTRODUCTORY REMARKS.

THE success and utility of this publication will depend, principally, on the practical knowledge of its contributors. The title denotes the nature of the work; —embracing all those subjects calculated to promote a taste for rural studies and pursuits—including information on agriculture and its subsidiary sciences—the most improved methods of gardening and farming—descriptions of the best cultivated farms, and biographical sketches of distinguished agriculturists—and reviews of publications devoted to subjects coming within the province of the work. Its prospective character may be learned from the sources whence are ex-

mit, and decorated with no plumes, but presented in the unstudied attractions of native plainness.

Our expectations from public patronage are moderate. The fields where we expect to gather our fruits, do indeed lie before us in pleasing and delightful prospect; yet there intervene heaths and obstructions of briars and thorns. Among these we shall cheerfully and perseveringly toil, in full anticipation of eventually gaining an easy and free access to the bowers of plenty.

[For the N Y. Farmer and Horticultural Repository.]
HORTICULTURAL SOCIETY

240   Facsimile of the first number of the *New York Farmer*, New York, January, 1828

CHAPTER VI

THE HEYDAY OF THE OLD FARM

THE issues of the new agricultural press were read by farmers who lived in the last phase of the old husbandry before the methods and machines of the new day had altered the life of the countryside. From that time, thousands of years ago, when farmers, by cultivating the flood plain of the Nile, had made possible a vigorous and enduring civilization, farming had been largely manual labor. For probably fifty centuries, as civilization crossed the boundaries of Egypt, spread into Asia and Europe and came finally to America, the simple tasks of sowing, plowing, reaping, and threshing underwent but little fundamental change. Then in the nineteenth century came revolution. The old farm which persisted almost to the close of this century marks the end of the old order in America.

Its methods or tools were not so primitive as those of the ancients. There had been much advance and progress was being made with constantly increasing rapidity. But the time had not yet come when the machine had taken the place of hand labor on the soil as it had already done in the factories. The farmer, like the old-time artisan, took pride in his handiwork. He lived, moreover, in a day when the countryside was broad and the cities small and far away. The greater part of the people of America were farmers like himself. He knew no other calling and aspired to none. If he were ambitious, he went West where land was cheap and bought up a large holding. But he remained a farmer and was content.

Farming conditions were better in the nineteenth than in the eighteenth century. The stagnation which resulted from complete loss of contact with a market had disappeared. Turnpikes were built throughout the eastern states until a loose network of improved highways covered the farming districts. After the completion of the Erie Canal in 1825, canal building became almost a craze. The farmer's products were hauled in the little canal boats to the population centers of the coast. New machines were appearing but were not in common use. Slowly the practice of fertilization was spreading and the land, impoverished by the exploitation of the pioneers, was bringing forth better crops. Some of the basic ideas of the men who at the end of the eighteenth century had led the way in agricultural improvement were spreading among the common folk of the soil.

In spite of the changes, the old farm was still in the stage of the handicrafts. But the craftsmen were no longer serfs or peasants as for so many centuries they had been in Europe and Asia. The rough struggle for life in America, the isolation, the development of the self-sufficient farm had produced a husbandman, independent and self-reliant. He had shaken off the peasant heritage. He was the American farmer, a new type in the history of husbandry. Intellectual and social isolation made him conservative; in his communities persisted the traditions of the past. But the great task of turning a wilderness into a nation kept his face turned toward the future.

THE VILLAGE OF CATSKILL

THE eighteenth century merged imperceptibly into the nineteenth in the little country villages of America. The passing years were not without change, here and there an old house burned or was torn down and replaced by a new one. Those that remained assumed a venerable aspect that gave a settled and stable appearance to the whole village. A stranger coming in the 'twenties or 'thirties into a hamlet like Catskill would feel

241   From N. P. Willis, *American Scenery Illustrated in a Series of Views by W. H. Bartlett*, London, 1840

that he had entered a community whose roots lay deep in the past. The rawness of the frontier had worn off, but the customs and the outlook of the country folk of New England, New York, or Pennsylvania in the time of President Andrew Jackson did not differ greatly from those when Crèvecœur attended the winter frolics of his neighbors.

THE STAGE AND THE TURNPIKE

BETWEEN the villages near the seaboard turnpikes, in the first decade of the nineteenth century, began to take the place of the rough roads which had been used in colonial times. Turnpike companies were organized by the farmers of the locality and the merchants of the towns and cities that were affected. The improved roads were built by private enterprise. At toll gates the traveler paid for his use of the highway. It was

242   From *The Ladies' Home Journal*, March, 1901, painting by W. L. Taylor.
© Curtis Publishing Company

the turnpike and the later canal that, crossing and recrossing the back-country, put its isolated people in closer touch with the village markets and brought new life into stagnant areas. Over the new roads rolled the great stage coach of an older day, carrying passengers, perhaps, from Philadelphia to New York. Young bloods went to ride with the maidens of their choice in the carriages that were the luxury of the time.

243   From a photograph by the United States Department of Agriculture

THE RURAL CENTER

THESE quiet country villages have persisted into the twentieth century, little centers for the life of the farms about them. To the superficial observer they seem alike, groups of houses clustering about a store or two. Yet each has its atmosphere. Many of their people are farmers who, when the vigorous years of life passed, turned over the work in the fields to younger hands and came to town to live. The rest, like the merchant and the carpenter, are dependent for their livelihood upon the surrounding farms. The churches are country churches and on the Sabbath the deep tones of their bells carry far out over the farms calling the families to worship. Such villages are far removed from the European hamlets where the farmers' homes are huddled close together and from which the husbandmen go out each morning to work in their fields.

244   From a photograph by Rudolf Eickemeyer

THE AMERICAN FARMSTEAD

As the nineteenth century opened, the countryside of the North assumed an aspect that it has retained into the present. The highways were bordered by small farms, in size from fifty to two hundred acres. On these the farmer's house and barns were built. Here was his business and his home. He drove two or three miles to town to do his trading, to get his mail, to have his horses shod or to go to church. Of life beyond the horizon of his little community he knew little. He visited the far-away city perhaps a half dozen times in a busy life.

245   From a photograph by the United States Department of Agriculture

THE INDEPENDENT FARMER

THE shift from village life to that of the scattered farmsteads brought into sharp relief the home as the center of rural life. Out of this isolation developed a cohesive and self-reliant family group. Owner of his own land, with the shaping of his destiny in his own hands, the American farmer of the nineteenth century outgrew the peasant's state of mind. In his thoughts stirred the new ideas which he got from his farm paper. He was animated by a spirit of progress which was furthered by the annual exhibition of the agricultural society of which he was a member. He confidently expected his children to go forward to opportunities and achievements that had been beyond his reach.

246   From a lithograph by Currier & Ives, 1864, after the painting *A Cold Morning*, 1862, by G. H. Durrie

247   From a photograph by courtesy of Malcolm Keir

THE ABANDONED FARM

Not all farmers were successful. Here and there, particularly in New England, may still be found desolate shells whose rooms no longer echo the cheerful sounds of family life. There were many shiftless and ignorant husbandmen whose buildings fell into decay and whose farms were sold under foreclosure. There were others who never rose above the status of "hired men" or at best of tenants. Dirty children played about their squalid shacks and in thriftless dooryards. In rural communities these folk formed a separate stratum, a group below the substantial husbandmen who had achieved independence.

248   From *The Cultivator*, Albany, 1848

AN IMPROVED FARMHOUSE

The heyday of the old farm came in the 'forties and 'fifties. Well-to-do farmers aspired to no little pretension. Houses took on a certain rural elegance. The picture represents a type of house advocated by one of the best farm papers in New York State and widely copied in the rebuilding of homesteads.

THE OLD LADY WITH THE CUP

ONE needed but to look into the faces of these farmer folk of the nineteenth century to appreciate the inherent soundness of the rural population. Perhaps they were uncouth; their manners suffered from isolation. Perhaps they were uneducated; early nineteenth-century schools were far from adequate. But the better folk had a native intelligence and a stability that bespoke dignity and worth. And withal, in spite of very many and very pronounced human weaknesses, they were in the main a kindly and an upright people governing their lives in accordance with the dictates of a simple faith.

249   From a photograph by Rudolf Eickemeyer

250   From a photograph by Rudolf Eickemeyer

THE FIDDLER

A TYPE to be found in every country community was the fiddler who played at the country dances. The busy life of the farm gave little time for the culture of the world beyond the bounds of the neighborhood. But in the housewife's little beds of old-fashioned flowers about the yard, in the designs of her patch-work quilts and rag rugs, and in the fiddling of her husband an inherent love of the beautiful that was part of their racial heritage sprang into a somewhat stunted life. Fiddlers were not common and sometimes traveled miles to the merry-makings over which they presided.

My playin's only middlin' — tunes I picked up when a boy —
The kindo' — sorto' fiddlin' that the folks calls "cordaroy";
"The Old Fat Gal" and "Rye-straw", and "My Sailyor's on the
    Sea",
Is the old cowtillions I "saw" when the ch'ice is left to me;
        So I plunk and plonk and plink,
        And rosum-up my bow
        And play the tunes that make you think
        The devil's in your toe!
            — JAMES WHITCOMB RILEY, *Neghborly
                Poems*, © 1891–1925.
Used by special permission of the publishers, The Bobbs-Merrill Company.

THE "RUBE"

ISOLATION and individualism bred types that came to be called "hayseeds" and "rubes"; rough, provincial, tobacco-chewing, cider-drinking rustics. They knew nothing of the fine clothes of the city; coarse shoes or leather boots in summer and felt boots in winter served equally well for most occasions. They spoke the farmer's vernacular with the farmer's inflection. They were only the more striking of the country folk. Frequently they were numbered among the thrifty and well-to-do. They have inspired the conventional farmer figure of literature and the stage, Ezekiel Biglow of Lowell's *Biglow Papers*, David Harum, and Solon Shingle, a Yankee of the early theater.

251   A Yankee Farmer, Vermont, from a photograph by
        Rudolf Eickemeyer

252   One of The Old Folks at Home, from a photograph by
Clifton Johnson

THE FARMER AND THE BIBLE

THE two important books of the farmer-folk of the mid-nineteenth century were the Bible and the almanac. The former offered the cure for the ills of the soul, the latter for those of the body. Both were studied frequently and with care. The Bible, moreover, contained on its fly-leaf a list of names and dates, the family record of joy and sorrow. In its great pages, black with massive type, the tired mother found a message that gave meaning to the dreary round of work that was her life.

254 From a photograph by Rudolf Eickemeyer

THE "HAYSEED"

WHITTIER and Riley were peculiarly the poets of the "old farm," the one for New England and the other for that region of vigorous life where many elements were blended, the valley of the Ohio. Both have depicted the picturesque countryman with his idiosyncracies and his rugged virtues. Riley's lines set forth a characteristic which was the foundation of his whole life and which was the peculiarity that set the American farmer apart from the servile husbandmen of Europe.

> I tell you what I'd ruther do —
>   Ef I only had my ruthers, —
> I'd ruther work when I wanted to
> Than be bossed 'round by others; —
>   I'd ruther kindo' get the swing
>   O' what was *needed*, first, I jing!
>   Afore I *swet* at anything!
> — JAMES WHITCOMB RILEY, *Neghborly
>   Poems*, © 1891–1925.
> Used by special permission of the publishers, The Bobbs-Merrill
> Company

253   From a photograph by Rudolf Eickemeyer

A TYPE OF BY-GONE DAYS

THE time was to come after the Civil War when the farmers thought of themselves as a group apart in the national population. But in the first half of the nineteenth century, in the heyday of the "old farm," they were not conscious of themselves. They were the Americans and most Americans were like them. They had the virtues of conservatism. Whig or Democrat, they were loyal to the parties which they espoused and looked with disfavor upon the man who vacillated between the two. Much modern unthinking party loyalty traces its origin to these farm communities.

SPRING PLOWING

THE yearly round of farm life changed little with the merging of the eighteenth into the nineteenth century. In fall and spring the husbandman followed the plow day after day. The heavy, monotonous work taxed his physical endurance and retarded his intellectual development. He remained conservative, and often narrow. But the variety of his work, the thought required in the management of his acres and the sale of his produce, and the stimulus which flowed from independence prevented stagnation. Only in the settlements far removed from a market did progress disappear and life sink back upon a dead level of monotony.

255   From the painting by William Steeple Davis (1884–). © by the artist and in his possession

THE HAYMAKERS

JOHN BURROUGHS of the Catskills was a child of the "old farm" and, for him, it never lost its poetry. With rare perception he saw and voiced the exhilaration of its ordinary labor. Haying was the period of storm and stress in the farmer's year: "It is a thirty or forty days' war, in which the farmer and his 'hands' are pitted against the heat and the rain and the legions of timothy and clover. Everything about it has the urge, the hurry, the excitement of a battle. . . . The Americans are — or were — the best mowers. A foreigner could never quite give the masterly touch. The hayfield has its code. One man must not take another's swath unless he expects to be crowded. Each expects to take his turn leading the band. The scythe may be whetted as to ring out a saucy challenge to the rest. It is a great ignominy to be mowed out of your swath."

256   From a photograph by Rudolf Eickemeyer

257   From a photograph by Rudolf Eickemeyer

DRAWING HAY

"How full of pictures, too! — the smooth slopes dotted with cocks with lengthening shadows; the great, broad-backed, soft-cheeked loads, moving along the lanes and brushing under the trees; the unfinished stacks with forkfuls of hay being handed up its side to the builder, and when finished, the shape of a great pear with a pole in the top for a stem. Maybe in the fall and winter the calves and yearlings will hover around it and gnaw its base until it overhangs them and shelters them from the storm. Or the farmer will 'fodder' his cows there, — one of the most picturesque scenes to be witnessed on the farm, — twenty or thirty or forty milchers filing along toward the stack in the field, or clustered about it, waiting the promised bite. In great, green flakes the hay is rolled off, and distributed about in small heaps on the unspotted snow. After the cattle have eaten, the birds — the snow buntings and red-polls — come and pick up the crumbs, the seeds of

258   From *Harper's Weekly*, Aug. 30, 1879, after a drawing by W. M. Cary

the grasses and weeds. At night the fox and owl come for mice." — JOHN BURROUGHS, *In the Catskills*, 1911.

HARVEST TIME

HARVEST was also a period of hurry and excitement. When the crops were in, the rhythm of the flails echoed through the barns. As the nineteenth century grew older, threshers appeared to expedite the work. But they were not common until the century was well advanced.

CORN HUSKING IN THE FIELD

Corn harvest followed that of wheat and oats when October frosts touched the long leaves with brown. The labor of this season was typical of the hand labor of the old farm. The farmer, his boys and a hired man or two went into the fields armed with corn hooks. Slowly they worked their way back and forth along the rows cutting the stalks and piling them into great shocks to be hauled to the barn for winter husking. When time pressed or labor was scarce, the farmer was forced to content himself with husking — stripping the ears from the standing stalks. The corn harvest was slow and tedious work, but the bins filled with the yellow ears were ample reward. They held out the prospect of fat animals during the winter season to come.

CORN HUSKING IN THE BARN

Corn was husked with a simple peg which the farmer whittled from a splinter of hardwood. It was one of the many home-made tools that were necessary in the farm activities. In the next two decades noisy machines could be heard clanking in the fields and barns. Among these were the corn binder and the power-driven husking

259   After the painting, 1834, by W. S. Mount (1807–68), courtesy of A. P. Buffet

machine. They marked the passing of the "old farm" where the husbandman had worked largely with his hands. Their advent brought new problems, new points of view, a new civilization to the American country-side.

260   From a lithograph by Currier & Ives, 1861, after the painting by Eastman Johnson (1824–1906)

261   From *A Book of Drawings by A. B. Frost.* © 1904, P. F. Collier & Son Co., by permission of the Dodge Publishing Co.

PIGS

No farm was complete without its pigpen. Swine were an important source of food supply for the farmer's family. In the spring the pigs were left to wander in the orchards and fields where grain was not growing. But before they were set at liberty, rings were put in their snouts to prevent the depredations which were sure to follow unrestricted rooting. In the fall the hogs were brought back to the pen and fed bountifully with corn and grain. Then, when winter had fully come and the days and nights were cold, the hogs were killed.

Fat sides of pork hung in the out-houses where the bacon was stripped off, the sausage was ground and the hams were shaped for barrels of brine. In due time the hams and the sides of bacon were lifted from the liquid and hung from the sooty cross poles of the smokehouse. Underneath them a smudge was built and carefully tended for many days until the meat, fragrant from the smoke, was fully cured. "Butchering time" was a time of plenty when choice cuts of "tenderloin" graced the farmer's table. Yet little of the meat was eaten fresh; the greater part was preserved in one way or another, to be used, some of it, as late as the harvest season of the following summer.

THE COVERED BRIDGE ON A COUNTRY HIGHWAY

THE harvest ended, the farmer turned his thoughts to hauling his produce to mill or market. Few of the highways, aside from the turnpiked main roads, were improved. In the spring they were trenched with ruts and oozy with mud. In the winter, sometimes for weeks, they were buried under deep drifts of snow. In

favored localities turnpikes were built and the farmer on his way to the village stopped at the tollgate to pay his pennies. In the main, his facilities for transporting his produce to market were poor. The covered bridge meant a safe passage all winter and protection to the bridge itself from the crushing weight of snow drifts. The roof and sides protected the planks and girders against exposure to the weather. Such a structure was a marked advance over the rude bridge which the colonial farmer had thrown across the streams.

262   From a photograph by Clifton Johnson

HAULING LOGS

In the winter woods the farmer's ax rang clear, strewing the snow with clean chips. The year's supply of wood must be worked up. There were logs to be drawn on bob-sleds to the saw-mill. The farmer always needed lumber for repairing his buildings and fences. Perhaps, in the spring, he would put up a new and larger barn to take the place of the old one.

THE BARN–RAISING, A SOCIAL AND CO–OPERATIVE EVENT

THE barn-raisings, which were in the beginning an adjustment to frontier conditions, lingered until near the middle of the nineteenth century. The afternoon was the time chosen. "The forenoon was occupied by the carpenter

263   From the painting by Paul King (1867–) by courtesy of the artist

and the farm hands in putting the sills and 'sleepers' in place. . . . When the hands arrived, the great beams and posts and joists and braces were carried to their place on the platform, and the first 'bent,'

as it was called, was put together and pinned by oak pins that the boys brought. Then pike poles were distributed, the men, fifteen or twenty of them, arranged in a line abreast of the bent; the boss carpenter steadied and guided the corner post and gave the word of command, — 'Take holt, boys!' 'Now, set her up!' 'Up with her!' 'Up she goes!' . . . Slowly the great timbers go up; louder grows the word of command, till the bent is up. . . . In every neighborhood there was always some man who was especially useful at 'raisins'. He was bold and strong and quick. He helped guide and superintend the work. He was the first one up on the bent. . . . He was as much at home up there as a squirrel." — JOHN BURROUGHS, *In the Catskills*, 1911.

264 From *The Ladies' Home Journal*, April, 1901, painting by W. L. Taylor. © Curtis Publishing Company

265   From a photograph by Clifton Johnson

THE DIVINING ROD

THE superstitions of an earlier day lingered on into the nineteenth century. The farmer, preparing to dig a well, provided himself first with a "divining rod," a crotch, preferably, of witch hazel. Back and forth across the area which he had selected he would trudge, holding the ends of the crotch in his hands. Slowly the stick leaned forward, through no conscious effort on his part, until the crotch pointed straight down. He would mark the point and approach it from every quarter. Each time the rod would turn and point to the earth. It had "found water" and the well was dug. Not everybody is a "douser"; it is a gift not wholly denied, even to this twentieth century.

RURAL MANNERS

CARLYLE thought Americans bores. Mrs. Trollope felt that they were boors as well. It is true these farmers had few intellectual interests outside their own small communities, at most a little dash of politics and religion. The jackknife was an indisputable aid to the difficulties of conversation. These men were engaged in subduing a wilderness. They dealt single-handed with the earth and

266   From the painting *Coming to the Point*, by W. S. Mount, in the New York Public Library

the elements. They had little time for speculation, yet in a very real sense they felt that they were laying the foundations of a great nation.

267   From *A Book of Drawings* by A. B. Frost.   © 1904, P. F. Collier & Son Co., by permission of the Dodge Publishing Co.

THE SICK COW

FARM life could be caricatured as well as sentimentalized. Few men have seen the foibles, the rustic oddities and the comical side of country folks with clearer and more kindly eye than A. B. Frost. Yet in his drawings is a truth that gives them more than passing value. The typical farmer of the nineteenth century counted his animals almost as members of his household. Sickness among them touched his heart as well as his pocketbook. In most cases he had to depend upon himself to diagnose the ailment and effect its cure.

THE YANKEE PEDLAR

WITH the eighteenth century had passed the self-sufficient farm. More and more as the new century progressed the farmer came to depend upon the market for the sale of his goods and the purchase of his wares. The enterprising Yankee pedlar brought the market to his door. The "tin wagon" and the "wood wagon" bumped over the country roads from farm to farm leaving behind many things the housewife badly needed, sold often at prices that had little relation to their actual cost.

268   From photograph of the painting by Thomas W. Wood (1823–1903), courtesy of the Wood Art Gallery, Montpelier, Vt.

269   Detail from the painting by Alfred C. Howland (1838–1909), in the Layton Art Gallery, Milwaukee, Wis.

DRIVING A BARGAIN

BUT the farmers themselves were not without shrewdness. Almost from the beginning they had to contend with tricky land agents, and defective titles, and the wily country merchant who, in the words of Crèvecœur, "sells for good that which perhaps he knows to be indifferent, because he also knows that the ashes he has collected, the wheat he has taken in may not be so good or so clean as it was asserted. Fearful of fraud in all his dealings and transactions, he arms himself therefore with it; strict integrity is not much wanted as each is on his guard in his daily intercourse and this mode of thinking and acting becomes habitual." Nowhere did this old code of the frontier persist longer in its pristine purity than in the gentle art of "swapping horses" and other live stock.

270   From *Harper's Weekly*, Nov. 26, 1870, after a drawing by John Bolles

THE TRAVELING TINKER

MOST of the itinerant mechanics who made the rounds from house to house passed with the eighteenth century. But the tinker remained. He came in either winter or summer as his work brought him from place to place. When he left, the housewife's pots and pans were mended and in shape for another year. If, for a long time the wanderer failed to appear, the farmer himself became a tinker. With the tinker there persisted the scissors grinder and the umbrella mender, reminiscent of the vanished eighteenth century.

THE VILLAGE POST OFFICE AND COUNTRY STORE

COMMERCE and the mails brought the farmer and his family to the general store in the little country village. Over its battered counters passed the goods that the family needed, dishes, cloth for shirts and dresses, lamps that burned whale oil or, later, kerosene, groceries in exchange for the butter, eggs, and poultry from the farm. The steady increase in the variety of the goods which the country merchant offered was the measure of the decline of the old-time, self-sufficient farm.

271   From photograph of the painting, 1872, by Thomas W. Wood, courtesy of the Wood Art Gallery, Montpelier, Vt.

THE COUNTRY STORE AS A SOCIAL CENTER

THE cast-iron stove, red on cold winter days, and the coal scuttle which served as cuspidor were the center of the group that made a club of the country store. Stories of adventure, successful deals, news, politics, and religion were but some of the topics bandied back and forth. In these impromptu gatherings the great difference between urban and rural life was daily made clear. Nothing in the life of the little neighborhood escaped notice. Few things could long be concealed. The affairs of no one were solely his own concern. Of never-ending interest were the strength and frailties of human kind.

272   From *The Ladies' Home Journal*, March, 1900, painting by A. B. Frost.   © Curtis Publishing Company

273   From photograph of the painting, about 1870, by Thomas W. Wood, courtesy of the Wood Art Gallery, Montpelier, Vt.

THE VILLAGE BLACKSMITH

THE blacksmith's shop a little way down the street was also a center of congregation. The local tavern was a third. In these places the monotony of heavy daily labor and the isolation of the farmstead were relieved. In the barroom of the tavern the heavy drinking of the previous century still found its votaries. Here came often the farmer's wife, when her shopping and visiting were done, to help her drunken husband to the seat in the "platform" wagon and to drive home through the gathering dusk. For her the village offered no place of congregation. If she had a club, it was her church with its "Ladies Aid" and its "Missionary Society." At the meetings or at the sewing bees she had her opportunity to contribute to and absorb the current news of the doings of her neighbors.

274   From *Harper's Weekly*, July 6, 1867, after a drawing by Charles J. Bush

THE FOURTH OF JULY

THERE were special seasons and holidays when the country people were called together. In the nineteenth century the Fourth of July was one of these. From far and near the farmers and their families came to celebrate in democratic fashion the birth of national independence. There were speeches, refreshments and whiskey. It was a time when folks who saw each other but once or twice a year met again and renewed acquaintance. There was marching and dancing, and the local politician was pleased to address a few words to his constituency.

275 From *A Book of Drawings by A. B. Frost.* © 1904 P. F. Collier & Son Co., by permission of the Dodge Publishing Co.

THE CIRCUS

At some time during the summer the circus came to a larger neighboring town. Over the country roads it wound its dusty way from village to village, terrifying the horses that had the ill fortune to meet its bears or elephants on the highway. For the country folk the circus was the one great entertainment of the year. To many the blare and tinsel under the great tent was life's chief consolation. There were others who felt the circus sinful, who shunned its sights and kept its glaring posters off their barns and fences. For the farm boys and girls it was a transport of flawless joy.

THE RETURN FROM THE COUNTY FAIR

In the autumn came the county fair. For three and sometimes four days the farmers from miles around drove to the fair grounds to see the exhibits, to watch the horse races, and to visit with folk from distant

parts of the country. Proud women watched the placing of the premium tags on their handiwork. The men made the rounds of the pens of animals to observe and comment on the judging. Local dealers had booths and tents where the new agricultural machinery that was coming into vogue was demonstrated and explained by honey-tongued agents. Could Elkanah Watson have lived in the 'fifties and 'sixties he would have seen his Berkshire System developed beyond his fondest hopes.

276   From *Harper's Weekly,* Oct. 25, 1873, after a drawing by W. M. Cary

277   From *A Book of Drawings* by A. B. Frost. © 1904 P. F. Collier & Son Co., by permission of the Dodge Publishing Co.

"THE ARKANSAW TRAVELER"

THE country people of the North were as fond of the dance as were the old planter aristocracy of Virginia. To be sure the discipline of the Methodist Church forbade this frivolity and there were many communities in which a strong religious sentiment either suppressed it or drove it into unseemly places. But in the average country neighborhood dancing was taken as a matter of course and a good fiddler was in demand. Hornpipes were not unknown, but the clog was a general favorite while the fiddles vibrated "The Irish Washerwoman," "Old Zip Coon," "The Arkansaw Traveler" and a host of other lively tunes.

278   From *Harper's Weekly*, Nov. 13, 1858

THE COUNTRY DANCE

PERHAPS the country dances of the North were not so elegant as those of old Virginia but they were entered into with as much zest. No dancing master taught the young swains and maidens to make of the Lanciers a thing of grace and beauty. As the fiddler, with violin held under his chin or resting on his knee, sang out the calls, "Balance corners!" and "Salute your partner!" the couples stamped and scraped and whirled with the rhythm of the dance, to which the old folks, too, kept time. What was lost in grace was more than made up in hearty vigor, and the breathless fiddler, when the set had ended, was greeted by a storm of applause.

279   From *Harper's Weekly*, Nov. 13, 1858, after a drawing by Winslow Homer

KISSING GAMES

There were games as well as dances at the country parties. "Blind Man's Buff," rough and strenuous, was a favorite early in the century. "Pop-Goes-the-Weazel" and the husking bee were popular for a longer time. For the husking the company assembled on the barn floor lighted with flaring lanterns. The red ear was the prize sought for. He who found it might kiss the girl beside him while she, with becoming modesty, must resist his efforts. Singing, jokes, and rough pranks added to the fun while the farmer's work was being done. So old customs lived to grace the heyday of the farm and passed only when the more polished manners of the later nineteenth century began to make themselves felt in the countryside.

THE SURPRISE PARTY

In the nineteenth century, as in the eighteenth, winter was the time when social life found scope. At night along the frozen roads jingled the bells of the teams drawing great bob-sleds with a noisy party of merry-makers. Farmers bundled their families into their sleighs and drove over to spend the day with a neighbor. Now and again a surprise party would burst into an unsuspecting farmhouse for a dance or a frolic. Play as well as work was vigorous. The farmer, absorbed in the activities of his community, rarely sensed that he was out of touch with the centers of thought and culture of the nation. His work, his home and the neighborhood of which he was a member satisfied the longings within him. He was content.

280   From *Frank Leslie's Illustrated Newspaper*, March 7, 1874, after a drawing by
Joseph Becker

281   Pitching Quoits, from a photograph by Clifton Johnson

COUNTRY SPORTS

THE farmers had few competitive games. Wrestling, jumping and foot races were common; such sports as were tests of individual skill or prowess. Organized teams in which the members must sometimes sacrifice a brilliant individual exhibition in the interests of team play were unknown. It is doubtful if the young men of the farming communities would have taken kindly to them because of the emphasis which the whole community life put upon individualism. The farmer and his sons were taught by their environment to be independent but they were not trained in co-operation. If called to war, they must undergo a great mental readjustment before they could accept with complacency the rigors of military discipline. Perhaps this is the reason why the small farmers of the North, in contrast to the planters of the South, have had little interest in military things and have tended to the belief that an army picked up after an emergency arose would be sufficient to meet all occasions.

282   A French Wrestling Match, from *Frank Leslie's Illustrated Newspaper*, Sept. 13, 1873, after a drawing by Joseph Becker

283 From *A Book of Drawings by A. B. Frost.* © 1904 P. F. Collier & Son Co., by permission of the Dodge Publishing Co.

THE GAME BETWEEN THE SQUIRE AND THE POSTMASTER

CARD playing was common and euchre and poker were favorites. But, like dancing, this amusement was looked at askance by many church people who thought that cards and gambling were inseparable. There was no taboo on checkers, however. This was a man's game and numbered the best minds of the neighborhood among its devotees. To be the champion checker player of the village was to achieve distinction.

284　　　　　　　　From *Frank Leslie's Illustrated Newspaper*, Jan. 15, 1876

THE SPELLING MATCH

PERHAPS nearest to a game organized into teams was the spelling match, yet even here the victory sought was individual championship. The one who could "spell down" the rest was a person of some consequence. Through the spelling contests the country folk became familiar with long words whose meanings they sometimes did not understand and whose only useful purpose in their lives was to compass the defeat of an adversary.

285   From *A Book of Drawings by A. B. Frost.*   © 1904, P. F. Collier & Son Co., by permission of the Dodge Publishing Co.

HOME FROM THE LEGISLATURE — THE DAY OF RECKONING

POLITICS were of perennial interest to the independent, individualistic farmer of the nineteenth century. In every sense he was a democrat jealous of his rights and standing in awe of no man. The more ambitious among his number sought election to the state legislature very often because the salary seemed considerable to men whose actual money income was still small. The scene might well represent the aftermath of a legislature's vote to increase the pay of its members at the expense of the taxpayers.

286   From *Outing*, Sept., 1907, after a drawing by Oliver Kemp, reproduced by permission

AROUND THE CIDER BARREL

IN the winter the cider barrel, which had been put carefully in the cellar after the apple harvest, was tapped and its quality tested. But the use of strong liquor was declining among the farmers as among other people of the nation. The much ridiculed temperance societies of the early nineteenth century proved that they had come to stay, and a sentiment against drunkenness set in. No longer was wine or rum or beer the inevitable accompaniment of social gatherings. Though cider persisted longest of the beverages made on the farm, in the 'forties and 'fifties its use was no longer universal.

AT THE MAPLE SUGAR CAMP

"ONE of the features peculiar to this country, and one of the most picturesque of them all, is sugar-making in the maple woods in spring. This is the first work of the season, and to the boys is more play than work. In the Old World, and in more simple and imaginative times, how such an operation as this would have got into literature, and how many legends and associations would have clustered about it! It is woodsy; it is an encampment among the maples. . . . How the tin

287   From *Harper's Weekly*, May 4, 1867, after a photograph

buckets glisten in the gray woods; how the robins laugh; how the nuthatches call; how lightly the thin blue smoke rises among the trees! The squirrels are out of their dens; the migrating water-fowls are streaming northward; the sheep and cattle look wistfully toward the bare fields; the tide of the season, in fact, is just beginning to rise." — JOHN BURROUGHS, *In the Catskills*, 1911.

288   From a photograph by Rudolf Eickemeyer

HOME FROM THE VENDUE

IN the spring also came the vendues when homes were broken and goods were sold. Perhaps the family was "going West." Perhaps the father had died and his wife was going to live with one of her children. The farmers gathered for the sale, swapped stories as they looked over the belongings that were offered and bid in the things they wanted. When the vendue was over wagon-loads of miscellaneous tools, furniture and utensils jogged over the rutty roads.

289   From *Harper's Weekly*, Aug. 19, 1876, after a drawing by E. A. Abbey

EASTER MUSIC IN CHURCH

THE country church was strong in the heyday of the old farm. A vigorous, if usually uneducated, clergy called upon their parishioners to hate sin and serve God. Sectarian interest and rivalry were keen. Methodists, Baptists, Presbyterians, Campbellites and a host of other denominations competed for membership until even the tiniest hamlets rarely had less than two churches. Winter revivals were of almost yearly occurrence. As the people flocked to the meetings and caught the emotionalism of the hour, excitement ran high. In the early days of the century on the frontier men and women had swooned and fallen in convulsions at the camp-meetings. By the middle of the century, however, such violent manifestations of the "coming of the Holy Ghost" had disappeared. But the revival which awakened the quiet, isolated community into new life and turned its thoughts into new channels was an institution that the country needed. So it lived on and flourished bringing, in spite of all its extravagances, many blessings to the solid folk of the countryside.

290   From photograph of the painting, about 1870, by Thomas
W. Wood, courtesy of the Wood Art Gallery, Montpelier, Vt.

THE DIFFICULT TEXT

SECTARIAN differences of ritual and creed sharply divided not only the clergy but the congregations in the little country villages. Religious disputes were as keen as those of politics. Rival ministers with little intellectual background often attacked one another in doctrinal sermons. For some folk the difference between "immersion" and "sprinkling" was nothing less than the difference between heaven and hell. The Bible was read in the implicit faith that its every word had proceeded out of the mouth of God. This old faith still flourishes in the American countryside. The violence of sectarian animosities disgusted some active-minded persons who, by sudden transition, passed from ardent worship to a free thinking that bordered on infidelity.

291   From *Frank Leslie's Illustrated Newspaper*, April 15, 1871

THE MINISTER'S WOODEN WEDDING

PERHAPS the minister received a hundred dollars a year, perhaps as much as five hundred. His little congregation was poor and the resources of the community were divided between two or more denominations. From time to time the pastor received "donations" to which the farmers came with wagons loaded with the produce of their acres. The clergyman sometimes eked out his meager living by doing a little farming himself. Life for him had many unpleasant features. He was a servant of a congregation often bristling with self-satisfied individualism. He must not antagonize the deacons or the members. The dominant democracy of the country folk too often undermined the authority of their ministers and left them helpless before the whims of the people. Rarely educated men, they were almost invariably facile exhorters whose sermons repeated the well-worn doctrines of their particular sect.

THE COUNTRY DOCTOR

SERVANT also of the community was the country doctor who mended the hurts and cared for the sick among its people. He called no hours of the day his own; no roads were too bad nor storms too fierce for him to try to reach the stricken household. At times he faced emergencies in a lonely house among the hills with what resourcefulness and courage he could summon and with no fellow practitioner to call to his aid. Perhaps a dread scourge, like smallpox, broke out and he had to fight it single-handed. Better than the minister he knew the sins of the community and held his tongue. Exposure, long hard rides on winter nights, and the worry and responsibility of his calling often broke down his resistance. Sometimes before the prime of life had passed he heard the call, "Physician, heal thyself," and could not.

292   From *Harper's Weekly*, 1888, after a drawing by J. Macdonald

293   From a photograph by Clifton Johnson

294 From a photograph by Rudolf Eickemeyer. © Campbell Prints, Inc.;
                    New York

THE COUNTRY BURYING GROUND

WHEN life flickered out, there was little ostentation in the country funeral. The neighbors and relatives gathered in the stricken home. The country preacher spoke of the deceased; there was prayer and singing. Then the procession of carriages moved slowly along the highway to the little burying ground where the one who had gone was laid to rest. As the minister, in the last rites, cast earth upon the casket, there were almost none who did not share his simple faith.

> Yet love will dream, and Faith will trust,
> (Since He who knows our need is just,)
> That somehow, somewhere, meet we must.

THE BAREFOOT BOY

BUT youth came on to take the places of those who had gone. Rarely did the poet of the farmer express more beautifully the sentiment that for him surrounded the farm of the old days than in his famous lines to the farm boy.

> Blessings on thee, little man,
> Barefoot boy, with cheek of tan!
> With thy turned-up pantaloons,
> And thy merry whistled tunes;
> With thy red lip, redder still
> Kissed by strawberries on the hill;
> With the sunshine on thy face,
> Through thy torn brim's jaunty grace;
> From my heart I give thee joy, —
> I was once a barefoot boy!
> —JOHN G. WHITTIER.

THE BOX–TRAP

THE pleasures of the country youth of the nineteenth century were drawn from the life about him. For him there was no baseball until the old farm had almost passed away. Many of the sports and pastimes of his city cousin are even yet strangers to him. Like his father, he early learned to hunt. The box-trap, built of boards, was a triumph of his skill with saw, hammer and jackknife. He set it, baited with an ear of corn, in the barn to catch the rats that burrowed in the bins of grain. He set it in the woods and took rabbits which he proudly brought home for his mother to cook. The open country, rather than the

295   From a lithograph, 1850, by Goupil & Co., after the painting, 1839, by W. S. Mount, by courtesy of A. P. Buffet

paved street, was his playground. As he grew older, he learned to hunt with his father but, in those days, before the advent of the Boy Scouts, he acquired little knowledge of woodcraft. The old farm was far removed from the frontier. Its life was only vaguely reminiscent of that lived on the edge of the wilderness.

CHILDREN AT SCHOOL

IT was the almost universal ambition of the farmer that his children, particularly his boys, should have advantages denied him in the more primitive times in which his own youth had fallen. In the fall, when the forest was a blaze of glory, his "young uns" trudged a mile or a mile and a half to the district school. The children grew up with the country and often achieved a station in life to which their fathers had never aspired. A host of men have come to American public life from a farm background.

296   From the painting *Snap the Whip*, by Winslow Homer, in the Butler Art Gallery, Youngstown, O.

297   From *The Ladies' Home Journal*, Feb., 1901, painting by W. L. Taylor.
                   © Curtis Publishing Company

THE DISTRICT SCHOOL

ALL ages came to school in the winter, the little tots side by side with their brothers and sisters who were eighteen or twenty or even more. There were rowdies aplenty and the tough birch rod was frequently needed. When the autumn farm work was over, some young bloods came to school with little other motive than to test the mettle of the master. If he could be driven from his school, it was a triumph indeed. All grades studied and recited in the rough schoolroom where the benches bore marks of many surreptitious jackknives. A few terms in the district school was all the schooling that most of the nineteenth-century farmers had.

THE VILLAGE DEPOT

THE new industrialism that followed the Civil War drew into the great city more and more of the young men of the countryside. The little engine with its train of painted wooden coaches brought a new world into the country villages. The old isolation began to break down. The people and manners of the city became more familiar to the country folk. The city folk spoke contemptuously of the farmers as "rubes" or "hayseeds." The farmers began to think of themselves as a group apart. The coming of the railroad marked the beginning of the end of the old farm.

298   From *Harper's Weekly*, Aug. 15, 1868, after a drawing by E. L. Henry (1841–1919)

"AFTER THREE YEARS IN THE CITY"

AFTER the middle of the nineteenth century when the boy grew to manhood the home ties that the farm life had made so strong were broken more and more often in a peculiar sense. The young man left the home and the community in which he had been reared and plunged into an environment strange alike to him and to those with whom his life had been cast. The father and mother must watch the youth go off into a world which they knew not, and must

299   From *A Book of Drawings by A. B. Frost.* © 1904, P. F. Collier & Son Co., by permission of the Dodge Publishing Co.

look forward to the time he would return, molded for good or ill by the new life. In either event he would be a stranger to their ways. Parting from such a boy was an experience which the earlier farmers had rarely been called upon to face, a quite different thing from sending a boy off to buy a farm and take a wife in a neighboring county.

The city did not always deal kindly with those who sought their fortune in its throbbing life. There were many who gave up the rugged independence of the farm for a cheap job in a store or a factory. Caught by the glamour of the town, they wasted their slender substance and their opportunities in a life of trivial consequence. Frost's drawing shows a transformation all too frequent.

THE PASSING OF THE OLD FARM

As the nineteenth century drew to a close, the passing of the old farm often became a grim reality. House after house was left desolate and abandoned. Others were turned over to tenants who shared with the owner the meager income from the acres. The children who had played about the door-step were gone, some west to the plains of Iowa or Kansas, others to the city. The father, worn out by heavy work, had died. The aged mother, left alone, gave up the old home to which she had come as a bride, where her babies had been born and whose rooms were hallowed for her by the death of her loved ones. Parting with the only life she knew, with heavy heart she followed her son into the strange terrors of the city.

300   From *The Ladies' Home Journal*, June, 1901, painting by W. L. Taylor.
© Curtis Publishing Company

CHAPTER VII

THE COTTON KINGDOM

THE life and the ideals of the plantation communities of the South stood in marked contrast to those of the farming neighborhoods in Pennsylvania or Ohio. There a rough equality in wealth and social position fostered a democratic spirit. Isolation threw the people of the country district back upon themselves and rustic manners and speech, contrasting with the ways of the city, were the result. But the social system of the South was founded on inequality, the gradations running all the way from the chattel slave to the wealthy planter, the owner of thousands of acres. Ideals of aristocracy gave tone to the community life, even though it was an aristocracy constantly recruited from the common farmers whom the spread of cotton-growing over the lower South had raised to affluence. The plantation was isolated but the wealth of the owner enabled his family to travel, to the coast cities, to resorts in the mountains, to fashionable Saratoga. Inheriting the dignified traditions of eighteenth-century Virginia and Carolina, the cotton planter was polished and urbane. Yet, as much as the northern farmer, his life was centered in the soil.

Cotton was king in the lower South and the crop was raised to the exclusion of almost everything else. Mules and even food were brought down the rivers from Kentucky and the farms of the Northwest. In the upper South, north of the cotton belt, a more diversified agriculture was the rule, although tobacco surpassed other crops in Virginia and Kentucky. But the plantation system with negro slavery extended to this climatic border region and bound the border states to the southern civilization.

Like earlier landed aristocracies in Europe the planters easily and naturally assumed political and military leadership in the communities of which they were the most important economic factors and over the social life of which their wives and daughters presided. Many sons of the South, reared in the habit of command, became officers in the army and navy. In the decades before the Civil War the influence exercised by the representatives of the southern civilization in the councils of the nation was wholly out of proportion to their numbers. The relatively simple economic foundations of their section made its needs easy to determine and to demonstrate. Successful planters proved themselves also successful politicians. They represented an agricultural interest which was often in conflict with the growing commercial interests of the North and also often at variance with the needs of the small farmer of the North. But with all its importance this divergence of interest was not the primary cause which brought about the destruction of the civilization of the South. The institution of slavery, which in the South was a solution of the labor problem and of a race problem of which slavery itself was the cause, aroused the bitter hostility of the people of the North. The time came, in 1861, when the ideals of free labor and slave labor clashed in open conflict and slavery was plucked out of American life in the fiery ordeal of war.

ELI WHITNEY, 1765–1825, INVENTOR OF THE COTTON GIN

In 1792, after his graduation from Yale College, a young New Englander, Eli Whitney, made his first trip into the South, expecting to take a position as teacher in Georgia. There he became acquainted with Mrs. Greene, the widow of General Nathanael Greene who, next to Washington, had been the ablest American commander during the Revolution.

While staying at the Greene plantation near Savannah he observed the difficulty of separating the seed from the cotton fiber. Slaves worked for hours at the tedious labor of pulling the seeds from the white balls that came from the cotton fields. An idea for a machine occurred to him. "There were a number of very respectable gentlemen at Mrs. Greene's," he wrote his father, "who all agreed that if a machine could be invented which would gin the cotton with expedition, it would be a great thing both to the country and to the inventor. In about ten days I made a little model, for which I was offered, if I would give up all right and title to it, a Hundred Guineas. I concluded to relinquish my school and turn my

301   From the portrait by S. F. B. Morse (1791–1872) in the School of Fine Arts, Yale University

attention to perfecting the machine. I made one before I came away which required the labor of one man to turn it and with which one man will clean ten times as much cotton as he can in any other way before known,

302   Model of Whitney's cotton gin in the United States National Museum

and also cleanse it much better than in the usual mode. This machine may be turned by water or with a horse, with the greatest ease, and one man and a horse will do more than fifty men with the old machines."

Such was the beginning of the cotton gin, America's greatest contribution to the series of inventions which made the Industrial Revolution possible. In 1794 Whitney received a patent for his contrivance. He formed a partnership with one Phineas Miller and undertook to manufacture gins at New Haven, but the demand outran the possibility of his supplying it. Local blacksmiths in the South built crude machines, and manufacturers infringed upon the Whitney patent. After long legal battles, on the whole successful, Whitney in disgust turned to the making of firearms.

THE OLD–TIME COTTON GIN

ARKWRIGHT and Hargreaves, in England, with their machines for spinning and weaving, had laid the foundation, before the close of the eighteenth century, for the English textile factory. The demand for wool and cotton became very great. Whitney's timely invention made possible the commercial production of cotton in the southern states. Within a decade after his first machine was built, cotton was the corner stone of the economic foundation of the lower South.

303   From *Harper's Weekly*, Dec. 18, 1869, after a drawing by W. L. Sheppard

It falls to the lot of but few men to influence so vitally the industrial structure of nations.

THE GIN HOUSE

THREE years after the invention of the gin the South produced 8,000,000 pounds of cotton. In the twenty-five following years this increased twentyfold and the growth continued. Cotton dominated the South. The institution of slavery, which some Southerners had begun to feel was on the point of dying out, gained new life and became the universally recognized labor system of the cotton plantation.

304   From the painting by Harry L. Hoffman (1880?–) in the Art Institute of Chicago

THE WEST VIRGINIA MOUNTAINEER

BUT the cotton kingdom was not a homogeneous unit. The wooded ridges of the Appalachians were thrust into its heart. In the eighteenth century, when a flood of immigrants began to go west from the states along the Atlantic seaboard, some of the settlers had turned aside and had climbed, step by step, up the valleys of the mountain streams and built their cabins in the uplands. They carried with them into the mountains the language, the ideas and the customs of colonial America. They held them fast through the years that saw the rise and fall of the planter aristocracy living on the plains beneath. In the lofty clearings of the mountain folk progress ceased.

305   From Henry Howe, *Historical Collections of Virginia*, Charleston, 1845

A CABIN HOME IN THE MOUNTAINS

THE people of the mountains on their sidehill farms lived simple, hard lives, lighted by the faith in God and His Holy Word their fathers had received from the earnest preachers of the eighteenth-century back-country. The husbandman was usually a hunter also and eked out with his rifle the products of his field. A long and

difficult journey separated the mountaineer from the plains country and the broad plantations. Few ventured it. For the most part the mountain folk knew but vaguely of the life beyond their wooded valleys. Much of the little they heard they did not like. Their deep-rooted independence rebelled against the standards of aristocracy which ruled the cotton planters. But in the life of the South these hill men were of no great consequence and the planters passed them by with scarcely a thought.

306   From a photograph by the United States Department of Agriculture

307 Ozark Mountain Types, from a photograph by Clifton Johnson   308   A Mountain Home, from a photograph by Clifton Johnson

OZARK MOUNTAIN SETTLEMENTS

West of the Mississippi the Ozarks, like the Appalachians, drew settlers to the shelves perched high on the mountain slopes. Here also the mountaineers formed a group apart from the lowlanders of Missouri and Arkansas.

THE WHISKEY STILL — WEST VIRGINIA

The mountain folk distilled their corn and fruits into strong liquors as their forefathers had done in western Pennsylvania in the time of Washington. They resented the activities of the excise-men as deeply as did the "whiskey boys" who fought Hamilton's excise tax. They resented also the political domination of the planter and disliked the slave system which supported him. Legislative representatives of the mountain districts sometimes fought boldly the extension of the plantation system. But such occasional efforts were futile. Mountain life remained foreign to that of the plains and the mountain people were quite unable to influence the development of the lowlands.

309   From *Harper's Weekly*, Feb. 5, 1870, after a drawing by W. L. Sheppard

A MOUNTAIN TEAM

OVER roads so poor as sometimes to be almost impassable the mountain folk hauled whiskey, their chief product of export, down to the people of the plains. Commercial isolation through all the first half of the nineteenth century kept the men of the mountains and the plains apart. When finally war came between the North and South, the mountaineer, still thinking the thoughts of his eighteenth-century ancestor who had first settled in the upland valleys, followed the cause of the Union.

LOG HOUSE IN THE GEORGIA FORESTS

NOT all the people in the lowlands were planters. Broad bands of sandy and infertile land broke up the plains. In these regions, where the planter would not go, lived the "piney woods" folk, who owned a negro or two and raised a bale of cotton a year. Known in different localities as "crackers," "hill-billies" or "sand-hillers," these poorer whites were found all over the southern lowlands in the less desirable regions. On the richer soil where the plantations clustered, many small farmers owning from ten to twenty negroes worked their holdings in the midst of large estates. Sometimes, where the soil was thin, these farmers used it up, "cleaned, cropped and cleared out," in the homely phrase, moving on to virgin soil farther west. This blend of planter and small farmer formed one of the striking characteristics of the old cotton country in the days of slavery. In part it was the result of the newness of the business of cotton raising.

310   A Mountain Road, North Carolina, from *Picturesque America*, New York, 1872, after a drawing by Harry Fenn

311   From Basil Hall, *Forty Etchings from Sketches Made with the Camera Lucida in North America*, Edinburgh, 1829

312   From *Harper's Weekly*, July 31, 1875, after the painting by Thomas W. Wood

THE POOR WHITE

An English barrister, Alexander Mackay, was traveling by rail in South Carolina in the 'forties when he was approached on the rear platform of the railway car by one of the lesser Southern whites. "His face, which had a sickly pallor about it, was strongly lined, and marked with a mingled expression of shrewdness and cunning which gave it some fascination, at the same time that it bordered on the repulsive. He was becoming prematurely gray, his hair sticking out from his head as strong and crispy as catgut. I instinctively shrunk from him as he approached me, for I saw a large capital note of interrogation in each of his little and restless light blue eyes. . . . So approaching me still nearer, he put a finishing pressure upon the tobacco which was between his teeth, and the remaining juice of which he vehemently squirted over the platform of the succeeding carriage. Having done this he bent his head forward, opened his mouth wide, and the reeking quid fell at my feet. . . . 'Good day, stranger,' broke upon my ear. . . . 'Good day,' I replied, glancing at him at the same time; but he was not looking at me, for his eye was so vacantly intent upon the wilderness before us, that, for the moment, I doubted his having addressed me at all. . . . 'I'm a Scotchman myself,' he added, fixing his eye upon me again. I was sorry to hear it, but looked unmoved, simply replying by the monosyllabic ejaculation, 'Ah.' 'Not exactly a Scotchman,' he continued, correcting himself; 'for I was born in this country, and so were my father and grandfather before me.' 'Then you have a longer line of American ancestors than most of your fellow-countrymen can boast of,' I observed. 'We don't vally these things in this country,' said he in reply; 'it's what's above ground, not what's under, that we think on. Been long in this country, stranger?' . . . 'How long d'ye think you'll stay in this free country?' he asked, baffled in his cross-examination as to my objects and pursuits. 'Until I'm tired of it,' said I. 'When will that be?' he inquired. 'Perhaps not till I'm homesick,' I replied. 'That'll be very soon,' said he; 'for most Europeans get homesick mightily soon after comin' here.' 'You give but a poor account of your country,' I observed. 'You're mistaken, stranger,' he remarked. 'I don't mean homesick.' 'You said homesick,' rejoined I. 'But I meant sick of home,' he added, in a tone of great emphasis; 'for they can't be long in the midst of our free institootions without agettin' dead sick of their tyrannical governments.'"—ALEXANDER MACKAY, *The Western World; Travels in the United States in 1846-7*, London, 1849.

IN THE "PINEY WOODS," MISSISSIPPI

In rickety carts, over unimproved roads almost impassable in the wet season, the "piney woods" people brought their cotton or their butter and eggs into the plantation towns to exchange for the few "store goods" they could afford. Many of them were cousins of rich planters, many others hoped their children would rise to the aristocracy. Quite possibly the planter west of the mountains sprang from these poorer people and was too democratic in his manner to insist much on class distinction. Moreover, if he were in politics, as so many

313   From a photograph by the United States Department of Agriculture

planters were, he must look to the poorer people for votes to support him. High and low were thus dependent upon each other, and the lower South, save for the mountain people and the slaves, was a unit.

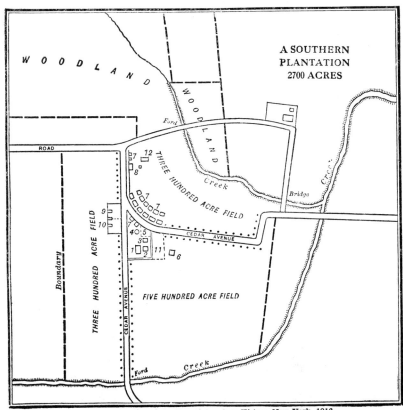

A SOUTHERN PLANTATION

In the fertile stretches from Virginia to Texas lay the cotton belt of the 'forties and 'fifties. Here were to be found many plantations laid out with house and outbuildings close together, backed by the cabins of the slaves, and on all sides the broad, rich fields of cotton under the warm sun. In the map, 1, represents the planter's house, 2, his kitchen, 3, the smokehouse, 4, the well, 5, the garden, 6, the plantation cemetery, 7, the slave quarters, 8, the overseer's house, 9, stables and lot, 10, the barns and barnyard, 11, an orchard, and 12, a gin house.

315   A Planter's Home, Alabama, from *Ballou's Pictorial*, April 19, 1856

THE HOME OF THE PLANTER

THE planter's house was the center of the plantation life. Sometimes it was a mansion, large, dignified and luxuriously appointed. Again it was scarcely more pretentious than the farmhouse of the Northern farmer. Yet its owner was an aristocrat, the master of his acres and the welfare of his slaves. Between the two yawned an impassable gulf.

SLAVE QUARTERS, SOUTH CAROLINA

NEAR the mansion clustered the slave cabins, a tiny negro village. "Matings among the slaves were encouraged within the plantation group, though not strictly confined within its limits. The planter expected his future laborers in the main to be born, reared and trained on the place. His obvious method was to promote family life among the slaves, and to insure the care of children. Here his wife had special functions. The master's household gave lessons to the slaves, whether by precept or example, and the play-time intermingling of white and black children contributed a positive link of domestic interrelation. The plantation was not merely a seat of industry, but was permanently and patently a homestead." — ULRICH B. PHILLIPS, *American Historical Review*, July, 1925.

316   On a Plantation, Eastern Virginia, from Henry Howe, *Historical Collections of Virginia*, Charleston, 1845

317   From a photograph by Clifton Johnson

PLANTATION LIFE — THE CALL TO LABOR

WHEN the busy season was on, the plantation day began
before sunrise. A bell rang sharply or a horn was blown.
By sunrise or a little after, breakfast must be cooked and
eaten and the men and women bending to their work in the
fields. At noon dinner was brought to the field and a two-
hour rest was customary. Then the work was resumed until
the waning light sent the negro "driver" and his charges
home for supper. In the dusk of the summer night the
fires in the broad fireplaces gleamed through the chinks
in the log walls of the slave quarters or lighted the yard
beyond the open door. Within could be seen the preparation of the corn cakes and bacon for the evening meal.

THE SLAVE–GANG IN THE FIELD

THE slaves were divided into gangs each in the charge of a
driver, the whole group under the watchful eye of the overseer. The former went first to the fields and laid out
"tasks" for each slave, which must be accomplished during
the day. During the hours of work he constantly urged on
the laborers. He carried a whip which he sometimes used.
Upon the overseer and the driver fell the heavy task of
accomplishing something with workers who had no incentive. At best the planter could not hope to get out of
a slave the work which a free white laborer would normally
perform.

318   From *Harper's Weekly*, Feb. 2, 1867, after a drawing
by A. R. Waud

319   From *Harper's Weekly*, Feb. 2, 1867, after a drawing by A. R. Waud

320   Plowing for Cotton, from *Harper's Weekly*, Feb. 2, 1867, after a drawing by A. R. Waud

LABOR IN THE COTTON FIELDS

CLUMSY hoes and plows were almost the only implements used on the plantation. "Such hoes as you use at the North," remarked a planter, "would not last a negro a day." The plows were drawn by mules, or, occasionally, oxen. Horses were not hardy enough to endure the rough treatment and lack of care which they received from the common field hands. On some plantations the "drivers" at night flogged the slaves who failed to complete their tasks. On others the practice was forbidden. Some flogging, however, was inevitable, for the slaves were lazy and artful in devices to escape their work. The wise overseer used special rewards as well as the lash to urge on his people. Slavery, even though it insured a supply of labor, was not, over a long period, an economic success. It flourished in the South while the soil was new and still rich. Even before the Civil War, the cotton fields of Alabama and Mississippi were showing the deterioration which had already overtaken the tobacco plantations of Virginia. A few far-sighted observers foresaw the time when the institution must be modified and perhaps die out. But social as well as economic factors entered into the problem, and the planter was appalled at the prospect of a minority of whites living in the midst of a multitude of free negroes. He clung to slavery as the only institution able to protect his home.

321   Hoeing the Young Plants, from *Harper's Weekly*, Feb. 2, 1867, after a drawing by A. R. Waud

322   A Cotton Field, from a photograph by the United States Department of Agriculture

THE COTTON HARVEST

AFTER weeks of growth and cultivation the cotton fields showed white. The slaves were then set to the task of picking. Old and young joined in. The snowy fiber was packed in bags and carried off to the gin house.

323   Cotton Picking, from *Harper's Weekly*, Feb. 2, 1867, after a drawing by A. R. Waud

THE PLANTER AND HIS OVERSEER

WHEN the crop had been harvested, the overseer could feel that the heaviest part of his responsibility was at an end. If his wages were wholly or in part dependent upon the cotton he produced, he had, in all probability, been a hard taskmaster and had by means of the drivers forced the slaves in his charge to the utmost of their capacity. If he worked on a salary, he was usually more lenient. Good overseers were hard to get. They were usually young men anxious to earn some money in order to start out for themselves. Frequently they were the sons of the "piney woods" folk seeking to escape the hard struggle for life on poor soil.

324   From *Harper's Weekly*, Feb. 2, 1867, after a drawing by A. R. Waud

GINNING AND BALING

AFTER the picking, the cotton was "ginned" and baled. The cotton press with its great sweeps which the mules pulled slowly round was a picturesque feature on every plantation. The press and the gin were the most complicated pieces of machinery that the plantation boasted.

325   From *Harper's Weekly*, Feb. 2, 1867, after a drawing by A. R. Waud.
Ginning the Cotton

The Cotton Press

HAULING THE COTTON FOR SHIPMENT

LOADED on the mule carts the bales of cotton were carried over rutty dirt roads to the nearest point of shipment. There was little improvement of highways in the South. Roads are costly and the plantations were separated by considerable distances. Horseback riding was frequent. The unimproved roads seemed sufficient to meet the needs of the simple economy of the plantation country. Even in 1861 much of the cotton kingdom was a new country less than a half century old. The roads and bridges were in part an aftermath of the rough conditions of the frontier.

326
From *Harper's Weekly*, May 12, 1866, after a drawing by Edwin Forbes

SLAVES SHIPPING COTTON BY TORCHLIGHT

FROM the plantations the highways led to the navigable streams. On these the river steamboats churned from landing to landing picking up their loads of cotton. Perhaps the river was the Alabama or the Tombigbee, whose boats docked at Mobile; perhaps it was the great Mississippi gathering the cotton from a wide area into the warehouses of New Orleans. The cotton country was dependent upon its highways and its rivers for the transportation of its staple crop.

327   From J. S. Buckingham, *The Slave States of America*, London, 1842

A SUGAR PLANTATION, LOUISIANA

IN the moist, hot climate of the lower Mississippi sugar cane flourishes. What cotton has been to Alabama, sugar has been to Louisiana. Very early sugar mills appeared and sugar plantations were laid out. Neither the institution of slavery nor the plantation system required essential modification to fit the requirements of the crop. The picture, drawn after the war, well represents the conditions of the old slave days, the drove of slaves, the overseer, the broad open spaces and the simple mill.

328   From *Harper's Weekly*, Oct. 30, 1875, after a drawing by A. R. Waud

329   A Slave Auction, an unfriendly cartoon from *Harper's Weekly*, July 13, 1861, after a drawing by Theodore R. Davis

THE SLAVE TRADE

SLAVE trading was inevitable where slavery existed. If a planter died or went into bankruptcy a readjustment in the plantation affairs was more than likely to involve the sale of some of its negroes. Moreover, on the impoverished tobacco lands of Virginia the increase in slaves was beyond the labor needs of the communities. The surplus must be disposed of or slavery would become an intolerable burden. This was a condition that called into being the professional slave trader who bought negroes in the upper South and sold them to the cotton planters of Georgia, Alabama and Mississippi. So long as slavery was considered to be an institution based on a sound moral foundation and beneficent alike for blacks and whites there could be no criticism of the work of the slave trader. He was as necessary as the trader in any other commodity.

A SLAVE AUCTION IN VIRGINIA

THAT the Abolitionists in the North should direct their attack particularly against the slave trade was as inevitable as that the trade itself should exist. It seemed an infamous traffic in human souls. A picture of a young woman on the block sold to the highest bidder to satisfy his lust was a common Northern representation of the slave auction. The appeal of such an argument was powerful. It helped materially in the creation of that feeling of hostility to slavery which ultimately brought the nation to civil war. The Southerner deeply resented the imputation of his northern antagonist and undertook a frank defense of slavery.

330   From *The Illustrated London News*, Feb. 16, 1861

THE SLAVE DECK OF THE BARK *WILDFIRE*, 1860

IMPORTATION of slaves from Africa had been forbidden by the Constitution after 1808, yet through all the years of the rise of the Cotton Kingdom New England ship-owners had found it profitable to smuggle shiploads of foreign negroes into the South. In 1858, at the Southern convention, William L. Yancey, the orator of the Southern radicals, openly urged the importation of hundreds of thousands of blacks from the Dark Continent under a scheme that would circumvent the Federal law. But the Yancey plan did not become effective. Yet savage negroes from the Congo jungles were not unknown among the field hands of the plantations of the lower South who gathered on "ration day" to get their food allowance.

RATION DAY

EACH week the rations were given out to the field hands and the other slaves who were not house servants. A peck

331   From *Harper's Weekly*, June 2, 1860, after a daguerreotype

of corn meal and three or four pounds of meat, usually bacon, made up a customary weekly portion. A little salt and molasses were sometimes added. A man received one suit of coarse clothes, shirt and pantaloons, for winter; for summer, when the work was hard and the wear greater, he often got two suits.

332   From *Harper's Weekly*, Feb. 2, 1867, after a drawing by A. R. Waud

333   From *One Hundred Years of Progress of the United States*, Hartford, Conn., 1875

A "DARKEY" PRAYER MEETING

ON Sunday there was roll call on many plantations, when every slave must answer to his name. Then he was free to attend his own religious services, when they were not forbidden for fear of insurrection. The negroes loved the ecstasies of the religious service. They absorbed the ceremonies and the simple theology of the Christian religion and infused the new faith with the wild emotionalism that had characterized the religious practices of Africa. They swung their bodies and danced. A slave exhorted with many gesticulations and prayed; the congregation prayed and wailed. Across the fields of the plantation rang their spirituals.

334   From the painting, about 1872, by Winslow Homer, in the Cincinnati Museum Association

Dark clouds am risin',
Poor sinner stan's a-tremblin' —
Oh, yondah comes my Jesus now,
Don't yo' want him in youah soul?
At las', at las', at las'.
An' by-and-by, free grace, free
    grace, free grace,
Po' mourner fin's a home by-
    an'-by.
Pray hard, pray hard, pray hard,
An' bow low, bow low, bow low.
Po' mourner fin's a home at las'.
— ESSIE COLLINS MATTHEWS,
    *Aunt Phebe, Uncle Tom and
        Others*, 1915.

"SUNDAY MORNING IN VIRGINIA"

ON Sundays a servant from the "big house" who had learned to read might bring down a Bible to the cabins and read the thrilling Word of God. The thoughtful planter, reading the same Bible, which he believed to be inspired of God in every word, became convinced that slavery was a divinely appointed institution designed for the betterment of both races. Solemnly, in 1860, Dr. Benjamin addressed his New Orleans congregation: "Not till the last man has fallen behind the last rampart, shall it drop from our hands; and then only in surrender to the God who gave it."

335   From the painting by Winslow Homer, in the National Gallery of Art, Washington

"A VISIT FROM THE MISTRESS"

MANY times a fine intimacy and genuine affection grew up between master and slave. "It was not merely his quality as a laborer that made the Negro so necessary to the South," Booker Washington has said, "it was also these other qualities to which I have referred — his cheerfulness and sympathy, his humor and fidelity." The slave took his rank from that of his owner. House servants were of a different caste from the field hands and the negroes of a great planter looked down on those of the "poor white." No white could surpass Black Sambo in *hauteur* when his superior position was questioned.

"UNCLE DAVID"

UNCLE DAVID represents the type that helped to draw the races so close together. He was proud of "ole massa's" fine horses and limitless acres. He boasted of "ole massa's great house" and of "young massa's" dashing ways. Perhaps he was "ole massa's" body servant during the war and among those who prayed beside his grave. The passing years, which wrinkled his brow and bent his back, only served to deepen the respect and affection which the white folks had for him, and to strengthen the faith which, through life, had been his inspiration and comfort.

> Obah de ribah I soon mus' go,
> Weary ob waitin' froo all dis woe;
> An' when my journey is ended, I know
>   Dat de Good Shep'ahd will open de do'.

336   From a photograph by Essie Collins Matthews,
               Barnesville, Ohio

337   From a photograph by Essie Collins Matthews

"BLACK MAMMY"

Next to his mother, the Southerner of the old slave days gave his affection to Black Mammy. She had nursed him when he was a babe and had watched over him with solicitous care when he was old enough to run about. At bedtime she had told him stories, and had sung to him the weird songs of the slaves.

> Pray, chillun, pray! Oh, pray to de Lord
> Till yo' soul cross ober — pray, oh, pray!

She had helped to fix in his speech the inflection that set off the Southerner from the Yankee. She was proud of her handiwork and her reward was the love and esteem of a gallant heart.

THE FESTIVAL

"The simple, natural joy of the Negro in little things," wrote an ex-slave, "converted every change in the dull routine of his life into an event. Hog-killing time was an annual festival." When the work was over, the fiddle and banjo inspired the inevitable dance and the songs of slavery were sung again.

338   From Robert Criswell, *Uncle Tom's Cabin Contrasted with Buckingham Hall, the Planter's Home*, New York, 1852

339   From the painting by Winslow Homer, in the Metropolitan Museum of Art, New York

THE CARNIVAL

The carnival and the camp meeting were the mountain peaks in the life of the plantation negro. Joseph in his coat of many colors was not more proud than Jim bedecked for the carnival. Much of the charm of the plantation life came from its negroes. The master supervised and aided the "doings" which helped to make slavery tolerable.

THE HUSKING

The husking was a prelude to the Christmas festivities. After the corn was gathered the ears were thrown into a great pile. On a certain night the slaves of the neighboring plantations received an invitation to attend. Then the negro with a reputation as a song leader would climb to the top of the pile and lead, in a clear loud voice, a song of the husking season. Perhaps he improvised, but the dusky ring at the base of the pile caught the refrain and the wild, strange music from a blend of negro voices rang through the night.

Massa's niggers am slick and fat,
    Oh! Oh! Oh!
Shine just like a new beaver hat,
    Oh! Oh! Oh!

Refrain

Turn out here and shuck dis corn,
    Oh! Oh! Oh!
Biggest pile o' corn seen since I
   was born,
    Oh! Oh! Oh!

    —Booker T. Washington,
    The Story of the Negro, 1909.

340   From Robert Criswell, *Uncle Tom's Cabin Contrasted with Buckingham Hall, the Planter's Home*, New York, 1852, after a sketch by F. O. C. Darley

341 From *Harper's Weekly*, Feb. 21, 1880, after a drawing by A. B. Frost

A NEGRO FUNERAL

When death stopped the work of the slave, a little band of weeping mourners followed the rude coffin. Significant of the childlike emotionalism of the black folk were the wails of the women as the rude cart jolted down the lane. The negro in slavery days did not get far beyond the superstitions of the Congo. The voodoo doctor of Africa reappeared in America. It is true that the primitive ideas of life and death were given a Christian setting and that much of the barbarism had disappeared. But the mourners following the rough cart did not differ fundamentally from their tribal ancestors, who with great emotion celebrated the last rites for the one whose spirit had passed over into another world.

THE PLANTATION GRAVEYARD

Beyond the quarters was the little cemetery where the slaves slept after they had for the last time "laid down de shubbel and de hoe." There were plantations on which the same physician attended the sick, both black and white, and the same chaplain pronounced the prayer at the last rites of master and slave. On the plantations of fine traditions, such as were found everywhere throughout the South, the graveyard was a place of sorrow for both blacks and whites, to be cared for tenderly and entered with respect. In others it was a forgotten corner for the carcasses of human chattels worn out before their time by the ruthless exploitation of an overseer with a reputation for making many pounds of cotton.

342 From *Harper's Weekly*, Feb. 2, 1867, after a drawing by A. R. Waud

A PLANTATION HOUSE

THERE was an unmistakable stateliness about the "great house" of the plantation. Almost universally a broad porch shaded the rooms from the beating sun. Within the house ceilings "were high everywhere, and windows tall and wide; but carpets were of plain design where there were carpets at all. On the walls there were portraits of worshipful ancestors, a steel engraving of George Washington, a battle scene of the Revolution, and a painting of Calhoun or Clay addressing the United States Senate. Furniture was as a rule plain but somewhat massive. Of servants there were always plenty and to spare, for the number of servants rather than the elegance of the outfit advertised the wealth and dignity of the family." — WILLIAM E. DODD, *The Cotton Kingdom*, Chronicles of America Series, New Haven, 1920.

343   A Louisiana Planter's Home, from a photograph by Clifton Johnson

PLANTER ARISTOCRACY

THE planter's family moved in a dignified and aristocratic social life. The costumes of the men and women were not so brilliant as those of the folk of eighteenth-century Virginia. The nineteenth century had seen the prosperity of the Old Dominion decline as its fields wore out and the Virginia gentleman often appeared in somewhat shabby clothes. Throughout the cotton country rich raiment was not a necessary manifestation of the planter's position. On their plantations, separated usually by broad stretches, the Southern gentry enjoyed a quiet social life rich in human contacts and marked by a gentility of manners unsurpassed and perhaps unequaled in nineteenth-century America. The best of them were true aristocrats, who received the deference of their slaves in the manner of the gentry of England. Their ladies, mothers of many children, who supervised the servants and tended the sick in the mansion and the quarters, were the plantation's crowning glory.

344   From *Harper's Weekly*, Dec. 26, 1896, after a drawing by W. T. Smedley

345   From *Harper's Weekly*, Feb. 2, 1867, after a drawing by A. R. Waud

THE SATURDAY EVENING DANCE

THE negroes contributed their share to the social life of the planter family. On many plantations on Saturday evening, when the week's work was done, they would gather in the yard of the "great house" and dance to rhythms echoing down the dark aisle of trees that bordered the drive.

As I walked down the new-cut road,
I met the tap and then the toad;
The toad commenced to whistle and sing,
And the possum cut the pigeon-wing.
Along came an old man riding by:

Old man, if you don't mind, your horse will die;
If he dies I'll tan his skin,
And if he lives I'll ride him a-gin.
Hi ho, for the Charleston gals!
Charleston gals are the gals for me.
— *Slave Songs of the United States*, New York, 1867.

346   From *Harper's Weekly*, July 9, 1887, after a drawing by Horace Bradley

A SOUTHERN BARBECUE

THE barbecue was a community gathering bringing the great planters and the lesser white folk together. It was a time for greeting distant friends, a time for the planter politician to address his constituents and to shake the voters by the hand. And not the least of its attractions was the barbecue itself, a feast of delicately flavored fresh meat, which relieved the tedium of the smoked and salted meats that were the common fare of the southern table.

347   From *Every Saturday*, Sept. 16, 1871, after a drawing by A. R. Waud

GOING DOWN TO NEW ORLEANS

THE planters, unlike the farmers of the North, traveled far from home. Perhaps the family rocked and rolled along the rough country roads to visit relatives or friends in a distant county or a neighboring state. Perhaps a great Mississippi steamboat was hailed and the planter went down to New Orleans to the races. The mountains of North Carolina, the Virginia springs, the shore of the Gulf, and Saratoga all drew the planters for sojourns of varying lengths. Life was gay in such fashionable places as it was also in Washington, where the wives of the planter statesmen were so often the dominating figures in the society of the capital.

A CHRISTMAS VISIT TO THE OLD MASTER

BUT the stately life of the Old South ended in tragedy. For four years blue-coated armies marched and counter-marched through the heart of the Cotton Kingdom. Southern man power and wealth were dissipated in a fruitless attempt to found a new nation. When the war was over and the nightmare of reconstruction had passed, many an old plantation house was a crumbling ruin. The peculiar life of the Old South was gone; yet something of the old friendship between the races continued. The Southerner understood the negro as his northern contemporary never could. The Christmas visit of the ex-slaves to the old master is typical of that afterglow of patriarchal slavery which even yet has not completely faded.

348   From *Harper's Weekly*, Dec. 12, 1885, after a drawing by W. L. Sheppard

CHAPTER VIII

CATTLEMAN AND NESTER

URING the years in which the Cotton Kingdom was developing its peculiar civilization and, in the North, the old farm, still worked by hand tools, was passing through its last and greatest phase, the frontier moved steadily and rapidly westward. Explorers and trappers blazed the way and wandering prospectors in search of gold broadened the trail. But farmers, as on every previous frontier, followed close, carrying with them from North and South the ideals of the communities they had abandoned. They left the forest behind them and struck out on the open prairie. They crossed the Mississippi and slowly climbed the broad incline that ends in the foothills of the Rockies. They scanned the maps made in the middle of the century and found "Great American Desert" written large across the country to the east of the mountains, where the bison grazed and the wandering Plains Indians built their tipis. But news came of the rich valley bottoms that lay beyond the Cordilleras, and the settlers, passing the "American Desert," toiled over the mountains, and built their cabins in Oregon and in California. The Indians of the plains watched the long trains of canvas-covered wagons crossing their hunting grounds in the 'forties and 'fifties, little realizing the red man's day was passing.

After the Civil War the nation, though deeply wounded, turned its attention to this vast region of the West. The clattering railroad became the instrument of a swift advance. The country of the bison was invaded and the great herds melted away like snow. The redskin, in a last desperate fight, met the fate of the forest tribes to the eastward. The bison range became the "Cow Country" and the Indians, shorn of their old-time freedom, were confined to reservations. So the frontier and the red man passed from American history. The small farmer, the sheep herder, and the cattleman ruled the conquered wilderness.

But more than the railroad was necessary if the farmer was to follow close upon the heels of the hunter-pioneer of this last frontier. Within its borders lay nearly half the territory of the United States. Wheat fields that stretched as far as the eye could reach could not be harvested with cradles, nor could the grain from a million sheaves be beaten out with flails. The trains which bore the settlers to Nebraska and Dakota carried swift-cutting reapers and power threshers to subdue the prairie West. The farmer-pioneers who steadily climbed westward up the Great Plains were the harbingers of a new day.

349   Buffalo in Wichita (Okla.) National Forest, from a photograph by the United States Forest Service

THE PRAIRIE FRONTIER

THE frontier relentlessly moved westward. Pioneers crossed the Appalachians into Ohio, Kentucky and Tennessee, thence westward into Indiana and Illinois. Thomas Lincoln moved with the frontier and Abraham finally grew to manhood on the Illinois prairies. The railroad, new mode of transportation, was pushing its tracks into thinly settled country, partly on the strength of grants of land from state or government. Railroads wanted settlers and stimulated immigration. The soil, made up of sands and gravels, clays and loam left by the last broad glacier that overspread the continent, varied in quality but was, in general, deep and fertile. Without realizing it the pioneers of the 'forties and 'fifties were laying out their farms on one of the richest plains areas of the world. Time would quickly demonstrate that the prairie plains themselves were able to support a great nation.

"BREAKING" THE PRAIRIE

IN Indiana and Illinois the pioneers found that the plows which had served in the valley bottoms of New England or the hillsides of New York failed to subdue the sod of a thousand years. A new and heavier plow was developed for the "breaking" of the prairie. Up and down the long straight furrows, which neither stump nor rock obstructed, the frontiersman plodded day after day beside the straining teams. It was heavy work. But when the grass roots had been broken there lay upturned a soil, dark and rich with vegetable mold, which produced crops yielding more than a hundredfold.

THE

Illinois Central Railroad Company

OFFERS FOR SALE

OVER 1,500,000 ACRES

SELECTED

FARMING AND WOOD LANDS,

IN TRACTS OF FORTY ACRES AND UPWARDS, TO SUIT PURCHASERS,

ON

LONG CREDITS AND AT LOW RATES OF INTEREST,

SITUATED

ON EACH SIDE OF THEIR RAILROAD, EXTENDING ALL THE WAY FROM THE EXTREME NORTH TO THE SOUTH OF

THE STATE OF ILLINOIS.

———————

BOSTON:
GEO. C. RAND & AVERY, PRINTERS,
No. 3 CORNHILL.
1857.

350   From a circular of the Illinois Central Railroad Company, Boston, 1857

351   From *Harper's Weekly*, Sept. 23, 1871

352   From a circular of the Illinois Central Railroad Company, Boston, 1857

A PRAIRIE SCENE IN ILLINOIS, 1857

NEAT, white farmhouses dotted the prairie before the Civil War. Fields were laid out and fenced where corn and wheat grew luxuriantly. Past the farmhouses shrieked and rattled the little trains of the new railroad that was putting the frontier in touch with a market. The railroad brought more settlers; towns sprang up; and the acres of the first comers began to increase in value. The railroads pushed on into country little settled, hoping for the profits that would come as a result of future settlement.

353   From Maximilian, Prince of Wied-Neuwied, *Travels in the Interior of North America*, London, 1838–1843, after a drawing by Carl Bodmer

THE FRONTIER WEST OF THE MISSISSIPPI

BUT the restless frontier never stood still. Early in the century pioneers had pushed across the Mississippi. Lewis and Clark in 1804 had found the cabin of the aged Boone many miles up the Missouri River. In 1821, Missouri became a state. Eleven years later the German prince Maximilian, on his way into the Indian country of the Great Plains, found this settlement in the upper Missouri country and his artist, Carl Bodmer, sketched the scene on the spot.

THE COMING OF THE GERMANS AND SCANDINAVIANS

BEFORE either Illinois or Missouri had been filled with people, the rich lands of Iowa beckoned more settlers across the Mississippi. The collapse of the German Revolution of 1848 led to a great emigration of liberals from the Fatherland. The western lands of America were advertised in German villages and soon the Mississippi river steamers were laden with immigrants who had debarked at New Orleans. In the 'fifties the Scandinavians began to come to America. From farms and villages in the rugged northland they emigrated to the plains country of the upper Mississippi valley and to the lowlands that border the Red River of the North. They needed to make no adjustments to the rigorous climate. They understood and loved husbandry. Over two million Scandinavians have come to the United States; they and their descendants form a substantial part of the population of rural America. The Norwegians led the exodus and there are today half as many of them in America as in the homeland. The climax of the Swedish migration came in the 'eighties, but the stream still flows. Many folk have come from little Denmark.

Für westliche Einwanderer!
Iowa Land
im Thale des
Des Moines Flusses.

Die zu verkaufenden Grundstücke enthalten gutes Bauholz oder liegen in der Nähe von Holzland!

Ueberall darauf sich genügendes Holz zum Bau von Häusern und zu Bauwerken vor, welches zu billigen Preisen abgegeben wird!

Eine Million Acker
Zu verkaufen gegen Credit von der
Des Moines Navigation Compagnie.

354   From a broadside (no date) of the Des Moines Navigation Company

LAWRENCE, KANSAS, 1854

IN 1854 the rivalry between the free and the slave states became so keen that another territory, Kansas, was cut out of the Indian country with scant regard for the rights of the red men. From the beginning settlers poured into Kansas and villages sprang up almost over night. People came not merely to get land for themselves but to win the country for slavery or freedom. The struggle over Kansas brought many farmers to the country of the Great Plains but they remained along the eastern edge. There were but few farms in the tufted grass where the bison grazed.

355   From E. F. Caldwell, *Souvenir History of Lawrence, Kansas,* 1898, after a sketch by J. E. Rice

356   On the Oregon Trail, from *Harper's Weekly*, June 8, 1878, after a drawing by W. A. Rogers

EMIGRATION TO OREGON

SINCE the early 'forties long trains of white-topped wagons had rolled across the plains country over the Oregon trail to the Columbia valley. A new frontier appeared on the forested Pacific slope. In 1844 a thousand persons had set out for the long journey into the West. Thousands more followed. The vast unpeopled region called for settlers. The trains of covered wagons were the answer of the white man, dooming the Indian and blocking the future expansion of the Oriental into America.

357   Following the Trail Across a Stream, from *Harper's Weekly*, June 8, 1878, after a drawing by W. A. Rogers

AN INDIAN ATTACK

THE roving bands of Plains Indians who pitched their tents in the bison country watched with growing apprehension the trains of covered wagons that summer after summer passed through their domain. They had grievances. The white men killed the bison on which their lives depended. Sometimes a warrior was shot in a quarrel. At times the tribal fighting men swooped down on a wagon train or surprised it from a well concealed ambush. But the best the redskins could do was to harry the immigrants. They could not stem the advancing white invasion.

358   From the painting by Charles Wimar (1828–63) in the collection of the University of Michigan

THE FIRST SEASON IN OREGON

IN the Columbia and the Willamette valleys the great, travelworn trains came to rest. Rude cabins sprang up in scattered places in Oregon and the settler turned to the clearing of the forest as, perhaps, his grandfather had done in Pennsylvania or New York and his father in Ohio or Kentucky. Towering mountains on every hand and the weary road that led back home accentuated the isolation of this new frontier. It was to await the growth of the Republic before its day would come.

359   From *Harper's Weekly*, June 8, 1878, after a drawing by W. A. Rogers

360   From *Harper's Weekly*, June 8, 1878

THE SECOND SEASON

MORE than one American frontier was an isolated one. The Atlantic Ocean cut off the seventeenth-century pioneers from the homeland in Great Britain or in Europe. The dreary waste of the Appalachian mountains separated the settlers of Tennessee, Kentucky and Ohio from the seaboard states in the last years of the eighteenth century. Now, in the middle of the nineteenth, the Cascades, the Sierra Nevadas, the Rockies, the rough expanse of the Central Basin of Utah and Nevada, and the broad, sub-arid plains that stretched eastward under the rain shadow of the mountain ranges separated the farmers of the Pacific coast from the homes they had left far to the eastward.

But the soil of the Far West was rich. Crops were soon growing about the cabins. The loneliness passed as more settlers came. Even before the Mexican War Americans had spilled over the international boundary into California. They carried the methods, the habits and the point of view of the early nineteenth-century husbandman of the North to the slopes of the Pacific.

NOTICE TO IMMIGRANTS!!

As there are in our City a number of men with remarkable principles. who go among those who have newly arrived and offer to sell or lease to them the *Public Land* in and about this place, thus imposing upon the unsuspecting The latter are hereby notified that the vacant land in Sacramento City and vicinity, is open for *ALL*, free of charge ; but, they can make either of the following gentlemen a present of a few thousand dollars if they have it to spare Such favors are eagerly sought and ex-ultingly received by them In fact, some of them are so solicitous in this matter that if they are not given *something*, they will *almost not like it*, and even threaten to *sue* people who will not contribute to their support. Those who have made themselves the most notorious, are

Barton Lee	Prettyman Barroll & Co.,	Warbass & Co.,
Burnett & Rogers	A M Winn,	J Sherwood,
Hardin Bigelow,	S. Brannan,	James Queen,
Pearson & Baker	Hensley, Merrill & King,	Dr W G. Deal,
Thomas M'Dowell,	Conn. Mining and Trading Co.,	Eugene F Gillespie,
R. J Watson,	Paul, White & Co.,	T L Chapman,
J. S. Hambleton,	W M Carpenter.	Dewey & Smith,
Starr, Beusley & Co.,	R. Gelston,	E. L. Brown,
	John S. Fowler	

Sacramento City, June 14, 1850.

"Sacramento Transcript" Print.

By order of the Settlers' Association.

361   Facsimile of a broadside, 1850

FRONTIER LAND CROOKS

THERE had been land sharks on every frontier, who lived off the ignorance of the newcomers. They had carried on their trade even in colonial times in the region east of the Appalachians. They were as inevitable as the westward advance.

THE HOME OF THE BISON

THE wagon trains that lumbered across the Great Plains passed through the bison range. These American beasts had once roamed east of the Appalachians, but, as the frontier advanced, they had been pushed westward. After the Civil War they were concentrated on the plains between the Mississippi and the mountains, where often the soil was free from snow, partly because of small precipitation, and partly because of the warm chinook winds (so named from the Chinook Indians), which blow down from the highlands of Montana and Alberta. Vast herds browsed over this open country, a strange sight to the young farmers from the quiet eastern villages who were pushing westward to Oregon.

362   From the painting *A Snow Landscape with Buffalo*, by George Catlin (1796–1872), in the Royal Ontario Museum
of Archæology, Toronto

INDIANS HUNTING BUFFALO WITH BOW, ARROW AND SPEAR

THE life of the Plains Indians was adjusted to the bison, which furnished the red man with his food, the hides for his clothing and tipis, the thongs that he used for weapons and utensils, and with other necessities. The Indian's camp followed the grazing herds. He had no agriculture. Wandering tribes came frequently into collision, and war was almost as familiar as the chase. Hence the redskin of the plains was a war-

363   From the painting by George Catlin in the Royal Ontario Museum of Archæology, Toronto

rior unsurpassed by any of his race. Against the eastern edge of this bison country pushed the white frontier.

364   From the painting by J. H. Moser (1854–1913) in the United States National Museum

HUNTING THE BISON: A NEW SPORT

AFTER the Civil War came the railroad. On May 10, 1869, at Promontory Point, Utah, was driven the last spike of the Union and Central Pacific, the first line to bind the Atlantic to the Pacific. With the railroad came the protecting army and, after the soldier, the hunter. The huge herds of bison that grazed on the western plains afforded hunting unsurpassed. The army hunted; the farmers along the eastern edge of the range hunted; wealthy sportsmen came from the East to hunt. The destruction of the bison had begun.

365
From *Harper's Weekly*, Dec. 14, 1867

SHOOTING BISON FROM THE TRAINS

MORE railroads were built across the plains bringing more settlers and more hunters. At first the bison was killed for his hide and bits of choice meat. Then the hunter took only the tongue from the carcass of his game and, at night by the camp fire, laid out the number he had gathered during the day. The acme of the slaughter was reached when the huntsmen abandoned all thought of deriving any benefit from the slain beast and shot the animals from the windows of moving trains.

THE WOUNDED BUFFALO

FOR a time the plains became the feasting ground of carrion birds and animals. The destruction of the bison, like the cutting of the forest, was characteristic of the young nation. Americans were unbelievably wasteful of the wealth with which a lavish nature had endowed their land. Not until the frontier had passed was conservation seriously undertaken. Then a few tiny herds of bison were rescued, in time to prevent this most picturesque of American beasts from becoming extinct.

366
From the painting by Charles Wimar (1828–63), in the City Art Museum, St. Louis, Mo.

They fell by thousands,
They melted away like smoke!
Mile by mile they retreated westward;
Year by year they moved north and south
In dust-brown clouds;
Each year they descended upon the plains
In endless floods;
Each winter they retreated to the hills
Of the south.
Their going was like the ocean current,
But each spring they stopped a little short —
They were like an ebbing tide!
They came at last to meagre little bands
That never left the hills —
Crawling in sombre files from cañon to cañon —
Now, they are gone!
— HAMLIN GARLAND,
Prairie Songs, 1893.

THE RISE OF THE CATTLE BUSINESS

THE loss of the bison was not without its gain. The railroads that wiped out the bison herds made possible the cattle business. Early in the nineteenth century wandering cattle from the old Spanish ranches in Mexico had formed the nucleus for a herd of wild cattle on the warm Texan plains. As the years passed, a distinct type emerged and the Texas Longhorns, small, slim, rangy, almost as wild as the bison to the north of them, grazed in great herds over the level grasslands near the Gulf. With the cattle were herds of wild horses; the small, shaggy, hardy broncos that the Plains

367   A Texas Longhorn, from a photograph by the United States Department of Agriculture

Indian rode. Among the Texas Longhorns the American cow business had its origin and the broncos furnished an indispensable part of the cattleman's equipment. In Mexico, south of the Rio Grande, the cow

368   Lassoing Cattle, from an engraving for the American Bank Note Company

business was well established before the first Americans in the 'twenties and 'thirties pushed their settlements out on the Texas plains. The cow industry had originated in the Spanish civilization of Mexico. The equipment, the methods, and the terms which the cowboy used came from the broad, semi-arid *haciendas* between the Sierra Madre Oriental and the Sierra Madre Occidental where the herds of Spanish cattle roamed. But, if the Americans borrowed, they made the devices their own and were unsurpassed in riding and the use of the lariat.

369   Catching a Steer in Spanish California, from Alexander Forbes, *California; a History*, 1839, after a drawing by Capt. Smyth, R.N.

370   From the painting *Wild Horse Hunters*, by Charles M. Russell (1865-1926) reproduced by permission

THE FIRST AMERICAN COWBOYS

TEXAS Longhorns rarely wandered north of the present boundary of the state whose name they bore, but the wild horses, "Indian ponies" as they were known on the plains, grazed over the whole bison range. In the 'twenties Americans began "sifting" into Texas to plant cotton on the unoccupied lands. Some of them, coming into contact with the leisurely Mexican cattlemen, turned to living on the range, though as yet there was no market for their product. As a part of their business they caught and broke the horses that their calling demanded. In 1836 Texas became independent and, in 1845, was annexed to the United States. The Lone Star State owned the range on which the first American cattlemen, together with a growing number of Englishmen, rounded up their herds. Four years after the Stars and Stripes were hoisted above the Texan capitol, an army of adventurers plunged west across the plains in the California gold rush. They passed by the bison and the droves of "Indian ponies." An occasional gold-seeker, perhaps a natural horseman, saw an opportunity. So it was that in the 'fifties the northern cowboy came into being, but his job was catching and breaking wild horses to sell in the markets of the East. Yet he was a cowboy whether fortune called him to be a "cattle puncher" or a "bronco peeler." And he looked with antipathy and supreme contempt upon the "sheep-herder" who later wandered over the grasslands with his bleating flocks.

371   From the painting *The Bronco Buster*, by Frederic Remington
                                    (1861–1909)

BRANDING

FROM Mexico came the custom of branding and ear-notching by which the owner identified his property. The early branding iron was simply a straight poker called a "running rod" with which the cowboy "painted" on the animals the designs that registered his brand. Later, when the device of altering brands that was known as "rustling" caused the loss of many cattle, "set brands," recording the whole device in one touch and more difficult to alter, were introduced.

372   From a photograph by the United States Department of Agriculture

373   A Rancher's Cabin, Texas, from a Missouri Pacific Railway Guide, about 1875

BEGINNING OF THE COW COUNTRY

IN the 'sixties, when the first railroad crossed the plains, wealth beckoned the Texas cattleman. At last a way to market had been opened even if the rail-head was far to the north of his ranch. The cow country, as it was to be known for twenty years, sprang suddenly into being. But the Longhorns dressed little beef and their meat was tough. The cattlemen, led by the English ranchmen, many of whom had been breeders at home,

began to import Herefords. Not many years passed before the Longhorn was rarely seen; his place was taken by sleek, well-rounded, white-faced cattle in whose veins, however, ran some of the blood of their wild predecessors. Once established as a paying industry, ranching spread westward from the Missouri River to the Rocky Mountains and northward from Texas to Montana. The Texas plains, where the winters were mild and the grass plentiful, remained the chief breeding ground of this vast pasture land.

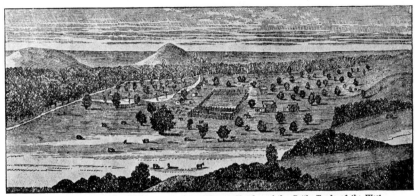

374   A Texas Ranch, from Joseph G. McCoy, *Historic Sketches of the Cattle Trade of the West and Southwest*, Kansas City, 1874, after a drawing by Henry Worrall

375   Winter Quarters of Cowboys, Kansas, from Joseph G. McCoy, *Historic Sketches of the Cattle Trade of the West and Southwest*, Kansas City, 1874, after a drawing by Henry Worrall

WINTER ON THE RANGE

Winter on the open range, be it north or south, was a time to test the mettle of any man. "Outriders" were sent to distant areas to guard the cattle. A cabin or a dugout served as shelter. When snow fell, the punchers drove the stock to sheltered spots where the herds could paw through to the grass beneath. But when a blizzard swept across the plains, the killing wind filled with blinding flakes, the danger was great. Then, in a bunch of huddled, frozen cattle, the "drift," a tragic, hypnotic march to death, might begin. "Abruptly, in sodden despair, with brain entirely dormant but muscles automatically working, some forceful steer started down to leeward, and behind him, in like condition, straggled the staggering herd. Each animal, keeping true to the wind's course, fought on till it dropped; and where it dropped it died. The numbed brutes fell one by one, first the weaker calves, then the stronger calves, each little tumbling body causing its attendant, anxious mother to stop and wait and perish beside a diminutive mound of snow. . . . [At last] the final sacrifice appeared in the frozen bodies of some grand bovine monsters, lying piled before the impassable barrier." — PHILIP ASHTON ROLLINS, *The Cowboy*, 1922.

376   Cattle in a Blizzard, from *Harper's Weekly*, Feb. 27, 1886, drawing by Charles Graham after a sketch by Henry Worrall

THE DAY'S WORK

THE cowboy's desperate attempts to break a "drift" and drive the herd to some safe cover were only part of the day's work. There were winters when some cowboys and thousands of cattle perished on the range. In the spring, the dugout was abandoned and, with "chuck wagon" to carry the food and "wrangler" to tend the mounts, the cowboys in small squads each under a boss set out to work the cattle of the range slowly toward the stockade or the protected

377 Cowboys Breaking Camp, from *Harper's Weekly*, Oct. 2, 1880, after a drawing by W. A. Rogers

valley that had been chosen for the round-up where the calves were branded. Weeks of hard and tedious riding followed, sometimes through parched country where the marching cattle filled the air with dust. Sweeping the cattle off the range and into the round-up area was an enterprise in which all the ranchers in the region joined and their cowboys worked the stock irrespective of ownership. There was much labor and little pleasure in such a life. Perhaps at night around the camp fire the punchers would recite in competition the labels on the canned goods carried in the "chuck wagon." With a five-cent fine for errors in punctuation and ten cents for a word, this presented a sporting proposition. But it was significant of the isolation of the cowboy's life. The settled family life of the snug eastern farms was rarely possible. Like pastoral nomads, which in a sense they were, the cowboys wandered for thousands of miles up and down the plains.

378   From the painting *Cattle Country*, by Maynard Dixon (1875–). Courtesy of the artist

379   From *Collier's Weekly*, Feb. 18, 1911, *The Stampede by Lightning*, painting by Frederic Remington (1861–1909).
© P. F. Collier & Son Co.

THE STAMPEDE

THE cattle of the plains were prone to panic. If a single leader took fright and with tail raised ("rolled," as the cowboys called it) dashed across the grasslands, nearby animals caught the contagion and joined in a mad rush of insensate terror. A stampede was on. The cow puncher urged his fleet "cayuse" to the head of the crazed column and with much profane yelling caused it to double back into the form of a letter "U." Then he forced the ends together so that the cattle began "milling" in a great circle. After a time the exhausted stock came to a halt and began to graze. To ride out a stampede in the blackest night over a country full of gopher holes or prairie-dog burrows took courage.

Woe to the man and woe to the steed
That falls in front of the mad stampede.

380   From the mural painting *A Texas Round-Up*, by Edward Holslag (1870–) in the First National Bank, El Paso, Texas.   © 1915, by the artist

381   From *Harper's Weekly*, May 2, 1874, after a sketch by Frenzeny and Tavernier

THE ROUND-UP

AT the round-up the cows were "cut out" of the mass of cattle each with a calf clinging to its heels. The calf was roped and dragged unceremoniously to the fire and branded with the mark its mother bore. Unmarked cattle were "mavericks" and were divided proportionately among the ranchmen participating in the round-up. The cattleman had a real respect for the cow that rushed, with head down, to the aid of its bawling calf beside the fire. Even a bellowing bull was not so dangerous.

382   From the painting *Jerked Down*, by Charles M. Russell (1865-). Courtesy of the artist

THE COW PONY

THE wiry, nervous, intelligent bronco was, in its way, as skillful as its rider. The cowboy had but to ride it into a "bunch of cattle," make clear to it which animal was to be cut out, and the little beast would practically do the rest. With the lariat wound tight around the "horn" of the saddle the "cayuse" would throw a steer of twice its weight. When a horse was branded, it was never handled in the same rough fashion. It was too valuable to justify taking risks with it.

"STRAYS"

At the round-up the "strays" which belonged to other ranchers than those participating were cut out and driven away in the direction of the head-quarters of their several owners. A man's brand was respected over the whole range. Sometimes brands were "doctored" and some-times calves were turned into "mavericks" by a single shot at the mother, but the code of the range was founded on honesty and was obeyed to a surprising extent.

THE "LONG DRIVE"

The round-up over, the "long drive" began which,

383   From the mural painting by Allen True (1861–). Courtesy of the artist

starting in Texas, often reached its end in Montana. One band of cowboys under a "trail boss" would take a "bunch of dogies" (yearling calves) northward to grow to maturity in Wyoming or Nebraska. An-other would drive a herd of steers to the railroad in Kansas. In the heyday of the cow country hundreds of thousands of cattle were driven out of Texas every year. The winding cattle trails were deeply incised in the plain. Day after day for weary weeks the cowboys drove their "bunches" northward. At night the stock would be turned aside to graze and rest, half a mile or so from the trail. During the hours of dark-ness the cattlemen in relays stood guard over their charges to prevent theft and to check an incipient stampede. Then it was that the cowboy sang to the cattle singularly profane and uncomplimentary verses set often to slow and solemn hymn tunes. The singing warned the nervous cattle of the approach of the patrolling cow-puncher and also identified him to other members of the guard.

Starting the river crossing was a nervous bit of work. The long line of straggling cattle must not rebound

384   From *Harper's Weekly*, Oct. 10, 1867, after a drawing by A. R. Waud

from the bank, for a stampede might result. So when the van of the column trotted down to the river, waded in and began to drink, the cattle-men picked two or three likely steers and, getting behind them, urged them quietly and skillfully into deep water. Swimming their ponies alongside, the punchers forced the selected leaders to main-tain a course across the river. The rest of the herd followed as a matter of course. Ere long the entire "bunch" had clambered up the oppo-site bank.

A SONG OF THE TRAIL

Your mother she was raised way down in Texas,
Where the jimson weed and sand-burrs grow;
Now we'll fill you up on prickly pear and cholla
Till you are ready for the trail to Idaho.

Oh, you'll be soup for Uncle Sam's Injuns;
"It's beef, heap beef," I hear them cry.
Git along, git along, git along little dogies,
You're going to be beef steers by and by.

REFRAIN

Whoopee ti yi yo, git along little dogies,
It's your misfortune, and none of my own.
Whoopee ti yi yo, git along little dogies,
For you know Wyoming will be your new home.
— *Collected by John A. Lomax.*

385   From *Harper's Weekly*, May 2, 1874

"COW TOWNS"

THE prosperity of the cow country was dependent upon the development of refrigeration. The invention of the refrigerator car and the machine for making ice made possible the distribution of meat raised on the Great Plains and slaughtered in Kansas City or Chicago to the growing market in the East. One after another the transcontinental railways laid their tracks across the cattle country and "cow towns" grew up from Kansas to Canada. On the streets of these "cow towns" was epitomized the strange and vigorous life of the last West. A "pilgrim" from the East could have seen in Atchison and elsewhere hunters or prospectors buying equipment and setting out for the mountains. There were blue-coated soldiers fresh from the Civil War sent into the cattle country to pacify

386   Wichita, Kansas, from *Harper's Weekly*, May 2, 1874

the Indians. Nesters from the neighboring homesteads mingled with the cowboys from Texas or Montana.

Commercial men from the East were gambling their fortunes on the expected growth of the frontier and sharpers of all sorts lay in wait to part the unsophisticated from their money. Rude wooden buildings, with the inevitable false fronts, lined the streets and displayed the signs of the grocery and hardware stores, the banks, and the multitude of saloons. There were confusion, squalor, and vice, but with it growth and the promise of the future.

387   Atchison, Kansas, from *Harper's Weekly*, July 28, 1866, after a drawing by W. M. Merrick

388   Cattle in a Kansas Corn Corral, from *Harper's Weekly*, April 28, 1888, after a drawing by Frederic Remington

SHIPPING CATTLE TO MARKET

At the "cow towns" the beef steers from the range were loaded into the open-sided cars and a wheezy little locomotive hauled the train away to Chicago. At regular intervals along the route the cattle were released for a space, that they might arrive at the stockyards in good condition. In the caboose rode a group of cowboys, "bull nurses" in the vernacular of the plains, to handle the stock when out of the cars and to deliver the shipment to the buyer. At the end of the journey inspectors checked the cattle to see that no ranchman was selling animals that bore another's brand.

389   Loading Cattle at Wichita, from Joseph G. McCoy, *Historic Sketches of the Cattle Trade*, etc., Kansas City, 1874

390   From Joseph G. McCoy, *Historic Sketches of the Cattle Trade of the West and Southwest*, Kansas City, 1874, after
a drawing by Henry Worrall

CORN-FEEDING STEERS IN ILLINOIS

BOTH before and after the coming of the railroads there were herds that left the long trail midway between north and south and went east to Illinois. The corn and the blue grass of the rich prairie brought them into prime condition, and Chicago was distant but a short run.

391   From *Harper's Weekly*, Sept. 11, 1875, after a drawing by V. W. Bromley

THE "BEEF ISSUE"

THE United States government bought beef on the hoof to feed its Indian wards on the reservations. From time to time the "beef issue" was driven into the northern corrals for distribution to the redskins. The Indians waited outside the gates each to receive his allotment as the animals were driven slowly out. The cowboy, knowing well the habits of his cattle and seeing an opportunity both for profit and for revenge on ancient foes, all too frequently roused a steer and started a stampede toward the familiar grazing grounds.

392   From the painting *Cattlemen*, by Allen True in the Wyoming State Capitol

HIS PHILOSOPHY OF LIFE

THE cowboy lived in daily contact with a majestic and uncertain nature. His life was full of hazards. Yet his religion was little developed. The redskins about him were, in their savage way, a peculiarly religious people, but the "Westerner's" reactions to his environment and the risks of life gave scant outward heed to any Invisible Governing Power. "Sunday stopped at the Missouri River" in the language of the plains. The population of the cow country was too sparse and too much on the move to make organized religion possible. So the cow-puncher was thrown back upon himself in the development of the life of the spirit. Many were open scoffers. Widespread throughout the West was a vicious and vulgar parody on the Bible. Profanity was an indispensable part of the cattleman's vocabulary. When the possibilities of the conventional words and phrases had been exhausted, the puncher developed his own "private cuss-words." Yet the cowboy had faith in himself, in his fellow men and, in a vague way, in God. Out of this came the code that demanded honest and courageous living.

"At the foot of one of the noblest peaks in the Rocky Mountains lies a grave. Its occupant died in a stampede. All that was said at the interment came out hesitatingly and as follows: 'It's too bad, too bad. Tom, dig a little deeper there. Hell, boys, he was a man,' and presently, when the burial had been completed, 'Bill, we boys leave you to God and the mountain. Good-by, Bill. Damn it, Jim, look out for your bronc.'" — P. A. ROLLINS, *The Cowboy*, 1922.

THE COWBOY

THE cowboy was the last and in some respects the most picturesque of American frontier types. His life was centered in the cattle he herded and the horses he rode. If his courage and his physical endurance were great, his intellectual outlook was sharply restricted and his social development limited to adjustment to the rough and rigid code of the cow country. He was trained in observation, could take in with surprising quickness and accuracy the peculiarities of a bunch of cattle. He was suspicious of strangers, particularly the "tenderfoot," and judged a man by his ability to measure up to the cowboy's code. In speaking he compressed his ideas into the fewest possible words.

393   From the painting by Allen True in the Montana
National Bank, Billings, Mont.

394   From a lithograph by N. Currier, 1856, after the painting by A. F. Tait (1819–1905)

"THE LAST WAR–WHOOP"

THE Indians, good horsemen and fighters, were a menace to the cattleman almost to the disappearance of the old cow country. The last great Indian wars occurred in the heyday of the cowboy, and even after the red-skins were defeated and confined on reservations they remained persistent and dangerous horse thieves. Like earlier frontiersmen the cowboy faced the Indian menace as part of the day's work.

395   From the painting by Charles M. Russell, courtesy of the artist

"WHEN HOSS FLESH COMES HIGH"

THERE were white thieves as well as red ones on the plains. Thieving ranged all the way from the occasional "rustling" of the cattle of an unpopular ranchman to the depredations of thoroughly "bad men." Trailing an occasional horse thief was part of the cowboy's job. Trained by his work to constant and acute observation, he borrowed the Indian methods of following a trail and improved upon them. Reading a trail required intelligence of a high order, and taking a thief who had been run down was not a task for weaklings. As the whole life of the plains country depended upon respect for property rights in animals that often wandered far from their owners, the penalty for thieving, particularly horse thieving, was severe.

396   From *Picturesque America*, New York, 1874, after a drawing by F. O. C. Darley

ROPING A GRIZZLY

WITH ranches often as many as fifty miles apart and with plenty of hard work to be done there was little time for recreation. The cowboys had occasional horse races, sometimes with Indians. As among the farmers to the eastward, cowboy sports displayed individual prowess rather than team play. To rope a grizzly and with two or three lariats to drag it alive to camp was sport in keeping with the rough and dangerous life of the cattle country.

397   From a photograph by the United States Department of Agriculture

THE SALOON OF THE CATTLE COUNTRY

ISOLATION and the stern discipline of his work led the cowboy to excess when the strain was relaxed. Saloons and dance halls in the cattle towns along the trail invited to every sort of vice. They were the inevitable accompaniment of the frontier. The abandon with which the cowboy gave himself up to the pleasures that were offered was perhaps more picturesque but certainly no more complete than that of earlier frontiersmen on earlier frontiers. If he was quick on the trigger and ready for a gun fight, he had at least advanced beyond the stage where the victor in a frontier fist-fight gouged out the eyes of his fallen opponent.

398   From *Harper's Weekly*, Oct. 16, 1886, after a drawing by R. T. Zogbaum

"PAINTING THE TOWN"

"PAINTING THE TOWN" is the characteristic of the old-time cowboy perhaps most exploited by artists and story-writers. Like his Indian neighbor, the cow-puncher was fond of bravado. "Painting the town" was a noisy and usually harmless sport. The spirit in which it was done was reflected in that favorite song of the range, "The Old Chisholm Trail."

We hit Caldwell and we hit her on the fly,
We bedded down the cattle on the hill
    close by.

We rounded 'em up and put 'em on the
    cars,
And that was the last of the old Two Bars.

I'm on my best horse and I'm goin' at
    a run,
I'm the quickest shootin' cowboy that
    ever pulled a gun.

Foot in the stirrup and hand on the horn,
Best damned cowboy ever was born.

399   From a photograph by the United States Department of Agriculture

THE BARBED–WIRE FENCE

THE old cow country flourished when the open range was owned by no man; it came to an end when the plains were divided into private possessions. The invention of the barbed-wire fence spelled the doom of the open range. Before it appeared, however, "cattle kings" had risen above their fellows, like the feudal barons of the Middle Ages. They owned vast herds and employed great numbers of cowboys. For a time they controlled the destinies of the grasslands from Texas to Montana. When it became clear that the barbed-wire fence had come to the range to stay these men enclosed great areas, sometimes legally but often in defiance of the law. The enclosed ranch brought the long drive to an end and ushered in a new chapter of the cattle business.

From the painting by Maynard Dixon, by courtesy of the artist

"TWO OLD–TIMERS"

In the latter half of the 'eighties the cow country disappeared as suddenly as it had come into being. The range became overstocked, since any man could graze cattle on land that belonged to the government. The

401   From a photograph by Brady

railroad which had first brought the cattleman in touch with a market now carried a flood of settlers into the plains, whose purpose was raising crops rather than stock. The old-time cowboy who had ridden the long trail passed away as the cattle business became concentrated on the less picturesque but, on the whole, more profitable privately owned ranches. In this way the Great Plains passed out of the pastoral and into the agricultural stage of development.

GALUSHA A. GROW, 1824–1907, FATHER OF THE HOMESTEAD ACT

In the Homestead Act of 1862 an old dream of the small farmer of the North came true. Southern statesmen, anxious for the expansion of slavery into the unsettled West had, before the Civil War, opposed the policy of giving away the public domain. Grow, Congressman from Pennsylvania, had been brought up on the frontier by a widowed mother. It was fitting that he should sponsor the Homestead Act, which offered a free farm to every man who would settle on it and improve it. Democracy's ideal of equal opportunity for all was never more perfectly realized.

(1.)

HOMESTEAD.

APPLICATION }
No. —— }

LAND OFFICE at ——. ——,18

I, ——, of ——, do hereby apply to enter, under the provisions of the act of Congress approved May 20, 1862, entitled "An act to secure Homesteads to actual settlers on the public domain," the —— of Section ——, in Township —— of Range ——, containing —— acres.

LAND OFFICE at ——, ——,18 .

I ——, Register of the Land Office, do hereby certify that the above application is for Surveyed Lands of the class which the applicant is legally entitled to enter under the Homestead act of May 20, 1862, and that there is no prior, valid, adverse right to the same.

—— Register.

(2.)

HOMESTEAD.

(Affidavit.)   LAND OFFICE at ——,
                          (Date.) ——

I, —— of ——, having filed my Application No.——, for an entry under the provisions of the act of Congress, approved May 20, 1862, entitled "An act to secure Homesteads to actual settlers on the public domain," do

solemnly swear, that [*Here state whether the applicant is the head of a family, or over twenty-one years of age; whether a citizen of the United States, or has filed his declaration of intention of becoming such; or, if under twenty-one years of age, that he has served not less than fourteen days in the army or navy of the United States during actual war; that said Application No.—— is made for his or her exclusive benefit; and that said entry is made for the purpose of actual settlement and cultivation, and not, directly or indirectly, for the use or benefit of any other person or persons whomsoever.*]

Sworn to and subscribed, this —— day of ——, before ——.

[*Register or Receiver*] *of the Land Office.*

(3.)

MILITARY OR NAVAL HOMESTEAD.

APPLICATION }
No.—— }   LAND OFFICE at ——, ——, 186

I, ——, of ——, being in the —— service of the United States, do hereby apply to enter, under the provisions of the act approved March 21, 1864, amendatory of the Homestead act of May 20, 1862, and for other purposes, a certain tract of land, which —— is hereby authorized to designate, at the foot of this application, as my Homestead, and which I agree to hold as my own selection.

ATTEST: ——, Commanding officer at ——.

402   Facsimile of a circular of the General Land Office, Sept. 17, 1867

APPLICATION BLANKS FOR HOMESTEADS

FEW formalities were necessary to become an independent landowner under the Homestead Act. The homesteader must live on his acres for three years, but if he had been a soldier in the Civil War his term of service was subtracted from the requirement. He must improve his land by cultivation and equipment. The rich soil and the rolling swells of the Great Plains beckoned the struggling farmer of the East. "God done His best on that there land — His level best."

A SOD HOUSE, NORTH DAKOTA

WHEN the Civil War had passed, the railroads brought westward a flood of settlers and the agricultural frontier climbed steadily toward the towering Rockies. Settlers came in prairie schooners, the thrifty min-

gling with the thriftless; those who looked forward to success with those who looked back upon failure; Americans with the foreign-born. Some of them had been farmers; some were the derelicts of a score of other callings. The frontier was the "safety valve" of the nation whither the radical and the misfit, as well as the able and ambitious, might go to breathe the air of liberty and equality. From Kansas to Dakota on the treeless plains rose the sod houses of the first comers.

403   From a photograph in the collections of the State Historical Society
of North Dakota, Bismarck, N. D.

404

From *Picturesque America*, 1874, after a drawing by F. O. C. Darley

EMIGRANTS CROSSING THE PLAINS

WE cross the prairie as of old
   The pilgrims crossed the sea,
To make the West, as they the East,
   The homestead of the free.

We're flowing from our native hills
   As our free rivers flow;
The blessing of our Mother-land
   Is on us as we go.

We go to plant her common schools
   On distant prairie swells,
And give the Sabbaths of the wild
   The music of her bells. — JOHN GREENLEAF WHITTIER

405

From Edward King, *The Great South*, 1874

A KANSAS FARMYARD

AGAIN in Kansas and Nebraska, in the Dakotas and Oklahoma, came the heavy work of breaking the prairie sod. For long autumn days men plowed acre after acre while the winds of the approaching winter swept over the swells of the plains. The railroads left lumber at the prairie stations and the homesteaders replaced the sod huts with frame houses.

406   From W. M. Thayer, *Marvels of the New West*, Norwich, Conn., 1890

A DAKOTA WHEAT FARM

NESTERS the cattlemen contemptously called the settlers who came out to the plains. Yet with growing apprehension the rancher watched the wheat fields and the barbed-wire fences creep farther and farther westward into the cattle range. Each year saw a westward advance. War flamed up between the homesteader and the cattleman. Again and again the nester was driven off, his fences cut and his buildings burned. But he returned. Law and numbers were on his side. The open range that stretched from Texas to Dakota was doomed. One after another the runways of the Long Drive were plowed under. The Little Fellow had come to stay.

407   From an etching *Wolves on a Buffalo Trail*, by Peter Moran in the United States National Museum

THE SCOURGE OF THE PLAINS

THE pioneer homesteader faced a host of enemies besides the cattleman. Wolves prowled in the night, killing his stray animals. Coyotes brought terror to his farmyard. Gophers and prairie dogs each in their own way made harder the task of the settler. In 1874 came the great plague of grasshoppers. The sky was darkened with clouds of the insects swarming from their breeding places at the foot of the Rockies. They settled down upon the fields and meadows. They covered the ground. When they passed, green fields had been turned into a desolate waste and the earth lay seared under a blistering sun. The folk who could not afford to buy food for themselves and their animals packed up their belongings and with sad hearts started on the long journey back home. Even on the open plains where the forest was not an obstacle the settler must fight against a hostile nature.

408   From *Harper's Weekly*, March 28, 1868, after a drawing by Theodore R. Davis

RUNNING THE "FIRE GUARD"

THE greatest of the terrors of the open country was the prairie fire, in the words of Garland, the poet and story-teller of the plains folk:

A curving, leaping line of light,
A crackling roar from lurid lungs,
A wild flush on the skies of night —
A force that gnaws with hot red tongues,
That leaves a blackened, smoking sod —
A fiery furnace where the cattle trod.

Prairie Songs, Chicago, 1893.

The farmer who had not prepared against the danger by leaving naked furrows about his fields must work fast when the black smoke cloud lifted itself above the horizon. If he chanced to be away at the mill or at market, he might return to find his crops wiped out and his home a smoking ruin.

409   From *Harper's Weekly*, Jan. 16, 1886, after a drawing by Charles Graham

"BANKING UP" FOR WINTER IN DAKOTA

HIGH up on the inland plains a thousand miles from the sea, the summer heat and winter cold are both intense. The small clapboarded houses of the early settlers were scant protection when an icy gale swept the frozen prairies. So, as days grew short in autumn, the prudent householder put a wall of sod about his house.

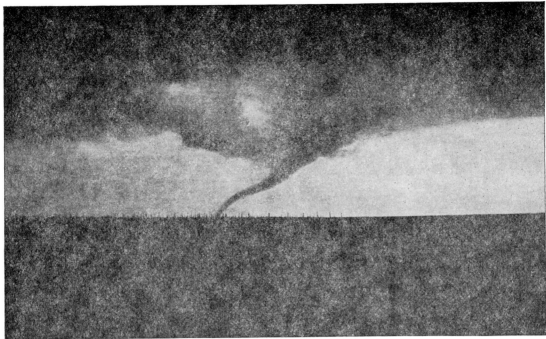

410   From a photograph by the United States Forest Service

THE CYCLONE

THE wind sweeps the unobstructed plains not less furiously than it lashes the waves of the northern Atlantic. It bends the trees that the settlers have planted and beats against their houses. Now and then it forms a column of madly whirling air reaching from the clouds to the ground. These "cyclones" struck terror into the heart of the homesteader as he watched them advance across the open country. The house of boards which he had built in place of the first sod hut could not stand against the black tornado. He built a cellar in which he and his family could take refuge when destruction crashed about them. After the storm had passed, came the long, hard task of reëstablishing the home.

411   A Cyclone Cellar, from a photograph by Clifton Johnson

412   From a photograph by the United States Department of Agriculture

THE WINDBREAK

THE windbreak of closely planted trees was a necessary adjustment to the storms of the plains. Set under the lee of a prairie swell and guarded by a thickset grove the new home of the farmer seemed snug and safe. The farmstead of the new day was a symbol of the victory of the nester over the obstacles that beset him.

413   From a photograph by the United States Department of Agriculture

CATTLE-RAISING ON THE HOMESTEAD

THE homesteader was quick to utilize the cattle of the plains. By divers methods he acquired a herd and marked them with his own brand. The cattlemen accused him of thievery. But he and his herds had come to stay. Barbed-wire fences guarded a property that helped him along the road to independence and prosperity. In time the nester supplanted the cattle king in the control of the plains.

MILES OF WHEAT

On the rolling prairie where the bison had cropped the bunch grass grew the corn and wheat of the homesteader. The rich soil brought forth abundantly. Wheat became the staple of the Northwest as cotton had of the South. In Minnesota or the Dakotas the traveler might, in the height of summer, look

414   From a photograph by the United States Department of Agriculture

out across the plain and see no end to the broad expanse of yellow wheat over which ceaselessly ran the waves which the wind made.

THRESHING ON THE PRAIRIE

In the autumn over the golden stubble where the spiders spread their webs sounded the roar of the thresher as the sheaves slid into the whirling cylinder. Wheat was king on the northern plains.

HARVESTING ON A BONANZA FARM

Before the rich soil had been impoverished by exploitive cropping the profits from wheat were large. In the 'eighties the "bonanza" farm appeared. The Dalrymple farm included fifty-five

415   From a photograph by the United States Department of Agriculture

thousand acres divided into tracts of about two thousand acres each. Battalions of plows broke the soil and long lines of reapers clattered around the fields of ripened grain. But the great farm was not so economical as the smaller one, and in time bonanza farms were broken up.

416   From a photograph by the United States Department of Agriculture

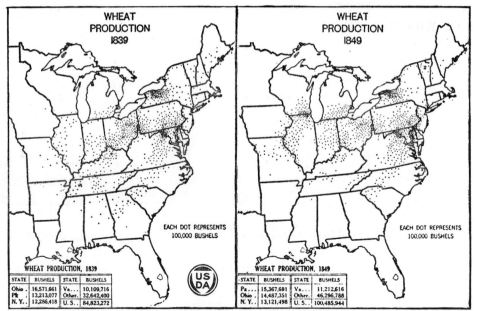

417   From a diagram in the 1921 *Yearbook* of the United States Department of Agriculture

THE ADVANCE OF WHEAT INTO THE OHIO VALLEY

THE westward march of wheat is one of the most striking phenomena in the agricultural history of the United States. In the seventeenth and eighteenth centuries wheat had been a common crop in the northern colonies. Wheat followed the westward advance of the farming frontier. In 1825 the Erie canal united Lake Erie and the Hudson River and offered cheap transportation across the mountain barrier from the Ohio valley to New York. In the 'thirties and 'forties the rich lowlands of western New York and southeastern Ohio were filling vast numbers of canal boats with yellow grain bound for the seaboard markets. In the older settlements the limestone country of Pennsylvania, Maryland and Virginia retained an ancient preëminence in wheat production. The 'fifties was a decade of railroad building during which for the first time Chicago was bound to the Atlantic coast by an all-rail route. Many farmers pushed into southern Michigan and Wisconsin and crossed the Mississippi into Iowa and Minnesota.

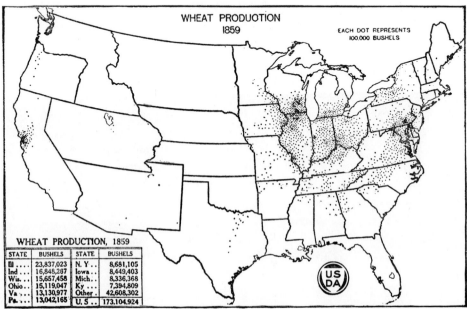

418   From a diagram in the 1921 *Yearbook* of the United States Department of Agriculture

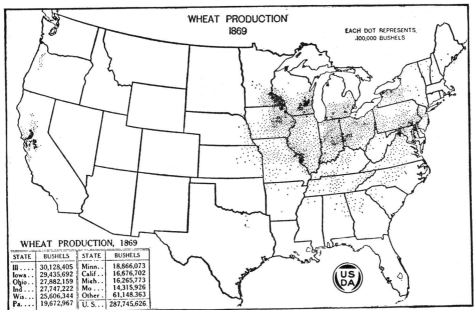

WHEAT PRODUCTION 1869

EACH DOT REPRESENTS 100,000 BUSHELS

WHEAT PRODUCTION, 1869

STATE	BUSHELS	STATE	BUSHELS
Ill	30,128,405	Minn..	18,866,073
Iowa..	29,435,692	Calif..	16,676,702
Ohio..	27,882,159	Mich..	16,265,773
Ind ...	27,747,222	Mo ...	14,315,926
Wis...	25,606,344	Other.	61,148,363
Pa....	19,672,967	U. S...	287,745,626

419   From a diagram in the 1921 *Yearbook* of the United States Department of Agriculture

THE MIDDLE YEARS OF THE CENTURY

WHEAT was an admirable crop for the prairie frontier. With the tough sod broken in the summer, the grain could be sown in the autumn. Thenceforth it required no attention until harvest the following July. The amount that could be planted was limited by what the farmer could harvest before it spoiled in the field. In the 'fifties, inventors of the reaper and binder were increasing vastly the acreage which one man could cut and shock. The threshed grain could at once be turned into money or could be held for a better market. So the farmer of the prairie frontier year after year planted his fields to wheat using the same exploitive methods that had worn out the soil of his seventeenth-century forefathers. The yields declined and prices fluctuated. Yet during the middle years of the nineteenth century wheat ruled in the valleys of the Ohio and the upper Mississippi while diversified farming only slowly worked its way in.

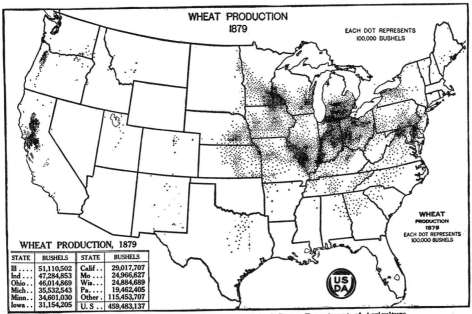

WHEAT PRODUCTION 1879

EACH DOT REPRESENTS 100,000 BUSHELS

WHEAT PRODUCTION 1879 EACH DOT REPRESENTS 100,000 BUSHELS

WHEAT PRODUCTION, 1879

STATE	BUSHELS	STATE	BUSHELS
Ill	51,110,502	Calif..	29,017,707
Ind ...	47,284,853	Mo ...	24,966,627
Ohio..	46,014,869	Wis...	24,884,689
Mich..	35,532,543	Pa....	19,462,405
Minn..	34,601,030	Other.	115,453,707
Iowa..	31,154,205	U. S ..	459,483,137

420   From a diagram in the 1921 *Yearbook* of the United States Department of Agriculture

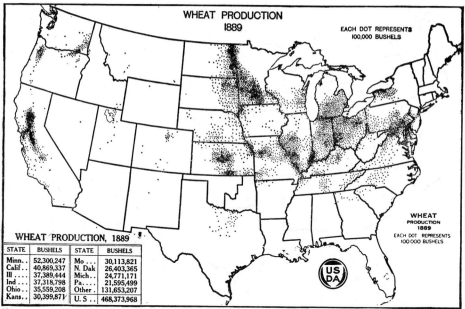

STATE	BUSHELS	STATE	BUSHELS
Minn..	52,300,247	Mo ...	30,113,821
Calif..	40,869,337	N. Dak	26,403,365
Ill	37,389,444	Mich..	24,771,171
Ind ...	37,318,798	Pa....	21,595,499
Ohio..	35,559,208	Other .	131,653,207
Kans.,	30,399,871	U.S ..	468,373,968

421   From a diagram in the 1921 *Yearbook* of the United States Department of Agriculture

WHEAT AFTER THE PASSING OF THE COW COUNTRY

THE maps for 1889 and 1899 show the areas of wheat raising after the disappearance of the old cow country. Iowa and Illinois were becoming the corn belt and wheat was moving into the valley of the northern Red River and into Kansas and Nebraska. The same soil-destroying practice of cropping a field with wheat year after year followed the frontier westward. The dots in the sub-arid region east of the mountains show how far the nesters had pushed into the cattle country. The black areas on the Pacific coast should be contrasted with those on the map for 1859. The growth of the Far West was keeping pace with that of the Great Plains. Low prices and occasional poor crops in the late 'eighties and the early 'nineties brought suffering to the farmers of the wheat country out of which came the Populist movement and the battle of 1896 when the western farmers sought to overthrow the power of eastern capital.

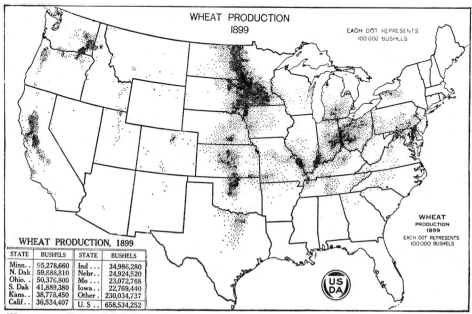

STATE	BUSHELS	STATE	BUSHELS
Minn..	95,278,660	Ind ...	34,986,280
N. Dak	59,888,810	Nebr..	24,924,520
Ohio..	50,376,800	Mo ...	23,072,768
S. Dak	41,889,380	Iowa..	22,769,440
Kans..	38,778,450	Other .	230,034,737
Calif..	36,534,407	U.S ..	658,534,252

422   From a diagram in the 1921 *Yearbook* of the United States Department of Agriculture

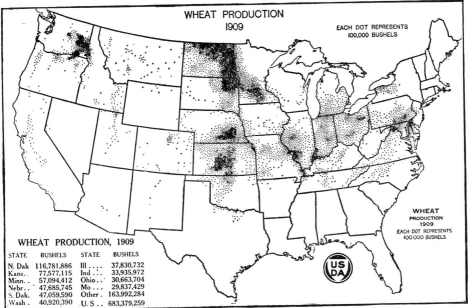

WHEAT PRODUCTION
1909

EACH DOT REPRESENTS
100,000 BUSHELS

WHEAT
PRODUCTION
1909
EACH DOT REPRESENTS
100,000 BUSHELS

WHEAT PRODUCTION, 1909

STATE	BUSHELS	STATE	BUSHELS
N. Dak	116,781,886	Ill	37,830,732
Kans..	77,577,115	Ind ...	33,935,972
Minn..	57,094,412	Ohio,.	30,663,704
Nebr..	47,685,745	Mo ...	29,837,429
S. Dak.	47,059,590	Other .	163,992,284
Wash .	40,920,390	U. S ..	683,379,259

423   From a diagram in the 1921 *Yearbook* of the United States Department of Agriculture

WHEAT IN THE TWENTIETH CENTURY

THE frontier has passed and the westward march of wheat has been halted. The "dry farmer," whose peculiar methods produce a crop where rainfall is scanty, has invaded the cattle range from Texas to Montana. Irrigation has carried wheat to the desert and to arid mountain valleys. With the disappearance of virgin soil, the unchallenged rule of wheat is passing even in its last and greatest strongholds. Diversified farming, which preserves and renews the land, is steadily driving out the wasteful and uneconomic single-crop system of the wheat country. But before the completion of the change, the wheat farmers, harried by depression, in 1924 rose once more to challenge the East. The problem of the future is to develop wheat raising in rotation with other crops in the regions where the soil and climate are favorable in such a way that the yield may be maintained, the soil conserved, and the farmers freed from the dangers that follow dependence upon a single product for their income.

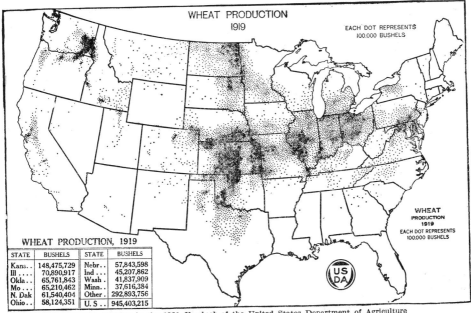

WHEAT PRODUCTION
1919

EACH DOT REPRESENTS
100,000 BUSHELS

WHEAT
PRODUCTION
1919
EACH DOT REPRESENTS
100,000 BUSHELS

WHEAT PRODUCTION, 1919

STATE	BUSHELS	STATE	BUSHELS
Kans..	148,475,729	Nebr..	57,843,598
Ill	70,890,917	Ind ...	45,207,862
Okla..	65,761,843	Wash .	41,837,909
Mo ...	65,210,462	Minn..	37,616,384
N. Dak	61,540,404	Other .	292,893,756
Ohio..	58,124,351	U. S ..	945,403,215

424   From a diagram in the 1921 *Yearbook* of the United States Department of Agriculture

425
From a photograph by the United States Department of Agriculture

RANCH BUILDINGS IN ARIZONA

THE disappearance of the bonanza farmers and the old-time cattle kings meant that the two industries of farming and cattle raising had passed out of the uncertain formative period and had become stabilized. Long before the twentieth century opened the last frontier had disappeared. The farms did not advance westward to the foot of the mountains. In the rain shadow of the Rockies the rainfall is too light for raising crops save by the recent and laborious methods of dry farming. Here on the old range and in the semi-arid country of New Mexico and Arizona are the cattle ranches of the new day.

426
From a photograph by the United States Forest Service

SHORTHORNS ON THE PLAINS

GONE are the wild, rangy Texas Longhorns. Stocky, well-shaped cattle, Herefords and Shorthorns, browse on the western plains. The old-time cowboy has also disappeared, now that the long drive is no more. The wild, free life of the frontier has given place to the quieter ways of civilization.

427   A Watering Place, Kansas, from a photograph by the United States Department of Agriculture

THE NEW RANCH

NOT all the picturesqueness has passed with the old ranch life.   The new ranch has also its wildness, its open spaces, its charm.   Sleek, purebred animals come down to the watering places.   The cow ponies are enclosed in the rough branding corrals until the cattleman needs them.   And over the plains where the swells rise

and fall the cattle graze on a thousand hills. The nester and the dry farmer have lessened the area of the old cow country. Vast numbers of cattle from the western pastures are sold in Iowa and Illinois for fattening. The rich corn belt supplements the dry and unimproved range. And steadily, as the years pass, the mounting population of the cities of both East and West demands more meat and hides. The cattleman busies himself to meet the demands of a growing market.

428   Corrals, Arizona, from a photograph by the United States Department of Agriculture

429   Cattle on Native Pasture, Kansas, from a photograph by the United States Department of Agriculture

SHEEP AND HERDER

BEFORE the old free range was broken up and cattle were raised under fence, the cattleman faced an enemy as dangerous as the homesteader. Flocks of sheep began to graze on the plains watched over by herders who lived in little covered wagons.

430   From a photograph by the United States Department of Agriculture

SHEEP RAISING

IN the sub-arid regions of the mountain states and in the green parks high on the mountain sides were the sheep ranges. When the herders took their flocks out to the open cattle country east of the Rockies, there was war. The feud between the cattlemen and sheepmen was long and bitter. There were already too many cattle for the range, and the sheep cropped the grass closer than other animals. "It is a pathetic spectacle to see parts of the Old West in which sheep steadily have been ranged. They utterly destroy all the game; they even drive the fish out of the streams and cut the grasses and weeds down to the surface of the earth. The denuded soil crumbles under their countless hoofs, becomes dust and blows away. They leave a waste, a desert, an abomination." — EMERSON HOUGH, *The Passing of the Frontier*, The Chronicles of America Series, Vol. 26, New Haven, 1920.

431   From a photograph by the United States Forest Service

432   From a photograph by the United States Forest Service

SHEEP IN A NATIONAL FOREST

SHEEP raising under fence was inevitable. Since the creation of the national forests it has become customary to allow sheep to range in them under a charge of so much per head. The old feud between the sheepman and the cattleman passed with the disappearance of the open range. The sheep industry, like farming and the cattle business, has become stabilized.

CATTLE IN A NATIONAL FOREST

INTO the national forests have also come the cattlemen. High up on the mountain sides where the forests break into open parks, graze herds that help to supply the ever-growing market of the East. Cattle raising, like agriculture, has adapted itself to the peculiarities of the American environment. The herdsman has found out the places where he can raise his animals with greatest profit.

433   From a photograph by the United States Forest Service

CHAPTER IX

THE CLANKING OF MACHINES

A SINGLE century sufficed to carry the American frontier from the western foothills of the Appalachians to the surging Pacific. The world had never seen so swift a settlement of so vast an unoccupied domain. America had land in superabundance and covered it with a thin veneer of people. But, in the process, the old husbandry of the scythe and hoe, of the ox team and the stone wall, was abandoned, and the skill which was the pride of the old farm was forgotten. When the nineteenth century closed, save for the war-wrecked South and occasional isolated uplands or tracts of infertile soil, a new husbandry ruled the American fields.

It chanced that in the latter half of the eighteenth century a remarkable group of inventions had profoundly altered the economic life of England. The influence of this industrial revolution was soon felt in the young and vigorous United States. The factory system and the machine took the place of the manual skill by which for countless generations the material things of life had been manufactured. Natural forces hitherto unused were harnessed to the drive wheels of the factories. Each year brought new machines or refinements of old ones. Americans, though as a rule less well trained in science than their English contemporaries, nevertheless proved themselves an inventive people. In the early years of the century, when American ironmasters were building their small stone forges in the forested limestone country of Pennsylvania and New York, when Fulton was perfecting the steam engines which drove his boats on the Hudson and the Mississippi, and when engineers were building the Erie Canal, some Americans turned their thoughts to the requirements of agriculture. Here, if anywhere, machines were needed.

America had insufficient man power to cultivate its vast possessions of fertile soil, and immigration did not make good the lack. Yet the frontier drew like a magnet. It offered independence to the many, and to the few wealth and power. To increase the productive capacity of the individual husbandman, to make it possible for him to do more work with less help became the central problem of American agriculture. The answer in the middle years of the nineteenth century was a group of machines that revolutionized husbandry and profoundly affected the farmer's life.

The change did indeed amount to a revolution. The old farm with its hand methods to a considerable extent passed away. The farm of the new day became more and more an enterprise involving large capital investments. The rapid changes which came with the introduction of the new machinery broke down the traditional rural conservatism which had already been modified by the adjustments to life on the new continent. The state of mind of the peasant was left far behind; the coming of the machines in the nineteenth century prepared the way for the wide application in the twentieth of the principles of a new science of agriculture to the farms of America.

434   From the *Universal Magazine*, London, 1748

TYPES OF EARLY ENGLISH PLOWS

THE husbandman's labor is to cultivate the soil. The plow is his basic tool, the symbol of his craft. During many generations English farmers developed different types of plows for the varied soils of the Kingdom. Many improvements were made in the eighteenth century when methods as well as tools were being revolutionized. Americans watching the developments across the sea were stimulated to effort, but they worked out their own peculiar problems in their own way. They adjusted the plow to American needs.

THE COLONIAL PLOW

THE eighteenth-century American farmer cultivated the soil with a wooden plow which had an iron point and some iron plates for turning the furrow. The one-handled plows left the husbandman a free hand for driving his team. Two handles enabled him to hold the tool more firmly to its work. The picture shows a plow which was probably the handiwork of a local blacksmith.

435   From an exhibit in the State Museum, Albany, N. Y.

436　　From *The Growth of Industrial Art*, Washington, 1892

THE NEWBOLD PLOW

THE first important American experimenter was Charles Newbold, of New Jersey. In 1797 he completed and patented the first iron plow cast in a single piece. But the farmers of the day were conservative and suspicious. The belief spread widely that a cast-iron plow poisoned the soil so that only weeds would grow. With a bitterness deepened by the loss of his small fortune in his attempt to introduce his improvement, Newbold saw his work rejected by the people whom he hoped to benefit.

THOMAS JEFFERSON'S PLAN FOR A MOLDBOARD

NEWBOLD was not the only eighteenth-century American who turned his mind to the plow. In 1799 Thomas Jefferson published a scientific discussion on the proper shape for a moldboard, the part of the plow which elevates and twists the soil ribbon. He worked out his theories by mathematical calculations. Jefferson believed that if the most efficient shape could once be determined all plows could be built to conform to it. This would put an end to the shallow scratching which had injured the colonial farms. Jefferson's work is significant not only of the spirit of progress which marked the end of the eighteenth century but of the caliber of the men who were seeking to promote the interests of agriculture.

The upper part of the figure shows Jefferson's calculations on the basis of which James Mease made his sketches.

JETHRO WOOD'S PLOW

JEFFERSON corresponded with Jethro Wood, a Quaker from New York state, regarding his moldboard. In 1819 this gentleman patented an improved cast-iron plow. Newbold's plow had been cast in a single piece; Wood's was so devised that the parts which were subjected to the greatest wear could be replaced. The Wood invention fell upon favorable times. The agrarian awakening at the end of the eighteenth century had begun to break down the farmer's conservatism. Inventors and manufacturers began to copy the new tool. The iron plow rapidly became popular and, by 1825, was in general use. Wood, like so many inventors, spent his substance in defending his rights and died impoverished and disappointed. But he left a rich heritage to his fellow-countrymen.

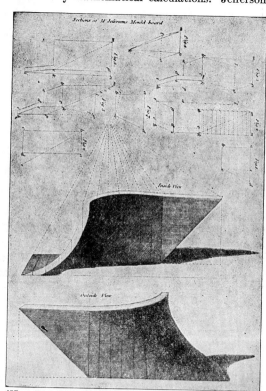

437　　From the *Domestic Encyclopedia*, Philadelphia, 1803, after a drawing by James Mease

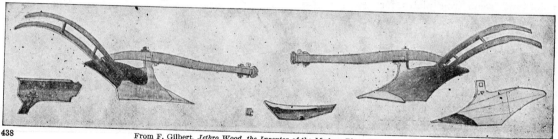

438

From F. Gilbert, *Jethro Wood, the Inventor of the Modern Plow*, Chicago, 1882

THE NEW IRON PLOW

THE plow was the first of the farmer's implements to be affected by the spirit of discovery and invention which had brought about the industrial revolution in the last half of the eighteenth century. For centuries the wooden plow had been handed down from generation to generation, scratching the soil from which the husbandman wrested a meager living. Then in a single decade all was changed. The old "bull plow" practically disappeared from the fields of America. "Yankee inventiveness" turned to the improvement of the nation's basic industry. Patent followed patent as plows of new designs were hurried on the market. At county and state fairs plowing matches were held to determine the best makes. The substitution of the iron for the wooden plow came in the same years that Watson's Berkshire System was spreading rapidly over the country. The two profoundly changed the mental outlook of the husbandman. New ideas as well as new tools were put to work on American fields. The ancient occupation of husbandry was passing into a new epoch.

RUGGLES, NOURSE & MASON'S SUPERIOR WORCESTER PLOWS.

THE American Institute at their Fair, held at New-York, for the whole Union, and the Massachusetts Charitable Association at their Fair, held at Boston, each awarded to Ruggles, Nourse & Mason, medals for the best and most perfect plows; and at the plowing matches of the Agricultural Society in the justly celebrated agricultural county of Worcester, in 1837, '38, '39, and '40, all the premiums for the best work in the field, were awarded to competitors using Ruggles, Nourse & Mason's plows.

In addition to the above, the New-York State Agricultural Society, at their Fair, held in Albany, in September last, awarded the premium for the best plowing to John Keeler, (see Cultivator, vol. IX, p. 178,) who on that occasion used one of the above plows.

A complete assortment of them, including Side Hill, Subsoil, and Corn Plows, Cultivators, Straw Cutters, &c. for sale at manufacturer's prices, by

Feb. 24, 1843. PRUYN, WILSON & VOSBURGH, 39 State st. Albany.

439 An Advertisement for the Eagle Plow, from *The Cultivator*, Albany, March, 1843

Plowing on the Old Farm. © Rau Studios

441   From *Harper's Weekly*, May 9, 1868

THE PRAIRIE SOD PLOW

"Why, thar ain't no stumps to plow around!" exclaimed
the pioneers, looking out for the first time across the
open prairie. But the tough sod balked the best
implements of the day. So there developed the great
prairie-breaking plow with wooden moldboard plated
with iron strips. The teams of many straining oxen,
the drivers with their whips and singsong calls, the
strong man at the handles, blended into a picture that
with but slight changes might serve to depict the
villeins of medieval England turning the soil of their
arable fields.

THE STEEL PLOW

Much of the prairie soil was a heavy loam which clung
to the iron-shod moldboard. John Deere, who set
himself to rectify this fault, was typical of that group
of early nineteenth-century Americans who made such
astonishing mechanical contributions to the life of their

442   John Deere, 1804–1886, Father of the Steel Plow, courtesy
of Deere & Company, Moline, Ill.

times. Born in Vermont of humble parents, Deere started life equipped with a common-school education
and a thorough knowledge of the blacksmith's trade. Like other enterprising young men he cast his lot with

443   Part of an early Deere Plow, courtesy of Deere & Company, Moline, Ill.

the frontier and, in 1837, set up his shop at
Grand Detour in Illinois. He observed that
the prairie plows worked badly. He built a
plow with moldboard of steel which, polish-
ing itself, would not become caked with
loam. Twenty years after starting his
frontier shop, in 1857 John Deere made ten
thousand plows. Yet even this was but a
beginning. The time came when Deere was
numbered among the greatest plow makers
in the world.

444

Courtesy of the Oliver Chilled Plow Works, South Bend, Ind.

THE OLIVER CHILLED PLOW

In spite of improvements the farmers had difficulties with the early iron and steel plows. They were brittle and their surfaces were roughened by blow holes which formed when the casting was made. It fell to the lot of a Hoosier, James Oliver, to devise a method which would do away with both of these imperfections. In 1869, the first Oliver plow with a chilled steel moldboard was produced. The modern plow had come into being. Since that time the sole task of the inventor has been to improve the details of the implement.

STEAM PLOW ON PATTERSON'S FARM, NEW JERSEY

In the same year that Oliver brought out his improved plow, Colonel William C. Patterson, owner of a thirty thousand acre estate in New Jersey, tried out a steam plowing equipment which he had imported from England. Although the plowing was satisfactory, it was too clumsy and costly to be practicable. Its only significance lies in showing the experimentation that was necessary in the evolution of the modern power plow.

445

From *Harper's Weekly*, July 24, 1869

446   A Gang Plow with Horses, from a photograph by the United States Department of Agriculture

THE GANG PLOW

THE gang plow, turning two or more furrows, which was one of the features of the Patterson outfit, has become a part of the equipment of the modern farm. On some land and in small fields the old single plow is still the most economical. The plowman who walks and holds his plow to the furrow has not disappeared. But more and more, on the better farms of America, the gang plow turns the soil. This device, like so many of the nineteenth-century agricultural inventions, makes it possible for one man to till more soil. It was an attempt to increase production per man, an adjustment to a situation in which vast areas of fertile land were covered with a sparse population.

447   A Gang Plow with Tractor, from a photograph by the United States Department of Agriculture

448   The Disk Plow, from a photograph by the United States Department of Agriculture

THE PLOWS OF THE TWENTIETH CENTURY

ON the rich, level lands of the prairie plains, where embedded roots and stones offer no obstruction, massive modern plows have appeared. Some are merely revolving disks; others are of the moldboard type hitched in great gangs. The ox and horse have been supplanted by the steam or gasoline tractor. Slowly back and forth across the level, treeless fields move these iron monsters guided and controlled by a single hand. Such machines and methods represent the acme of extensive agriculture. The old world has never seen such farming. It is far removed from the husbandry of the peasant farms of Russia, of the crowded lowlands of China and India or even of the thickly settled plains of France and Germany.

449   Disking with a Steam Tractor, from a photograph by the United States Department of Agriculture

450   Courtesy of the Oliver Chilled Plow Works

TURNING THE PRAIRIE

ON the medieval manor some three or four men and six or eight oxen labored together to turn a single furrow across the arable field. To-day the husbandman has harnessed to his plow the same mighty natural forces that have made industrial civilization possible. The man who owns and uses such tools is far removed from his stolid peasant forefathers; he is much more than a mere tiller of the soil.

451   From a photograph by the United States Department of Agriculture

THE SPIKE–TOOTH HARROW

PLOWING must be followed by harrowing before the clods are broken and the surface fitted to receive a crop. In the early days of settlement before the stumps were fully cleared from the fields a triangular harrow shod with vertical wooden pegs was dragged over the plowed land. As time went on and the stumps disappeared, the triangle was replaced by a square and the wooden pegs by iron teeth.

452 From a photograph by the United States Department of Agriculture

THE SPRING–TOOTH HARROW

But the spike-tooth harrow, so great an improvement in its day, has gone, save for the great steel tools often used to prepare potato ground for this crop. The adjustable steel tool is now found on modern fields. On the prairie farms harrows are often hitched behind the great gang plows so that the two essential processes in the preparation of the soil are performed together. After the harrowing the farmer compacts the loosened soil with a roller.

453 From a photograph by the United States Department of Agriculture

THE DRILL

The drill has driven the picturesque broadcasting sower from the fields. As early as the eighteenth century experiments were made with machines that would plant the seeds at the proper depth and cover them with soil. Merely casting the grain on the surface was wasteful and resulted in uneven crops. The modern drill plants the seed grain where it can germinate, with fertilizer close at hand where the growing seedling can best use it. Variations of the grain drill are used for many different crops, — such as corn planters and potato planters. There are machines which facilitate the setting of tiny plants which are being transferred from the hothouse to the field. The drill is an improvement looking toward efficiency as well as the saving of labor.

454   From a photograph by the United States Department of Agriculture

THE CULTIVATOR

THE time-honored hoe was one of the tools of primitive agriculture. In England in the eighteenth century Jethro Tull taught the use of the plow to replace the hoe in guarding a crop from weeds. In nineteenth-century America the cultivator displaced the plow in the rows of beans and corn. The cultivator digs out the weeds between the rows, loosens the soil, maintains the dust mulch, and, when necessary, hills up the growing plants.

455   From a photograph by Rudolf Eickemeyer

CRADLING

THE farmer of the early nineteenth century laid aside the sickle for cutting grain and carried to the harvest field a clumsy cradle which was merely a scythe with a set of long curved wooden teeth parallel to it. Against these teeth the grain lay until the end of the swing, when it was dropped in a row convenient for binding. Both strength and skill were required to swing this early cradle throughout a hot July day. As a farmer feelingly remarked, it was "almost a trade by itself."

456   From *The Cultivator*, May, 1841

THE FIRST REAPER

AT best, cradling was slow. Before the eighteenth century closed men were turning their minds to the invention of a machine that would cut grain. But it was not until 1833 that Obed Hussey patented the first successful reaper. Triangular knives attached to a horizontal bar and vibrating between metal guards or fingers took the place of the sickle or the long-bladed cradle. A man seated on the machine watched the grain fall from the knives and raked it off into gavels which another bound into sheaves.

OBED HUSSEY, 1800–1860, INVENTOR OF THE REAPER

OBED HUSSEY, like his contemporary, John Deere, was typical of his generation. Born in Nantucket, he moved west to the growing town of Cincinnati. He was a mechanic with a turn for invention. He devised a machine to make pins and another to mold candles. Then came the reaping machine. With his clumsy reaper a demonstrated success, Hussey abandoned the West and moved to Baltimore. From time to time he made improvements as experience with his machine demonstrated needs. He became an important figure and his invention steadily won its way among the farmers of the East. In 1858, two years before his death in a railway accident, he invented a steam plow. With his reaper he made the name of Hussey a household word among the farmers of the North, but his fame never equaled that of a competitor who had independently produced a reaper involving many of Hussey's principles.

457   From a tintype in the possession of Miss Martha Hussey, Rochester, N. Y.

CYRUS H. McCORMICK, 1809–1884

ROBERT McCORMICK's lot in life was to live in the heyday of the old farm and to rebel against the manual tasks that made up so much of its routine. As he swung his heavy cradle about his grain fields in the Shenandoah valley in Virginia, the conviction burned within him that his work was a waste of time, that machinery, not human hands, should reap the harvest. His workshop became an obsession where he spent days and nights seeking to give reality to his dream of making a machine that would cut his wheat. He failed amid some shaking of heads on the part of his practical-minded neighbors. But he passed on his aspiration to his young son, Cyrus. As a boy, Cyrus worked in his shop beside his father. In his teens he saw his father's strange contrivance of whirling sickles make an inglorious failure. He discarded his father's ideas, thought out the principles which underlie the modern reaper and, in 1831, while but twenty-two, completed a machine that under the admiring eyes of his family cut the grain on his father's farm.

458   From a daguerreotype, about 1839. Courtesy of the
International Harvester Company of America

THE TESTING OF McCORMICK'S REAPER

A LITTLE later in the same season young McCormick gave the first public demonstration of a successful reaper. As his clumsy machine clattered about the field, the skepticism of the handful of farmers who had come to witness the attempt was changed to admiration.

459   From a lithograph, courtesy of the International Harvester Company of America, Chicago

THE SUCCESS OF THE McCORMICK REAPER

FOR three years after the first public demonstration at Steele's Tavern, McCormick, with practically no capital, worked in his father's shop perfecting his invention. In 1834, one year after Hussey, he secured his patent. McCormick, unlike his rival Hussey, was more than a mechanic. Time was to prove him one of the greatest business organizers and executives of his day. Whereas Hussey had turned his back on the prairie plains and had come east with his invention, McCormick left his quiet Virginia home and put his fortune to the hazard in the new West of the

460   McCormick's Cincinnati Factory, 1845, courtesy of the International Harvester Company of America

Ohio valley. He established a shop in Cincinnati where, in 1845, one hundred machines were built. But with the rare foresight of genius he saw in the little city of Chicago, numbering scarcely more than ten thousand souls, the strategic center of the West, and in the level grain fields of the prairie plains the great market for his invention. In 1848 his new factory on the shores of Lake Michigan turned out five hundred machines. Yet this was but the beginning of his triumphs.

461   McCormick's Chicago Factory, 1850, courtesy of the International Harvester Company of America

THE McCORMICK REAPER OF 1847

ROUGH and crude though they seem, McCormick's early machines were sturdy and well built. One man drove the team while another raked off the grain from the platform where it fell after the knives had cut it. Perhaps the farmer's wife raked the gavels together and bound the sheaves. Another man stood them up in shocks for curing. Then McCormick added a device for raking off the straw.

462   Courtesy of the International Harvester Company of America

463   Courtesy of the International Harvester Company of America

THE McCORMICK REAPER OF 1848

THE picture shows the machine that McCormick built the year after he moved his plant to Chicago. An automatic rake had been provided so that it was no longer necessary to have a man to pull the grain from the cutting knives. This was the machine that McCormick sent agents over the country to sell — on the installment plan, a method of marketing goods almost as revolutionary as the invention itself.

464   From *Harper's Weekly*, Aug. 1, 1857

A TRIAL OF REAPERS AT THE NEW YORK STATE FAIR, 1857

IN 1852 nine reapers entered the trials at Geneva, New York. Only one or two did fair work. Yet, though it was clear that the reaper was yet in the experimental stage, there was no doubt of its utility. Five years later at Syracuse the more than forty mowers and reapers entered showed that a reliable and serviceable machine had been achieved. For the progressive farmer the day of the cradle had definitely passed.

THE SELF-BINDER

SPEED in binding the grain was as essential as rapid cutting. Two Illinois farmers named Marsh substituted for the wooden platform on which the cut grain fell a moving canvas which carried the straw up to a man who gathered together the sheaves and turned them over to another to bind. From 1860 to 1874 the Marsh type of harvester was widely used. The contribution of the Marshes was vastly important. Then came McCormick's self-binder, binding the sheaves with wire. For ten years the new device and his magnificent selling organization made him master of the harvester situation. Then William Deering in 1884 brought out a binder

465   An Improved Reaper, 1875, courtesy of the International Harvester Company of America

which bound the sheaves with twine. He had purchased from John F. Appleby of Wisconsin an amazing invention of a mechanical device for tying knots. McCormick hastened to perfect a knotter of his own. The evolution of the reaper had come to an end. One man driving these new machines could accomplish all that eight men could do with the early reaper. Like the monster gang plow the binder is the product of the needs of extensive agriculture. The prairies of the upper Mississippi valley called both into being. William H. Seward once remarked that the binder made it possible for the frontier to advance each year twenty miles farther west.

466   An Early Type of Self-Binder, courtesy of the International Harvester Company of America

467   A Header at Work, courtesy of the International Harvester Company of America

THE HEADER

BUT on the broad areas of the western plains, where wheat fields sometimes stretch as far as the eye can reach, even the improved binder has given way to the header cutting its tremendous swath.

The great machine, drawn sometimes by many horses and sometimes by a tractor, clips the heads off the standing, ripened grain, leaving the straw to rot and be plowed under where it stood. Sometimes to the header a thresher is attached making one huge machine by which the grain is cut and prepared for mill. Twentieth-century folk are accustomed to the new machines. Yet for thousands of years the tools of the husbandman were the hoe and the sickle. They go back to the beginning of the age of iron. Then in the nineteenth century, in the lifetime of two generations, intricate machines were put to work on one of the world's largest and richest agricultural areas which had lain practically untouched through the long ages when man was rising from stage to stage of culture. Few economic revolutions have been so sudden and so profoundly important.

468   A Combination Header and Thresher, from a photograph by the United States Department of Agriculture

469   From a photograph by the United States Department of Agriculture

OLD-TYPE REAPER STILL IN USE

YET the old reaper was not abandoned. On the hilly fields of the eastern farms, covered perhaps with crops of buckwheat, it is often more economical than the more expensive machine. It may still be seen, with its great rakes for sweeping off the gavels, lurching over the fields on the smaller farmsteads.

470   Courtesy of the International Harvester Company of America

MOWING WITH SCYTHES

THE meadows have also seen a change. The scythe has passed away. The mower was a natural outgrowth of the reaper and many of the early machines were convertible and could be used for either purpose. In 1856 the patents of Cyrenus Wheeler brought into existence the modern two-wheeled mowing machine as distinct from the reaper.

471   Mowing Machine in Timothy, from a photograph by the United States Department of Agriculture

IMPROVEMENTS IN MOWING MACHINERY

To-day in place of the swish of the long clean blades of the scythes is the rattle of the mower with its staccato click as it turns the corners. Maud Muller no longer rakes "the meadow sweet with hay." Horserakes gather the dried grass into windrows ready for hauling. A few men and a few machines can do the work of many laborers. On the new farm with its new machines the plodding ox has small place. In his stead the horse and the tractor do the farmers' work. Unlike the automatic devices of the factory the new farm machines have not done away with the need for skill. Careful driving and close attention are required to keep the selvedge straight, the corners square, and to make no balks. The farmer is master of the tools he uses.

472   A "Side-Delivery" Rake, from a photograph by the United States Department of Agriculture

473   Pitching Hay the Old Way, from a photograph by the United States Department of Agriculture

HAY PITCHING OLD AND NEW

HAYING has always been heavy work. It is a race against the possible storm. The busy farmer with a succession of crops ripening at short intervals through the summer and fall cannot afford to dawdle over haying, which is the first crop of all. His timothy and clover must be in the barn before the rye and the wheat ripen. Yet the old method of loading hay may still be seen on smaller farms in the hot days of June and July. The windrows left by the horserake are piled into cocks for final curing and these are hoisted by hand forks to the top of the bulky load. The forks are unlike their ill-shaped forerunners of the eighteenth century, being well made and perfectly adjusted to their work. The hay loader saves time; with it the crop can be brought to the barn more quickly. But the work is still heavy. The machines which have come to the farmers' aid call for brains and skill in their management. But they have not eliminated the need for muscle. Farming is no job for weaklings. To the mental strain of managing a complex business enterprise is often added the physical exhaustion which comes from hard, manual toil.

474   A Modern Hay Loader, from a photograph by the United States Department of Agriculture

475   Haystacks and Stacking Outfit, from a photograph by the United States Department of Agriculture

HANDLING HAY

SOMETIMES the hay is stacked in fields to await the hay press. Sometimes it is put in the mow in the barn for fodder for the stock. On the old farm haying meant long days of tedious work with a hand fork. The cured grass must be pitched from the cock to the load, from the load to the mow and in the mow each forkful put in its proper place. To cut and haul even a moderate acreage required many hands. Much of the slow pitching of the old days is now done away with. Great one- or two-tined forks lift the hay from the wagon and carry it to the place where it is wanted in mow or stack.

Horse forks they are called because the hay is moved by a horse or team pulling the hay rope. A proud farm boy "drives off" the load. About the time of the Civil War the new devices for handling hay began

rapidly coming into use. The reaper and the iron plow had served in a measure to break down rural conservatism and attachment to old usage. The growing cities of an age of industrialism required many horses, for trucking, for pleasure driving, for hauling street cars. Eastern farms turned to the raising of hay to supply an increasing market. The demand for more and more hay made necessary the new devices. The horse fork made practicable larger barns wherein could be housed all the farmer's hay, thus saving the wastage that resulted from the weathering of the stack.

476   A Horse Fork at Work, from a photograph by the United States Department of Agriculture

477   Husking Corn in the Field, from a photograph by the United States Department of Agriculture

HARVESTING THE CORN

WHEN the sharp rustle of dried leaves announced that the corn was ripe, the early farmer went into his fields with his corn-knife, a modification of the sickle. He cut the ripened stalks by hand and stood them in great shocks beneath which the field mice built their nests. Sometimes he husked the ears in the field; or he drew the shocks to the barn for the winter days when the husking would be done on the barn floor. But new machines have appeared. Much corn raised in dairy sections is never husked but is cut before it is ripe by the corn binder and hauled green to the ensilage cutter beside the barn, by which ears and stalks are chopped into fine bits and stored in the great cylindrical silo. Ensilage is green food and is given to dairy cattle during the winter season when the pastures are dead or covered with snow. The development of the silo marks one of the greatest advances in modern milk production.

478   A Corn Binder, from a photograph by the United States Department of Agriculture

479   From a photograph by the United States Department of Agriculture

HUSKING CORN BY MACHINERY

In the corn belt, stretching from Ohio to Iowa, the raising of the grain which the redskins gave the whites has reached its fullest development. There is a world of difference between the methods of the squaws and those of the prairie farmers. The corn binder has replaced the old hand tool. In some localities the husking machine comes to the barn in the fall to husk the ears to be used for the fattening of livestock. Other machines, after the plan of the combination header and thresher, travel up and down the rows of the field dropping the husked corn into a wagon.

480   From *The Growth of Industrial Art*, Government Printing Office, Washington, 1892

THE PASSING OF THE THRESHING FLOOR

Machines have also replaced the weary beating of flails and the monotonous round of the animals on the threshing floor. Almost as old as agriculture itself are these two methods of separating the grain from the straw. The oxen of the early Hebrews trod out their wheat. But the time-honored flail and threshing floor passed for America in the century that saw so many machines added to the equipment of the farm.

481   An Eighteenth-Century Threshing Device, from *The Growth of Industrial Art*, Washington, 1892

EARLY ATTEMPTS AT THRESHING MACHINES

THE making of machines to thresh grain was early in men's minds. In the eighteenth century strange devices made their appearance. In general the earliest were built on the principle of the flail. They were simply machines to increase the amount of grain a man could beat out. Few of these schemes were practical nor were they widely used. "Threshing machines utilizing hand-power were introduced from Europe at the end of the eighteenth century and several of Scotch make were set up in 1802 in Pennsylvania, Delaware and New Jersey. . . . Small hand-power and horse-power machines of a number of makes were advertised in the agricultural press in the years 1820 to 1830." — PERCY WELLS BIDWELL AND JOHN I. FALCONER, *History of Agriculture in the Northern United States, 1620–1860*, Washington, 1925.

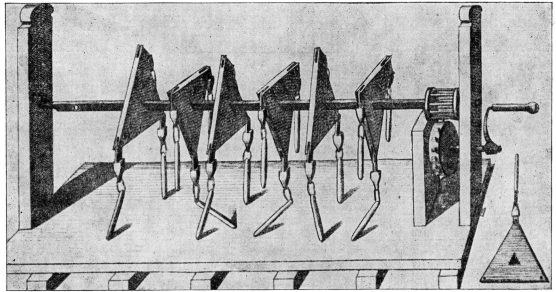

482   A Machine for Beating Grain, from *The Pennsylvania Magazine*, 1775

483   Pitt's Thresher, from *The Cultivator*, 1838

AN IMPROVED THRESHER

THE invention which made the thresher a success was an iron cylinder armed with teeth whirling in a toothed concave. Behind the cylinder was a device for shaking the grain from the straw and for winnowing the chaff. At first these machines were generally driven by a treadmill. By 1825 this type of thresher was in use on the farms of America. In 1855, at an international exposition in Paris, Pitt's thresher easily surpassed every competing European device. It proved its superiority to one English and two French machines as well as to six men working with flails. "Yankee inventiveness" had scored another triumph. Yet Pitt's thresher, small and clumsy, only dimly foreshadowed the vast and complicated machine that in a generation was to take its place on the farms of America.

484   From *Harper's Weekly*, Sept. 21, 1878, after a drawing by O. D. Steinberger

THRESHING IN THE FIELD, 1878

As time went on a new machine, the "sweep horse power," took the place of the smaller treadmill. Long arms projected from a revolving center and a team of horses was hitched to each. Hour after hour they plodded the circuit as a sailor walks the capstan. The artist has described the scene, which was sketched in central Ohio. "At these threshings some twenty men are required and, when a steamer is not used, about the same number of horses, besides an infinite number of children, who carry water and are 'kept lively' at other light work. The men are variously employed as feeders, band cutters, drivers, haulers, sackers, straw-diggers, stackers, etc. Neighbors usually help each other and have generally, in spite of the dust, what Westerners call a 'jolly good time.' The women are kept busy in preparation of the meals, for all hands are boarded and it is a point to have the bell ring or the horn blow exactly on time."

485   A Thresher with Traction Engine, from a photograph by the United States Department of Agriculture

THE MODERN THRESHER

As of old the threshing machine travels from farm to farm, drawn now by a steam engine or a gasoline tractor instead of laboring teams. When the "traction engine" puffs up the driveway past the barn and deftly backs the great thresher into place, the busiest moment of the farmer's year has come. Neighbors with forks over their shoulders gather in, one of the few modern survivals of pioneer coöperation and exchange of labor. The men are told off to their several tasks, some to bring up the sheaves, others to care for the straw, and the farmer himself to carry the grain to the bins. The long belt slaps as the engine starts and the machine begins to hum. The cylinder roars as the sheaves are fed into its spiked throat, and the thresher, in which great sieves are shaken swiftly to and fro, vibrates with its work. Everywhere sweaty, dust-covered men hurry to the accomplishment of the task. Perhaps the threshing lasts a few hours, perhaps, if the crop is large, two or three days.

486   A Thresher with Wind Stacker, from a photograph by the United States Department of Agriculture

487   From a photograph by the United States Department of Agriculture

SPRAYING THE ORCHARD

IN the orchards as well as on the fields have appeared the machines of the new day. Spraying devices with poison mixtures destroy the enemies of the fruit trees. In place of poor apples and stunted peaches full-formed fruit hangs on the branches when the picking season comes, when other devices aid in the grading and the packing of the crop. Horticulture has become a highly developed science and the successful fruit grower must have at his command a considerable equipment and body of knowledge. His orchard with trees set in straight rows and neatly trimmed suggests in its orderliness the evolution that has taken place since the days of the unkempt fruit trees scattered at random throughout the back lots of the farmer.

488   From a photograph by the United States Department of Agriculture

A DIRT HIGHWAY

THE new farm machinery must have lost some of its significance had the highway that passed the farmhouse been forgotten. Much of the isolation of the old farm of the earlier day was due to the little-cared-for dirt roads that lay between the farmstead and the market. Back and forth through the mud and over the ruts the farmer traveled with the things that he had to sell and the necessities that he bought at the store. A ten-mile trip to town and home again was an all day journey except in winter when the sleighing was good. Horse and driver were weary at the end. The dirt highway took a heavy toll in time and energy.

ROAD BUILDING

In the main the old highways were cared for by the farmers who lived beside them. Often the state law required the individual to work a certain number of days each year upon the road dragging the clumsy scrapers and smoothers over the rutty surface. On main thoroughfares, however, the turnpike early appeared.

In 1793, near Lancaster, Penn., the first American turnpike was built. During the nineteenth century many

489 A Farmer as Road-Mender, from a photograph by the United States Department of Agriculture

pikes were constructed in New England, in the eastern farming states and in the Ohio valley, by private companies that collected tolls from the persons who drove on them. Toll bridges were also built over the larger streams. But, good as they were, the turnpikes did not solve the farmer's transportation problem. They cut down the steeper hills and improved the grades. They gave the road a broad and rounded surface. But rarely were they made of stone. When the winter frost left the ground, they were as muddy as other roads. For a time about the middle of the century plank roads became popular, but the wooden surface ultimately proved unsatisfactory and was removed. Only a few main roads were turnpiked. The average farmer was condemned to poor bridges, steep grades, ruts, and mud. Rural America has never had the capital necessary to free itself from the incubus of the dirt road. Until the coming of the automobile and the building of roads by state and national governments, the farmer accepted mud, like the weather, as inevitable.

490   The Modern Paved Country Road, from a photograph by the United States Bureau of Public Roads

491   From a model built for the American Section of the Brazilian Centennial Exposition

THE MODERN HIGHWAY

WITH increasing rapidity, since the opening of the twentieth century, the improved highway with a hard, smooth surface and easy grades has been extended through the country districts. Sturdy culverts of stone and cement have replaced the little wooden bridges that so often gave way under a heavy load. The automobile owner of the city rather than the farmer forced the change. At first only the main thoroughfares were improved, but in recent years on the lesser roads to right and left the work of improvement in many states has gone steadily on. These highways of the first quarter of the twentieth century have brought changes in American farm life as significant as those which followed the great inventions of the nineteenth. With the coming of the "State road" and the automobile the isolation of the farm has passed.

492   From a photograph by the United States Reclamation Service

THE DESERT AWAITING RECLAMATION

SIDE by side with the building of new roads has gone the reclaiming of the desert areas of the West. Irrigation is almost as old as husbandry. Ditches built by Indians, who vanished long before the coming of the whites, still trench the deserts of Arizona and New Mexico and one of them a score of feet in depth, cut in rock for several hundred yards, carries the water of a modern irrigation project. The Mormons, coming into Utah in the 'forties, were pioneers in the irrigation of the dry valley bottoms of the mountain region. But aside from the Mormon ditches, the reclamation of the dry country awaited the time when the public domain was filled with farms and ranches and the frontier gone. Then state and national governments began to turn their attention to the sandy regions of the mountains and the southwestern desert, where little but the sagebrush and the cactus grow.

A NATURAL RESERVOIR

LITTLE snow-fed lakes lie high up in the mountain masses and from them swift streams tumble through rock gorges down the mountain sides. The high peaks comb the water from the moist winds and leave the lower areas dry and parched. To tap this source of moisture in the uplands and bring it to the flat lowlands beside the mountain base is the irrigation problem.

THE ARROWROCK IRRIGATION DAM IN IDAHO

THE large-scale development of the water resources of the mountains began in 1894 when Congress, through the Carey Act, gave to any state the control of a million acres of arid public lands within its borders. The state government then contracted with an irrigation company for the development of a certain district. The settlers on the reclaimed land bought their farms from the state and ultimately, after forming an association, took over the irrigation system. The law resulted in considerable development, but private enterprise was unwilling to undertake the vast outlays that were necessary if the water resources of the mountains were to be adequately utilized. In 1902, with the passage of the Reclamation Act, irrigation entered upon a new era. Under this law the Federal Government undertook the building of the works which were

493   From a photograph by the United States Forest Service

necessary for the reclamation of the desert lands of the West. Gigantic dams have been built to hold back great lakes; one of them, in New Mexico, is the largest artificial lake in the world. From these mountain reservoirs comes the water that brings life to the plains below.

494   From a photograph by the United States Reclamation Service

III—16

495   An Irrigation Flume in Washington, from a photograph by the United States Department of Agriculture

BRINGING WATER FROM THE RESERVOIR

Down the mountain sides the water slips in great flumes past steep cliffs, down sharp inclines and over deep ravines. Sometimes the flumes are great closed pipe lines and sometimes the water runs in open troughs. Here and there a lateral taps the main stream and diverts a part of the flood. In most cases the great cylindrical flume has replaced the open aqueducts which the ancients used in bringing water from distant reservoirs. These mountain pipe lines symbolize the perfection of man's adjustment of his agriculture to nature.

496   An Irrigation Lateral in Colorado, from a photograph by the United States Department of Agriculture

AN IRRIGATION DITCH IN IDAHO

The rushing water of the flume comes to rest in the broad irrigation ditches of the flat country. From these the farmers get their supply. The charges are so arranged that, in course of time, the husbandmen in the irrigated district have reimbursed the government for its expenditures and the money can then be used in the development of other projects. So the reclamation of the dry land is continued.

497   From a photograph by the United States Department of Agriculture

498   From a photograph by the United States Reclamation Service

FLOODING A FIELD IN WYOMING

Small canvas dams are placed in the main ditches distributing the water to any part of the field that the farmer wishes to irrigate. With an assured supply he is able to soak down his fields when they most need it. Though blasting summer skies yield him no rain, his crops push cheerfully forward to maturity, and a rich harvest crowns the summer's labor. The quantity of water to use and the proper time to apply it in order to get the best results, present problems the solution of which the ordinary farmer must leave to chance.

AN IRRIGATED FIELD

The holdings of the irrigation farmers are small and their fields intensively cultivated. Their homes cluster in villages like the vills of the ancient manors, and from these each morning the husbandman sets out to till his acres. Like the folk of the manors, these people have learned well the art of coöperation.

499   From a photograph by the United States Reclamation Service

500   Establishing the Umatilla Project, Oregon, from a photograph by the United States Reclamation Service

TRANSFORMING THE DESERT

MORE than nineteen million acres have been reclaimed from the desert, and the task is yet unfinished. To add so much to the food-producing areas of the world is not the least of our national achievements. The soil reclaimed is rich in plant foods which have not been leached out by the rains of the recurring seasons. Six years sufficed in the Umatilla Project in Oregon to produce trees higher than the ridgeboards of their owner's house. Irrigation, like improved machinery, is merely another phase of the application to the practical needs of husbandry of the knowledge which the investigators of science have amassed. It represents a closer and more intelligent adjustment to natural conditions. Yet it is but a small part of that larger adjustment to nature, the Science of Agriculture.

501   The Umatilla Project Six Years Later, from a photograph by the United States Reclamation Service

CHAPTER X

THE AGE OF SCIENCE

TO say that the outstanding achievement of western civilization in the nineteenth century was the acquisition of knowledge and the establishment of the reign of science is to repeat a commonplace. The material life of men was changed as never before in a like period. Commerce and industry were profoundly affected. Inevitably the ancient calling of the farmer felt the impact of the forces of the new day.

The group of leaders who, at the end of the eighteenth century, sought by study and experimentation to improve American husbandry believed that they were serving their country by bettering the methods of that calling which claimed the lives of the great majority of Americans. Yet, though their methods were sound, they were working largely in the dark. The meager "chymistry" of their day did not explain for them the composition of the soil or the foods which plants require nor did "natural philosophy" teach them much of the laws of growth and life. Scientific investigators were groping, seeking with difficulty to read the riddle of nature and these pioneers of the science of agriculture were doing what they could with the knowledge of the day. Livingston, in enumerating the "elements that go to the composition of vegetables, to wit, earth, air, fire, water," mirrored the ignorance which still surrounded even the most intelligent. Yet through just such efforts as theirs knowledge of the ways of nature was ultimately gained. They initiated in America the application of the principles of pure science to the problems of husbandry; they died ignorant of the full significance of their work.

More than half a century was to pass before the development of the science of American agriculture was seriously undertaken. The rich virgin soil of the Mississippi valley and of the Pacific coast dulled the incentive to better farming. If the fields of the East gave out, the farmer had but to move to the frontier to find better land awaiting him. Yet, during the years in which the American frontier was moving steadily westward, natural science was swiftly pushing back the boundaries of knowledge. In 1862, in the midst of the fiercest war in the nation's history and before the frontier had passed away, the national government sought to harness science to the plow. The result has been a revolution which has remade the American countryside.

But it has done more. With the Civil War the day passed when the American farmer, on his isolated and largely self-sufficient little homestead, could take thought only for his family. Industrialism was building great cities whose millions of people must be fed. America could not look abroad for any large amount of food. The strength and power of the nation lay, ultimately, in the hands of the men who tilled its fields. If agriculture failed to keep pace with industry, America was a house built on the sand. The improvement in agricultural practice begun by Jared Eliot and his eighteenth-century contemporaries made possible modern industrial America.

CONSIDERATIONS

ON THE

NECESSITY OF ESTABLISHING

AN

AGRICULTURAL COLLEGE,

AND HAVING MORE OF THE

Children of Wealthy Citizens,

EDUCATED FOR THE

PROFESSION OF FARMING.

By Simeon DeWitt

ALBANY:

PRINTED BY WEBSTERS AND SKINNERS,

AT THEIR BOOKSTORE, IN THE WHITE HOUSE, CORNER OF STATE
AND PEARL STREETS.

1819.

502   Title-page of a pamphlet in the New York Historical
Society

ROBERT HALLOWELL GARDINER, 1782–1864, FOUNDER OF THE FIRST AMERICAN SCHOOL OF AGRICULTURE

Two years after the publication of De Witt's pamphlet, Robert Hallowell Gardiner founded the Gardiner Lyceum. Heir to a large estate in Maine he had prepared himself for its management by travel and study in England and France. Chief among his many interests was a desire to promote better husbandry and raise the low standards of New England agriculture. Not without significance is the fact that the founder of the first American school of agriculture, like his forerunners, Bordley and Livingston, was a large landholder with means and vision. The time for securing adequate and continuous help from the state governments had not yet come.

AN EARLY SUGGESTION FOR AN AGRICULTURAL COLLEGE

THE pioneers who began in America the development of agricultural science saw clearly that, if their work was to go forward, it must be carried on in schools. In 1792 a professorship of natural history, chemistry, and agriculture was established at Columbia. Wrote Bordley, in 1799, proposing a plan for Pennsylvania: "The legislature may enjoin on these [country] school-masters, the combination of the subject of agriculture with the other parts of education. . . . And thus the youth of our country will effectually, and at a cheap rate, be grounded in the knowledge of this important subject. They will be easily inspired with a thirst for inquiry and experiment, and either never acquire, or soon banish, attachments to bad systems, originating in the ignorance and bigotry of their forefathers, which in all countries have been the bane of good husbandry." In 1819 Simeon De Witt, cousin of De Witt Clinton, published anonymously a pamphlet urging the establishment of an "Agricultural School of the State of New York." "Its primary object should be to teach the theory and practice of agriculture, with such branches of other sciences as may be serviceable to them: its secondary, to make improvements."

503   From the painting by Chester Harding (1792–1866), in the possession of Robert H. Gardiner, Gardiner, Me.

THE GARDINER LYCEUM

ON January 1, 1823, twenty students filed into the new, two-story, red brick building at Gardiner, Maine. They were enrolled by the principal, the Rev. Benjamin Hale. Two years later the student body had increased to a hundred and twenty and the corps of instructors had been enlarged. Then the Maine legislature became interested in a going enterprise and led the way for the states by appropriating for a number of years a thousand dollars annually to the school. But this Gardiner Lyceum was ahead of its time. The rich lands of

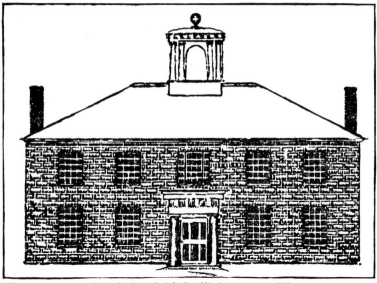

504   From the *Journal of the Franklin Institute*, Oct., 1895

the West drew the enterprising young men of the older sections to the frontier. The little school at Gardiner could not stem the westward-moving flood. In 1832, it closed its doors for want of patronage and support.

505   From S. L. Boardman, *Agricultural Bibliography of Maine*, Augusta, 1893, after a photograph made in 1865

EZEKIEL HOLMES, 1801–1865, AN EARLY TEACHER OF AGRICULTURE

A MEMBER of the faculty of the Gardiner Lyceum was a young physician, Ezekiel Holmes, "permanent instructor in agriculture." Holmes was one of that group of Americans which includes Crèvecœur, Thoreau, and Burroughs, lovers of nature and diligent students of her ways. He mastered the geology and botany of Maine as far as those sciences were developed. He knew the birds and fishes, was an able chemist and was acquainted with entomology. His life work was the application of the new sciences to the betterment of husbandry. Editor, for thirty-two years, of the *Maine Farmer*, member for eight years of the legislature, in constant demand as a lecturer in a day when Emerson was the greatest lecturer in America, Holmes perhaps more than other men molded the agricultural thought of New England.

506   From a photograph, courtesy of Pennsylvania Agricultural
College, State College, Pa.

DR. EVAN PUGH, 1828–1864, PIONEER IN AGRICULTURAL EDUCATION

WHILE Holmes was at the height of his influence, Bordley's dream for Pennsylvania began to come true. With Peters and Clymer he had worked for the founding of a state agricultural society "to propagate a knowledge of the subject." In 1850 the society came into being and nine years later, as a result of its activities, was founded the institution which has become Pennsylvania State College. In February, 1859, the first students crossed the campus "through the well-tromped mud of the breaking up of the winter frosts." Dr. Pugh was not primarily an agriculturist. His service was in guiding, as president, one of America's first colleges of agriculture through the difficult period of the Civil War, leaving behind him an institution founded upon principles of liberality.

FARMERS' COLLEGE, OHIO

ALTHOUGH the first school of agriculture had been built in Maine, the work was carried forward in the Ohio valley. In the winter of 1846–1847 Pleasant Hill Academy, a few miles from Cincinnati, was reorganized and christened Farmers' College, "the first American institution bearing the name of college and continuing through any series of years to give real attention to agricultural matters." For a time the enterprise throve. But, following the Civil War, when the new Homestead Act was stimulating the westward movement, interest waned and there was a gap of a few years. In 1884, Farmers' College changed its name and gave up its agricultural work.

FARMERS' COLLEGE.

507   From an engraving, 1862, courtesy of the Ohio Military Institute, Cincinnati

MICHIGAN AGRICULTURAL COLLEGE, 1857

ESTABLISHED by act of the legislature and opened in 1857 in a clearing three miles from Lansing, Michigan became the first of the modern agricultural colleges. It never joined with the University. "Applicants for admission as pupils," read the catalogue, "must have attained the age of fourteen years and must have acquired a good primary school education." The course of study "will embrace a wide range of instruction in English literature, in mathematics,

508   From a photograph, 1872, courtesy of Michigan Agricultural College

and in Natural Science. Special attention will be given to the theory and practice of Agriculture in all its departments and minutiae." In the years from the close of the Civil War to the end of the century when new colleges of agriculture were springing up in all the states under the stimulus of the Morrill Act, Michigan led the way and exercised a dominating influence on agricultural education.

509   From *A Memorial to John Pitkin Norton*, Albany, 1853

JOHN P. NORTON, 1822–1852, TEXT-BOOK WRITER

DR. PRIESTLEY, a contemporary of Livingston's, had been perhaps the first trained scholar to aid in the development of agricultural science. His approach had been through chemistry, which remained the scholar's approach through the first half of the nineteenth century. In 1850 John P. Norton, professor of analytical and agricultural chemistry in Yale College, when but twenty-eight years of age wrote his *Elements of Scientific Agriculture*, the best of a series of treatises which mirrored the growing knowledge of the day. Norton, trained under Benjamin Silliman, had studied agricultural chemistry in Scotland and Germany. His book had great influence. In 1855 its circulation reached ten thousand. But its author had died three years before, one of the first and ablest of that army of scholars who have brought the science of agriculture into being. Norton's most valuable work lay in applying the knowledge and principles of chemistry to the needs of agriculture. In due time other sciences, biology and geology, were also to make their contributions.

"EMERSON AND FLINT"

In 1862, the year of the Land Grant Act, George B. Emerson and Charles L. Flint published the *Manual of Agriculture*, the best of the early treatises. It sought to give the scientific reasons for the rotation of crops and other farm practices. Like Norton's book, this is one of the "great historic American text-books."

JONATHAN B. TURNER, 1805–1899

Jonathan B. Turner, graduating from Yale with highest honors, cast his lot immediately with the pioneers. In 1832, when Illinois was on the frontier, he became a professor in Illinois College. Failing health drove him to a farm. Turner fell in with Abraham Lincoln and taught him mathematics. The two young men, in the words of the tutor, "dreamed out together the hope for a new education in the practical

things of life." Turner, a man of great mental energy, wrote many books on agricultural and scientific subjects. His greatest achievement, however, was an address delivered at Granville, Illinois, outlining a plan for an "industrial university." It was deemed of such importance that it was published in the Patent Office Report of 1852, the bureau which was later to become the Department of Agriculture, being at that time a part of the Patent Office. This address and subsequent correspondence are believed to have been the chief inspiration of Senator Morrill for his famous Land Grant Act of 1862.

511   From a crayon portrait, 1892, in Illinois
              College, Jacksonville, Ill.

MANUAL

OF

AGRICULTURE,

FOR

THE SCHOOL, THE FARM,

AND

THE FIRESIDE.

By GEORGE B. EMERSON,
Author of a "Report on the Trees and Shrubs of Massachusetts,"
AND
CHARLES L. FLINT,
SECRETARY OF THE STATE BOARD OF AGRICULTURE,
Author of a Treatise on "Milch Cows and Dairy Farming," and "Grasses and
Forage Plants," etc., etc.

BOSTON:
SWAN, BREWER & TILESTON,
131 WASHINGTON STREET.
1862.
[Published under the sanction of the State Board of Agriculture.]

510   Title-page of Emerson and Flint's
              Manual, 1862

JUSTIN SMITH MORRILL, 1810–1898, AUTHOR OF THE LAND GRANT ACT

Justin S. Morrill, representative in Congress of Vermont, was a son and a grandson of a blacksmith. His formal education was got in a small "district school" with a term or two in an academy when he was fourteen. He became a successful merchant in the little town of Strafford and, after fifteen years, retired to a farm. But he loved good books and read them in his leisure hours. Such was the background of the man who became the author of the Land Grant Act of 1862 and guided its somewhat stormy course to its final adoption. "The Land Grant Act is probably the most important single specific enactment ever made in the interest of education. It recognizes the principle that every citizen is entitled to receive educational aid from the government and that the common affairs of life are proper subjects with which to educate or train men. Its provisions are so broad that the educational development of all future time may rest on it. It expresses the final emancipation from formal traditional and aristocratic ideas, and it imposes no methods or limitations. It recognizes the democracy of education, and then leaves all the means to be worked out as time goes on." — Liberty Hyde Bailey.

512   From the portrait, 1884, by G. P. A. Healy
             (1813–94), in the Corcoran Gallery of Art,
             Washington

513   Courtesy of Georgia State College of Agriculture

GEORGIA STATE COLLEGE OF AGRICULTURE

THE provisions of the Morrill Act were few and simple. Each state, if it met the conditions imposed, was to receive as many times thirty thousand acres of public land as it had senators and representatives in Congress. The sale of this land would provide funds that were to be invested. The interest thus obtained should be used to support a college of agriculture and the mechanic arts for which institutions the states should provide suitable buildings. So were laid the foundations of many of the state universities that have become so important a part of the educational system of the United States. Through the courses they offer, the farmer's son may look beyond the narrow limits of his farm and community and receive a professional training that not only enables him to further his own interests but to serve effectively the nation of which he is a citizen.

514   Courtesy of Cornell University

THE NEW YORK STATE COLLEGE OF AGRICULTURE, CORNELL UNIVERSITY

OUT of the Morrill Act, and the supplementary Act of 1890, have come the colleges of agriculture and the mechanical arts one or more of which is to be found in every state and one each in the Philippines, Hawaii and Porto Rico. Maine, influenced by Ezekiel Holmes, led the way in using the money which the Land Grant measure produced to found a separate institution and many states followed the example. In New York, Ezra Cornell, in 1867, established the university that bears his name, to which the state allotted the federal funds for the support of its colleges of engineering and agriculture. Cornell, under the leadership of its great president, Andrew D. White, was a pioneer in putting the new technical training on an equal footing with the old and well-established education in the liberal arts.

515   Courtesy of the College of Agriculture, University of Wisconsin

THE WISCONSIN COLLEGE OF AGRICULTURE

On the fields and in the laboratories of the agricultural colleges the science of agriculture has come into being. Investigators have pushed out the boundaries of knowledge and have trained a new generation of scholars to take their places. Teachers have passed on the new knowledge to growing numbers of students, some of whom have gone back to the farms and others, in turn, become teachers of agriculture in secondary schools or colleges. "Extension men" have carried the findings of the scientists to the farmers themselves and in their own communities have explained and demonstrated new principles and methods.

516   From a photograph by the United States Department of Agriculture

FARMERS INSPECTING EXPERIMENTAL FIELD WORK AT CORNELL

Not only has the college gone to the farmer but the farmer has been invited to the college. In many institutions farmers from all over the state are entertained for a week each winter and share in the benefits of lectures and demonstrations. Visits are made to the experiment farms that are managed by scientists. Over the whole nation the college of agriculture has become in very truth a "people's college."

517 From a photograph by the United States Department of Agriculture

THE AGRICULTURAL HIGH SCHOOL

GRADUATES of the colleges have gone out to the high schools and in their agricultural courses have brought to the farm boys and girls the rudiments of the science of agriculture, training them in improved methods, and preparing them to go on with their fathers' calling instead of seeking the city. When the full significance of this development is realized, it can be seen how far the American husbandman has advanced beyond the stage of the peasant.

SAMUEL W. JOHNSON, 1830–1909, DIRECTOR OF THE FIRST EXPERIMENT STATION

THE work of the Land Grant colleges was to learn as well as teach. In the new institutions the minute investigations of the ways of nature already well begun were carried steadily forward. These early efforts made clear the immensity of the task. Then Connecticut, in 1875, led the way in a new type of institution and established the first experiment station in the United States supported out of public funds. The state had recognized the importance of knowledge for the welfare of its people and the fact that knowledge is the product of unhurried, unremitting research. For twenty-three years Professor Johnson of Yale served as director of the Connecticut Agricultural Experiment Station, one of the great figures in that growing army of investigators whose work has revolutionized the agriculture of the nation.

518 From a photograph

From a photograph by the United States Department of Agriculture

THE MODERN EXPERIMENT STATION

In 1887 with the passage by the Federal Government of the Hatch Experiment Station Act, "the first really national system of experiment stations in the world came into existence." An experiment station was established in every state in connection with the Land Grant College. The Act completed the conception of the Land Grant College as a place of research as well as teaching.

ISAAC NEWTON, 1800–1867, FIRST UNITED STATES COMMISSIONER OF AGRICULTURE

Side by side with the colleges has worked the Department of Agriculture, established in 1862, the year of the Land Grant Act. Isaac Newton, a Pennsylvania farmer, had for twenty years been urging the establishment of the department. When at last his efforts were rewarded, he was honored by being made the first Commissioner of Agriculture. Under his direction began the organization of that great department which has ably met the need which he clearly saw for "a more thorough knowledge and practice of agriculture as an art and science."

JEREMIAH RUSK, 1830–1893, SECRETARY OF AGRICULTURE, 1889–1893

By 1889 the Department of Agriculture had so grown in importance that its head was made a cabinet officer. The portfolio fell to Governor Jeremiah Rusk of Wisconsin. Reared on the frontier in Ohio, Rusk understood from his own hard experience the frontier background of American husbandry. With energy and common sense he set his department at the service of the country. The frontier was practically gone; the monster city of the industrial era had come in East and West. It behooved the nation to take thought of its husbandry. The small farmer centered his attention on his few acres. The Land Grant colleges and experiment stations sought first to solve the problems of their localities. The Department of Agriculture is a gigantic effort on the part of the world's greatest agricultural nation to bring about the intelligent and effective adjustment of its farm folk to their natural and societal environments.

521 From a photograph, courtesy of the United States Department of Agriculture

522 From a photograph by the United States Department of Agriculture

DIPPING CATTLE

The Department of Agriculture whose field of activity reaches from the Atlantic to the Pacific and is backed by the power of the central government accomplishes things which the colleges cannot do. In many directions it works hand in hand with the state institutions; in others its activities are unique. It is the center of an organization reaching through the colleges and experiment stations to the local high schools and the county agent. Secretary Rusk undertook to fight the scourge of the cattle country, the hoof and mouth disease. The work has broadened until the Bureau of Animal Industry set itself to the task of studying and checking all dangerous animal diseases. One of its triumphs has been the discovery of the tick that causes cattle fever and the practical elimination of the disease, first through the practice of dipping and later through the development of a breed that resists the disorder. But equally important is the finding or developing of animals suited to the peculiar conditions of the grazing areas of the country, sheep for the mountain parks, beef cattle that will also make better milkers. Man works side by side with nature to hasten and perfect the world-old process of adaptation to environment.

523   From a photograph by the United States Department of Agriculture

MEAT INSPECTION AT THE PACKING HOUSE

WHEN the cattle, brought from the ranches to the packing houses, have been prepared for market, representatives of the Department of Agriculture inspect each carcass to safeguard the health of the nation.

524   From a photograph by the United States Department of Agriculture

A MODEL DAIRY

MILK production is a matter that has a bearing on the health of the people as well as on the purse of the farmer. Investigators, working through the agencies of the government and the agricultural colleges, have been seeking to develop breeds that would be most profitable to the dairyman and methods of handling the milk that would insure the purity of contents of the bottle that is left each morning at the doorstep.

A MOUNTAIN LION SHOT BY A GOVERN- MENT HUNTER

THE struggles of the pioneers against the dense forests and on the stony fields of the new country have been recounted many times in the nation's literature, but the almost equally bitter struggle against the living enemies of the farmer's crops and animals has largely been forgotten. The bounties which struggling colonial governments put on the

525   From a photograph by G. R. Williams, of the United States Biological Survey

heads of wolves and wild cats find their culmination in the thorough organization of the work of extermination undertaken by the national government. From bacteria to the largest mammals war is waged against hostile nature not in isolated frays but in nation-wide campaigns. Man has called to his aid all the weapons and devices that his intellect can devise to wipe out the organisms that are his enemies.

526   From a photograph by the United States Department of Agriculture

EXTERMINATING THE COMMON BARBERRY BUSH

THE picturesque wild barberry of the open fields has been found to be the intermediate host of the tiny organism that causes wheat rust. A killing dose of salt is dumped at its roots. Investigation has proved it to be an aid to the enemy, and it must go.

III—17

527   From a photograph by the Federal Horticultural Board

GUARDING AGAINST FOREIGN INVASION

At the seaports and along the international borders, agents of the Department of Agriculture inspect all immigrant plants and animals. When this innocent looking box from Brazil was opened by a Baltimore inspector, the small packages of cotton lint and seed that were among its contents were found to be infested with the pink bollworm in all stages of development. Had this package reached its destination, the cotton farmers of the South would have suffered incalculable injury.

528   From a photograph by the United States Forest Service

THE FOREST RANGER

Other guards climb the ridges of the mountains to watch for forest fires. In both the western and eastern mountains national forests have been set aside partly to conserve the timber and partly to hold in the soil the water from rain and melting snow and so keep a more even flow in the streams that head in the highlands.

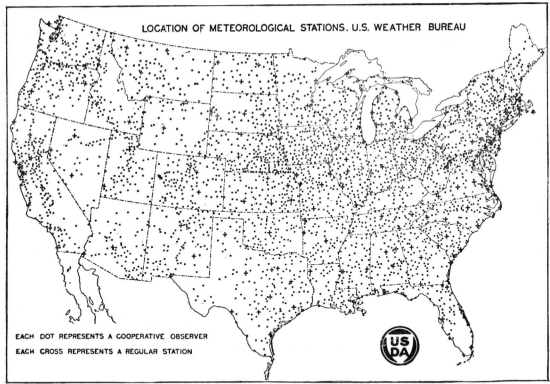

LOCATION OF METEOROLOGICAL STATIONS. U.S. WEATHER BUREAU

EACH DOT REPRESENTS A COOPERATIVE OBSERVER
EACH CROSS REPRESENTS A REGULAR STATION

529   Chart of U. S. Meteorological Stations, from the 1921 *Yearbook* of the United States Department of Agriculture

FORECASTING THE WEATHER

WEATHER is the perennial problem of the farmer. Untimely frosts kill his crops; rains rot the hay and grain that he has cut and not yet drawn. To know the weather probabilities for twelve hours in advance is to be prepared for more efficient planning. Gone are most of the old weather superstitions, of the new moon or the old, of Candlemas Day or St. Swithin's prophecy, that are part of the folklore that has come out of antiquity. Gone also is the influence of the old almanac that predicted the weather for three hundred and sixty-five days in advance. By newspaper, by telephone, or by radio the weather report comes each day to the modern farmhouse. The Department of Agriculture has scattered its weather stations over the country. In the difficult task of prediction many farmers coöperate. About four thousand five hundred unpaid observers have on their farms or ranches the rain gauge and the thermometer shelter which form the equipment of the volunteer coöperator. Each day these men furnish reports of temperature, rainfall, and weather to the climatological section centers in each state. From this information and that gathered at the regular stations the daily weather map and forecast is made. Science and coöperative effort have supplanted superstition.

530   An Outfit for a Coöperative Observer, from a photograph by the United States Department of Agriculture

531   From a photograph by the United States Department of Agriculture

BUILDING UP THE LEVEE IN LOUISIANA

WHEN the rains are heavy in the mountains and the streams rise in their narrow gorges, word is sent out to the lowlands. Along the lower reaches of the Mississippi levees are inspected with double care and piled high with sandbags against the coming emergency.

532   From a photograph by the United States Department of Agriculture

GUARDING AGAINST A FROST, OREGON

THE heaters burning in the Oregon orchard illustrate one service of the Weather Bureau in behalf of the farmer. In fruit-growing regions warnings of dangerous temperatures are sent out from the weather stations and specific information as to the time to begin firing. Weather bureau representatives are often on duty all night during critical periods. Annually hundreds of thousands of dollars' worth of fruit is saved.

A PLANT EXPLORER IN THE ANDES

In 1836 the United States Commissioner of Patents asked the various American consuls stationed in foreign countries to send home the seeds of valuable native plants. In place of this haphazard method experts now go to the four corners of the earth in search of plants to meet specific American needs. As a result more than thirty-four thousand new varieties have been brought to America. Kaffir corn that will grow on the semi-arid plains east of the Rockies was brought from South Africa. From Russia and Siberia came durum wheat for making macaroni. Explorers in Japan brought back a superior rice that now grows in a wide belt along the Gulf coast of Louisiana and Texas. Americans have not been content to take their environment as they found it but, ransacking the world, have modified it to meet their needs. The strength of American husbandry lies as much in this habit of intelligent adjustment as in rich soil and a favorable climate.

533   From a photograph by the United States Department of Agriculture

DR. SEAMAN A. KNAPP, 1833–1911

New plants, like new machines, were easy to introduce among the farmers; their utility is obvious. Getting the husbandman to accept new methods was quite a different matter. The horny-handed farmer sneered at the college scientist who undertook to tell him how to run his business. Pride of calling closed the mind of many a tiller of the soil. The first quarter of the twentieth century has seen the last phase of that ancient rural conservatism which has been the chief obstacle confronting every agricultural reformer. The greatest figure in the assault upon this wall of ignorance and sometimes bigotry was Dr. Seaman A. Knapp of the Department of Agriculture. Since 1892 the dread boll weevil, coming into the United States across the Rio Grande, had spread eastward at the rate of roughly forty miles a year, leaving devastation, poverty, and suffering. The South, but a single generation away from the Civil War and Reconstruction, saw in the new evil the blasting of its hopes. Under such circumstances Dr. Knapp, in 1904, was sent into Texas to combat the weevil with the gospel of better husbandry. Said the *Progressive Farmer:* "Dr. Knapp made one of the greatest original contributions to agricultural science in that he discovered not simply a new agricultural truth, but a new way of disseminating all the vast treasures of truth which others had developed. Grant that in learning from him the small farmer heard only what other men had been saying for forty years; the point is that they had been crying in the wilderness of ineffectuality while Dr. Knapp actually reached the ear and the heart of the man behind the plow. He actually carried the message to Garcia."

534   From a photograph, courtesy of the United States Department of Agriculture

THE COUNTY AGENT AND A FARM FAMILY

"THERE is something new in the land. A man, clad with no authority to compel, but armed with a knowledge of good farm practices, goes about his county counseling this man and that to reform his ways, to forsake his slip-shod and erroneous farm practices, feel a change of heart and help in the general movement for farm uplift. This man is the new county demonstrator. In rich counties, such as we see in Illinois, he is provided with an automobile and stenographer, he has his office in the courthouse whence

535   From a photograph by the United States Department of Agriculture

daily he sallies forth on missions of good import. Elsewhere he goes in vehicle or on horseback; the principle is the same. He is a man supposedly full of good practical ideas, and it is his mission to so modify the farming of his county that he will have earned his salary and a great deal more." — *The Breeder's Gazette.*

A DEMONSTRATION IN SELECTING SEED CORN

THE county agent is an outpost of the Department of Agriculture whence some of his salary comes. He also represents the agricultural organization of the state in which he works and is paid in part by it. But he is chosen by the farmers of the county under state supervision and is also paid by them. He is not a

specialist but a middleman between the specialist of the agricultural college or the experiment station and the farmer who works the land. He carries the knowledge of the one, to the farm of the other and, often, brings the two together. The office of the county agent is a busy center for the improvement of husbandry.

536   From a photograph by the United States Department of Agriculture

JUVENILE CLUBS — DR. KNAPP'S SUCCESSFUL IDEA

THE corn club was perhaps Dr. Knapp's greatest idea. He sought to reduce the dependence of the cotton country upon a single crop. He endeavored to persuade the southern farmer that, if properly raised, there was profit in the grain which the Indians had developed. Small corn fields and miserable yields characterized the land which the planter aristocracy once had ruled.

In county after county he organized the boys. Each boy as a member of a corn club pledged himself to raise a patch of corn in accordance with instructions supplied by the Department of Agriculture. Local pride was counted on to reward the most successful boy of the county, but the boy who led the state won a trip to Washington at the expense of the Department, where he received the personal congratulations of the Secretary of Agriculture and shook hands with the President.

The results exceeded the most optimistic expectations. In South Carolina with an average yield of less than twenty bushels to the acre, hundreds of boys averaged some sixty-nine bushels and, in 1910, one lad produced upon his acre no less than two hundred and twenty-eight bushels of corn.

537   The Corn Club, from a photograph by the United States Department of Agriculture

Knapp in this ingenious way had compelled farmers who would not learn of the agricultural expert to sit at the feet of their own sons. Elkanah Watson with all his intuitive knowledge of human nature never achieved a result such as this. Dr. Knapp demonstrated the permanent importance of boys' and girls' clubs in carrying the new agriculture to the old farmer.

But the significance of this successful new device was greater than merely teaching new methods to farm boys and girls. The coming of industrialism and the rise of the city since the Civil War had drawn thousands of young men and women off the farm and into the uncertainties of a new life. Corn clubs, calf clubs, pig clubs, and poultry clubs give to the younger generation a real vision of the possibilities of the farmer's calling, and the inspiration which leads to successful achievement. Perhaps it will result in lessening that loss to the farm of the brains and the enterprise which American agriculture can ill afford. Each year makes more clear the fact that the future welfare of America depends upon the character of its husbandmen and the quality of its agriculture.

538   A Member of the Poultry Club, from a photograph by the United States Department of Agriculture

539   Learning how to Select Eggs for Market, from a photograph by the United States Department of Agriculture

WORKING WITH THE HOUSEWIFE

THE interests of the house-wife are not ignored in this new movement for rural betterment. Side by side with the county agent works the woman in charge of the "home bureau", bringing the principles of domestic science to country women. The Smith-Lever Act of 1914, fathered by a Representative from South Carolina and a Senator from Georgia, made possible these public servants who labor to ameliorate the conditions of farm life and improve the nation's husbandry. This Act, little heard of outside the farm papers, has for its purpose the dissemination among the farmers of knowledge of their occupation and of how to improve their living conditions. Its direct instrument is the county agent, who may be found in the great majority of the three thousand counties of the nation. It provides that the national government shall appropriate money on condition that the states appropriate equal amounts. It is one of those measures which help to mark an epoch.

540   A Canning Club at Work, from a photograph by the United States Department of Agriculture

CHAPTER XI

THE FARMER OF THE NEW DAY

ON a clear June day in 1924 a biplane rose gracefully from its flying field on the edge of the Atlantic and turned its nose westward, following the path of the pioneers. It roared across the Appalachians, once a barrier, now covered with a network of lines that mark the railroads and the highways. Hour after hour it flew above the vast central lowland that lies between the Alleghenies and the western mountains. Its lone pilot looked down upon an endless succession of cities, villages, and farms green with many crops. Where once grazed gaunt herds of bison, swiftly moving trains shuttled back and forth from town to town. The afternoon came on and the drone of the propeller echoed through the cañons of the Rockies. Herdsmen in the national forests looked up, and farther down the mountain sides farmers turned from their irrigation ditches to gaze at the passing stranger. As evening approached, the snow-capped Cordilleras became but a distant blur on the eastern horizon and were finally lost to sight. The flier had crossed the Sierras and was gliding above the wheat fields and the vineyards and orchards of California. At the edge of night he came to rest on the shores of the Pacific.

Nowhere in this long flight from ocean to ocean was there a frontier; nowhere vast tracts of unoccupied land to be had for the taking by the venturesome or the elsewhere unsuccessful. The pilot, winging his solitary way from coast to coast, surveyed the vigorous life of the new day. He beheld America no longer merely a land of farms and forests. The green and yellow countryside he saw reaching up to urban centers. Spacious farmsteads and rich crops in the fields bespoke a new husbandry, while the dark lines of railroad and the shining highways led out into rural regions no longer isolated. From East to West was life and growth. He saw a mighty nation, still on the threshold of its career, surging toward a destiny which no man could foretell.

541   Hauling Cotton from a Southern Plantation, from a photograph by the United States
Bureau of Public Roads

542   From a lithograph issued by *The Prairie Farmer* in 1869

A TYPICAL
CARTOON OF THE
AGRARIAN CRUSADE

THE abnormal conditions of the Civil War sent the prices of northern farm produce soaring. When the war was over, the Homestead Act, aided by rapidly lengthening railroads, brought a vast expanse of rich prairie soil under cultivation. Overproduction followed close upon the advance of the frontier. In a time when industry and commerce were still prosperous farm prices fell and the farmer's family felt the pinch of hard times. When, in 1873, the nation was demoralized by a financial panic, suffering in the agricultural districts was intense. For the first time in American history the farmer began to think of himself as of a group apart. He felt that he was supporting on his weary shoulders the entire superstructure of civilization.

OLIVER H. KELLEY, 1826–1913, THE FOUNDER OF THE GRANGE

IN 1866, the Bureau of Agriculture sent one of its clerks, Oliver H. Kelley, through the southern states to discover the condition of the farmers. Kelley, himself an ex-farmer, returned with the determination to devote his life to improving the farmer's lot. He conceived and became the first organizer of a secret society, the Patrons of Husbandry. In 1867 the first "Grange" was founded; seven years later there were more than twenty thousand. The sudden rise of the Grange was reminiscent of the equally sudden expansion of the Berkshire societies (page 104). Each had its day and then declined almost as rapidly as it had grown. Each was the product of the unsettled conditions which inevitably follow a great war. The older organization had disappeared, leaving the county fair as its heritage. The Grange after a period of decline has once more become the most important organization among the farmers of the present.

543   From a photograph, courtesy of C. M. Freeman, Tippecanoe City, Ohio

THE GROWTH OF THE GRANGE

THE membership card of a Granger was the bond which united the farmers against the growing power of "big business." The countryman saw, as industrialism swept America, that only in unity of action could he make his influence felt.

544 Membership Card, in the collection of the Wisconsin State Historical Society

A GRANGE MEETING IN AN ILLINOIS SCHOOLHOUSE, 1874

WOMEN as well as men were admitted to membership and three offices, Ceres, Pomona, and Flora, were open to them alone. The order was designed to serve the social and intellectual needs of the farmer. A "lecturer" was charged with the duty of arranging programs which would supplement the ritual. In the meetings rang the new songs of the Grangers.

545 Charter for a Local Grange, in the collection of the Wisconsin State Historical Society

The farmer's the chief of the nation —
The oldest of nobles is he;
How blest beyond others his station,
From want and from envy how free:

His patent was granted in Eden,
Long ages and ages ago;
O, the farmer, the farmer forever,
Three cheers for the plow, spade and hoe:

546   From *Frank Leslie's Illustrated Newspaper*, Jan. 31, 1874, after a drawing by Joseph B. Beale

547   From *Frank Leslie's Illustrated Newspaper*, Oct. 18, 1873, after a drawing by Joseph B. Beale

GRANGE DEMONSTRATIONS IN ILLINOIS, 1873

THE optimism of some of the Grange songs was not borne out by the facts. The list of foreclosures in the panic year of 1873 is a long one. Hundreds of farmers saw the hard work of years go for naught under the auctioneer's hammer. Many such men, impoverished and embittered, looked to the Grange to right their wrongs. Grange meetings became centers of agitation where the farmers' wrongs, real and fancied, were heatedly discussed. Under the pressure of economic hardship they sought to analyse the causes of their troubles. To such discussions they brought little knowledge of general national conditions or of the laws of economics. Their mental horizon was limited to their own small communities.

Independence Day in 1873 was called the "Farmers' Fourth of July," and on this day assemblies of farmers in Illinois listened to the reading of a *Farmers' Declaration of Independence*, concluding as follows:

"We, therefore, the producers of the state in our several counties assembled . . . do solemnly declare that we will use all lawful and peaceable means to free ourselves from the tyranny of monopoly, and that we will never cease our efforts for reform until every department of our Government gives token that the reign of licentious extravagance is over, and something of the purity, honesty, and frugality with which our fathers inaugurated it has taken its place.

"That to this end we hereby declare ourselves absolutely free and independent of all past political connections, and that we will give our suffrage only to such men for office, as we have good reason to believe will use their best endeavors to the promotion of these ends; and for the support of this declaration, with a firm reliance on divine Providence, we mutually pledge to each other our lives, our fortunes, and **our sacred honor**."

548   From *Frank Leslie's Illustrated Newspaper*, August 30, 1873, after a drawing by Joseph B. Beale

THE GRANGE IN POLITICS

THE Grange was powerful in the states of the northern Mississippi valley. The South was still prostrate as a result of the war. The eastern farmer looked upon the farmer of the West as a rival and competitor. The distressed husbandmen of the prairie states, casting about for a cause for their ills, generally hit upon railroads. The single railroad which offered the only outlet for the country village wielded a powerful influence over its economic well-being. The farmer believed that rates were high to the point of extortion. He also believed that railroad management was corrupt. He fought the railroad with the only weapons he knew, the vote and the independent political party.

POLITICIAN—"Oh, I assure you this new party on my shoulders is of no weight. He will slowly disappear. He is, as a politician, an utter failure."

549   From *Frank Leslie's Illustrated Newspaper*, July 11, 1874

550   From the original in the collection of the Wisconsin State Historical Society

TRADING CARD OF A LOCAL GRANGE

THE activities of the Grange were not limited to politics. The trading card is typical of efforts at coöperative buying in a community. Certain stores offered the members of the local Grange a discount in return for the patronage of the Grange as a whole. Stores were established and run by the Grange itself in competition with local merchants, and there were efforts at coöperative selling. Almost without exception these ventures proved failures. The farmers had not yet learned the difficult art of successful combination.

THE GRANGE WRECKS THE RAILROADS

IN 1874 the Granger movement reached the zenith of its power, then rapidly declined. The farmer's individualism, the result of single-handed conflict with nature, and his inherent conservatism, the product of the isolation of the farm and the farming community, made his continued coöperation with his fellows difficult to the point of impossibility. But the power of the Grange did not wane until it had established for all time the right of the government to regulate public utilities.

551   From *Harper's Weekly*, Nov. 22, 1873, cartoon by Thomas Nast

552 From *Judge*, May 15, 1886, cartoon by Zimmerman, courtesy
of the publishers

"THE LEAKY CONNECTION"

THE rise of great cities after the Civil War furnished the farmer with growing markets for his produce. They also brought about a complicated system for the marketing of his crops. Slowly the existence of the "middleman" became clear to him. The farmer read in his journals the prices which city people paid for the things he raised. He compared these prices with those he received from the local dealer to whom he sold his products. The difference was often great. The conviction grew in the farmer's mind that he was being ground down by a system of distribution which took from him the profit that should legitimately be his. His resentment was deep not only because of the loss he thought he was suffering, but owing to a certain proud independence of spirit which was the outgrowth of his environment. An eastern cartoonist has vividly depicted the situation which led and is still leading to the development of farmers' coöperatives. To attack this system from a different quarter the farmer sought again and again to carry his fight into politics.

THE FARMERS' ALLIANCES

THE decline of the Grange was not the result of a lifting of the farmer's burden. In the 'eighties the old troubles of low prices and high freight rates still beset him. Organizations sprang up to take the place of the Patrons of Husbandry; two in the south, the Farmers' Alliance and the Agricultural Wheel, and in the north the Northwestern Farmers' Alliance. Though they were of value in furthering agrarian interests their combined accomplishment was not great. The cartoon represents the farmer vote cutting down political figures of both parties, including President Harrison, Republican, and ex-president Cleveland, Democrat.

553   From *Judge*, Aug. 16, 1890, cartoon by Victor Gillam, courtesy of the publishers

THE FARMER OF THE NEW DAY

"THAT WICKED LITTLE FARMER BOY"

By the end of the 'eighties, the western farmers, rendered desperate by hard times and mortgages unpaid, lost confidence in the two old parties. They thought that by increasing and cheapening the currency they would be better able to pay their debts; they demanded the free coinage of silver at a ratio to gold that would overvalue the silver. There were silver groups among both Republicans and Democrats. Twice, in 1878 and again in 1890, the farmer saw his favorite proposal of free silver blocked by a compromise which held the currency of the nation on a gold standard. When, with the passage of the Sherman Silver Purchase Act of 1890, the last congressional drive for free silver failed, the farmer thought more earnestly of throwing over the old parties and of organizing a party with which he could challenge the financial and business interests of the East. He was repeating the effort of the debtor farmers in the years following the close of the Revolution.

554   From *Judge*, Aug. 30, 1890 (not signed), courtesy of the publishers

THE PEOPLE'S PARTY

OUT of the hardships and suffering of the western farmers came in the 'nineties a crusade, the Populist Party. The hostile cartoonist has shown the farm leaders, Peffer and "Sockless" Jerry Simpson, working in harmony with the labor leader Powderly, and Ben Butler, a political nondescript of evil fame. The Populist Party included many elements most conspicuous of which was labor but, in reality, it was a western farmer's party. "Wall Street owns the country. It is no longer a government of the people, by the people and for the people, but a government of Wall Street, by Wall Street, and for Wall Street. . . . We want money, land, and transportation. We want the abolition of the National Banks, and we want the power to make loans directly from the Government. We want the accursed foreclosure system wiped out. . . . The people are at bay, and the blood-hounds of money who have dogged us thus far beware!"—MARY ELIZABETH LEASE, 1890.

555   From *Judge*, June 6, 1891, cartoon by Gillam, courtesy of the publishers

556　From *Judge*, Jan. 17, 1891, cartoon by Gillam, courtesy of the publishers

"THE NEW UNCLE SAM"

"We want money, land, and transportation. We want the abolition of the National Banks, and we want the power to make loans directly from the Government. We want the accursed foreclosure system wiped out." These demands of the western farmer were ridiculed by the cartoonist who represented the point of view of the East. Nearly a quarter of a century was to elapse before the Farm Loan Act enabled the husbandman to borrow efficiently for the cultivation and harvesting of his crop.

"COIN'S FINANCIAL SCHOOL"

The western farmers believed that the free coinage of silver would lighten most of their burdens. They recognized that to coin silver dollars at the ratio of 16 to 1 would depreciate the currency, but they were convinced that a depreciated currency would benefit them in their dealings with their creditors and they needed desperately a larger circulating medium. *Coin's Financial School*, written by W. H. Harvey in 1894, persuaded thousands of farmers in the west and south of the economic soundness of their position. Eastern business men charged that the farmer sought dishonorable repudiation and anarchy.

557　　　　　　　From W. H. Harvey, *Coin's Financial School*, Chicago, 1894, cartoon by Henry Mayer

558   From *Judge*, Oct. 10, 1896, cartoon by Hamilton, courtesy of the publishers

THE ELECTION OF 1896 — AN ANTI–BRYAN CARTOON

In 1896 the storm broke in one of the tensest and most momentous presidential campaigns in American history. The Democratic party swung to the free silver issue and united with the Populists. William Jennings Bryan became the standard bearer of the great crusade. He went from state to state in a mighty effort to rouse the people. "You shall not press down upon the brow of labor this crown of thorns," he declared at the Democratic National Convention, "you shall not crucify mankind upon a cross of gold." The Republicans under the great organizer, Mark Hanna, rallied to McKinley. With argument, ridicule, vituperation, and money they fought back the farmers.

THE DEFEAT OF THE POPULISTS

The western farmers, in advocating free silver, had pinned their faith to an unsound proposition. Eastern farmers did not follow the lead of their western brethren. Mr. Bryan lost the election. The Populist movement collapsed as the rising sun of prosperity brought peace and security to the homestead. There was to be no farmers' movement again until the cessation of the World War brought the West once more face to face with depression.

"THE LAST STRAW."

559   From *Judge*, Nov. 7, 1896, cartoon by Gillam, courtesy of the publishers

III—18

AGRICULTURE AND THE NATURAL ENVIRONMENT

THE rise and decline of the Populist movement came in the decade that saw the frontier pass away. With that momentous event the history of America entered upon a new phase. Free land was gone, and with it passed the trains of westward-moving settlers. Agriculture was the first of the great national industries to feel the change. To produce

560 Relief map of the United States, from the 1921 *Yearbook* of the United States Department of Agriculture

more food by merely moving into empty land was no longer possible. For the first time American agricultural leaders were compelled to survey the soil resources of the whole country and to increase the output of food for a rapidly mounting urban population by better adjustments to areas already laid out in farms.

They studied the physical map of the United States. In the vast mountainous region of the West husbandry was possible only here and there. The Appalachian uplands and the mountains of New York and New England contained great areas where farming was not practicable. In the southwest lay a desert and between the Rockies and the Sierras and Cascades rose rough and arid plateaus. The Great Plains, where the cow country had flourished, were deficient in rainfall. The important farming areas of the United States were limited to the Gulf and Atlantic Coast Plain, backed in the South by the Piedmont Plateau, the Prairie Plains of the upper Mississippi valley, and the rich lowlands of the Pacific slope. To these areas, varying greatly in soil and climate, the American farmer has adapted himself; the map of the agricultural regions shows his larger adjustments. The day of the westward march of wheat or corn or cattle has passed. Nature has determined the boundaries of the spring wheat area, the corn belt, the corn and winter wheat belt and the cotton belt. The future will see but little change.

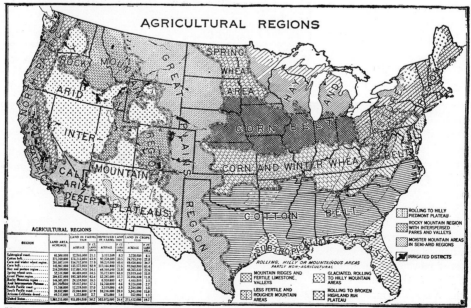

AGRICULTURAL REGIONS

REGION	LAND AREA ACREAGE	LAND IN FARMS 1920 ACREAGE	P. CT. LAND AREA	IMPROVED LAND IN FARMS 1920 ACREAGE	P. CT. LAND AREA	LAND IN CROPS 1920 ACREAGE	P. CT. LAND AREA
Subtropical coast	61,500,000	12,965,000	21.1	5,111,000	8.3	3,728,000	6.1
Cotton belt	275,760,000	176,213,000	63.9	97,238,000	33.5	74,755,000	27.8
Corn and winter wheat region	201,887,000	156,717,000	77.9	99,219,000	49.4	69,638,000	34.7
Corn belt	145,987,000	135,577,000	92.9	111,166,800	77.5	89,568,800	61.4
Hay and pasture region	214,209,000	117,001,502	54.1	64,365,690	31.8	48,365,810	22.6
Spring wheat area	52,516,000	44,489,000	84.5	35,272,000	68.0	29,019,000	55.8
Great Plains region	384,832,000	193,569,000	62.4	52,295,000	17.2	32,006,000	11.8
Rocky Mountain region	146,101,000	24,159,000	16.5	6,930,000	4.7	4,466,809	3.1
Arid Intermountain Plateaus	341,704,000	59,317,000	17.5	15,760,000	4.6	9,226,000	2.7
North Pacific coast	71,768,000	12,219,000	17.0	5,519,000	4.9	2,264,000	3.6
South Pacific coast	38,622,000	22,044,000	57.9	10,246,000	26.9	5,945,000	15.6
Arizona-California desert	49,717,000	1,323,000	2.7	675,000	1.4	552,000	1.1
United States	1,903,215,000	955,884,000	50.2	503,073,000	26.4	375,432,000	19.7

561 From the 1921 *Yearbook* of the United States Department of Agriculture

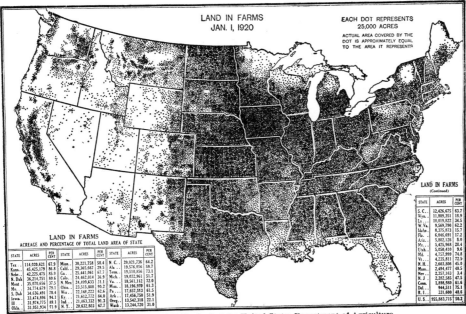

LAND IN FARMS
JAN. 1, 1920

EACH DOT REPRESENTS 25,000 ACRES

ACTUAL AREA COVERED BY THE DOT IS APPROXIMATELY EQUAL TO THE AREA IT REPRESENTS

LAND IN FARMS (Continued)

STATE	ACRES	PER CENT
S. C.	12,426,675	71.7
Wyo.	11,809,351	18.9
La.	10,019,822	34.5
W. Va.	9,569,790	62.2
Idaho	8,375,873	15.7
Fla.	6,045,691	17.2
Ariz.	5,802,126	8.0
Me.	5,425,968	28.4
Utah.	5,050,410	9.6
Md.	4,757,999	74.8
Vt.	4,235,811	72.5
N. H.	2,603,806	45.0
Mass.	2,494,477	48.5
Nev.	2,357,163	3.4
N. J.	2,282,585	47.5
Conn.	1,898,980	61.6
Del.	944,511	75.1
R. I.	231,600	48.6
U. S.	955,883,715	50.2

LAND IN FARMS
ACREAGE AND PERCENTAGE OF TOTAL LAND AREA OF STATE

STATE	ACRES	PER CENT	STATE	ACRES	PER CENT	STATE	ACRES	PER CENT
Tex.	114,020,621	67.9	Minn.	30,221,758	58.4	N. C.	20,021,736	64.2
Kans.	45,425,179	86.8	Calif.	29,365,667	29.5	Ala.	19,574,856	59.7
Nebr.	42,225,475	85.9	Ga.	25,441,061	67.5	Tenn.	19,510,856	73.1
N. Dak.	36,214,751	80.6	Colo.	24,462,014	36.9	Mich.	19,032,961	51.7
Mont.	35,070,656	37.5	N. Mex.	24,409,633	31.1	Va.	18,561,112	72.0
Mo.	34,774,679	79.1	Ohio.	23,515,888	90.2	Miss.	18,196,970	61.3
S. Dak.	34,636,491	70.4	Wis.	22,148,223	62.6	Pa.	17,657,513	61.5
Iowa.	33,474,896	94.1	Ky.	21,612,272	84.0	Ark.	17,456,750	51.9
Ill	31,974,775	89.1	Ind.	21,063,332	91.3	Oreg.	13,542,318	22.1
Okla.	31,951,934	71.9	N. Y.	20,632,803	67.7	Wash.	13,244,720	31.0

562

From diagram in the 1921 *Yearbook* of the United States Department of Agriculture

THE WORLD'S CHIEF AGRICULTURAL AREA

Outside the dry and the mountainous regions farmers have fenced in practically the total remaining area of the United States. Their holdings include wood lots and large amounts of what they call "waste land." To get a true picture of American producing areas, the map of the improved land within the farms must be put beside that of the farms themselves. These arable fields, taken together, form the greatest food- and fiber-producing area in the world. "Four countries are preëminent in quantity of agricultural production — the United States, Russia, China, and India — and at present the production of the United States is considerably greater than that of any other nation. The aggregate value (United States value) of the agricultural products of the Russian Empire just prior to the war was only about two-thirds that of our Nation, while the production of foods and fibers in China, which can only be guessed at, is probably also about two-thirds and certainly not over three-fourths that of the United States. The agricultural production in India is less than half that of our Nation. Only the British Commonwealth of Nations as a whole — India, Australia, New Zealand, South Africa, Canada, and the British Isles — approaches the United States in quantity of agricultural production, with an aggregate about nine-tenths that of the United States. The United States is not only the leading nation in agricultural production, but also it leads all nations in exports of agricultural products. The teeming populations of China and India require practically all the food produced and most of the fiber for home consumption, but in normal times Russia has ranked with the United States in value of agricultural exports." — O. E. BAKER, in 1921 *Yearbook*.

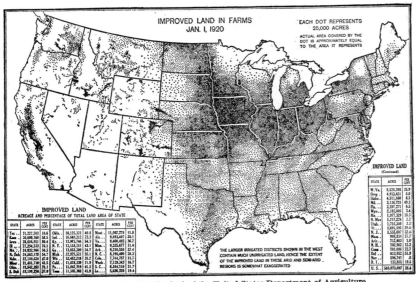

IMPROVED LAND IN FARMS
JAN. 1, 1920

EACH DOT REPRESENTS 25,000 ACRES

ACTUAL AREA COVERED BY THE DOT IS APPROXIMATELY EQUAL TO THE AREA IT REPRESENTS

THE LARGER IRRIGATED DISTRICTS SHOWN IN THE WEST CONTAIN MUCH UNIRRIGATED LAND, HENCE THE EXTENT OF THE IMPROVED LAND IN THESE ARID AND SEMI-ARID REGIONS IS SOMEWHAT EXAGGERATED

IMPROVED LAND (Continued)

STATE	ACRES	PER CENT
W. Va.	5,520,386	35.9
Oreg.	4,912,651	8.0
Idaho.	4,511,560	8.5
Md.	3,136,726	49.3
Fla.	2,297,271	6.5
Wyo.	2,192,005	3.4
Me.	1,927,329	10.1
N. Mex.	1,717,274	2.2
Utah.	1,715,380	3.3
N. J.	1,555,607	32.4
Mass.	998,834	21.7
Ariz.	712,863	1.0
N. H.	702,902	12.2
Conn.	701,056	22.8
Del.	653,052	51.9
Nev.	594,741	...
R. I.	132,855	19.5
U. S.	503,073,907	26.4

IMPROVED LAND
ACREAGE AND PERCENTAGE OF TOTAL LAND AREA OF STATE

STATE	ACRES	PER CENT	STATE	ACRES	PER CENT	STATE	ACRES	PER CENT
Tex.	31,227,503	18.6	Okla.	18,125,321	40.8	Mont.	11,007,273	11.8
Kans.	30,600,760	58.5	Ind.	16,580,212	72.3	Ala.	9,853,407	30.1
Iowa.	28,606,951	80.4	Ky.	13,965,746	54.3	Miss.	9,460,492	30.7
Ill	27,294,533	76.1	N. Y.	12,155,581	43.1	Calif.	9,325,677	31.4
Mo.	24,832,966	56.5	Ga.	12,055,309	34.7	S. C.	9,210,556	27.4
N. Dak.	24,543,178	54.7	Mich.	12,027,591	35.2	N. C.	8,195,409	26.3
Nebr.	23,109,624	47.0	Wis.	12,452,216	35.2	Colo.	7,744,757	11.7
Minn.	21,481,710	41.5	Pa.	11,947,919	41.9	Wash.	7,139,343	16.7
Ohio.	18,542,353	70.1	Tenn.	11,585,362	41.8	Va.	6,834,559	31.7
S. Dak.	18,199,250	37.0				La.	5,626,225	19.4

563

From diagram in the 1921 *Yearbook* of the United States Department of Agriculture

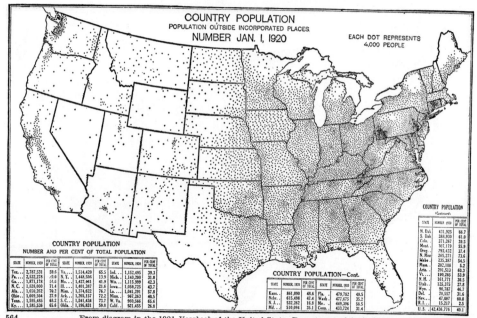

COUNTRY POPULATION
POPULATION OUTSIDE INCORPORATED PLACES
NUMBER JAN. 1, 1920

EACH DOT REPRESENTS 4,000 PEOPLE

COUNTRY POPULATION
NUMBER AND PER CENT OF TOTAL POPULATION

STATE	NUMBER, 1920	PER CENT OF TOTAL	STATE	NUMBER, 1920	PER CENT OF TOTAL	STATE	NUMBER, 1920	PER CENT OF TOTAL
Tex...	2,787,531	59.6	Va...	1,514,420	65.5	Ind...	1,152,495	39.3
Pa...	2,532,278	29.0	N.Y...	1,448,506	13.9	Mich...	1,140,208	31.8
Ga...	1,871,178	74.6	Mo...	1,427,441	41.9	Wis...	1,115,599	42.3
N.C...	1,828,000	71.4	Ill...	1,401,387	21.6	Iowa...	1,058,725	43.7
Ala...	1,650,262	70.2	Miss...	1,374,622	76.7	La...	1,041,291	57.8
Ohio...	1,609,504	27.9	Ark...	1,265,157	72.2	Minn...	967,263	40.5
Tenn...	1,595,485	68.2	S.C...	1,241,434	73.7	W.Va...	960,566	65.6
Ky...	1,585,536	65.6	Okla...	1,196,831	59.0	Calif...	521,455	26.8

COUNTRY POPULATION (Continued)

STATE	NUMBER 1920	PER CENT OF TOTAL
N. Dak.	431,925	66.7
S. Dak	388,930	61.0
Colo.	371,267	39.5
Mont.	307,179	55.9
Oreg.	793,432	37.4
N. Mex	265,271	73.6
Idaho	235,387	54.5
Mass.	202,108	5.2
Ariz.	201,513	60.3
Vt.	190,265	53.9
N. H.	161,771	36.5
Utah.	125,375	27.8
Wyo.	90,787	46.7
Del.	70,557	31.6
Nev.	47,087	60.8
R.I.	15,217	2.5
U.S.	42,436,776	40.1

COUNTRY POPULATION—Cont.

STATE	NUMBER, 1920	PER CENT OF TOTAL	STATE	NUMBER, 1920	PER CENT OF TOTAL
Kans.	861,090	48.6	Fla.	479,782	49.5
Nebr.	615,498	47.4	Wash.	477,675	35.2
N. J.	532,262	16.8	Me.	449,396	58.5
Md.	510,094	35.1	Conn.	433,724	31.4

564   From diagram in the 1921 *Yearbook* of the United States Department of Agriculture

THE WORLD CONTRIBUTION OF THE AMERICAN FARMERS

"The vast agricultural production of the United States requires the labor of about one-quarter of our gainfully employed population, whereas 85 per cent of the population of Russia is classed as agricultural, and probably three-fourths of the people of China and India derive their support from agricultural pursuits. Six and a half million farmers in the United States, assisted by a somewhat smaller number of farm laborers, probably less than 4 per cent of the farmers and farm laborers of the world, produce nearly 70 per cent of the world's corn, 60 per cent of the world's cotton, 50 per cent of the world's tobacco, about 25 per cent of the world's oats and hay, 20 per cent of the world's wheat and flaxseed, 13 per cent of the world's barley, 7 per cent of the world's potatoes, and 5 per cent of the world's sugar, but only 2 per cent of the world's rye and rice." — O. E. Baker.   In these figures the Department of Agriculture (1921 *Yearbook*) measures the world significance of the American farmer.

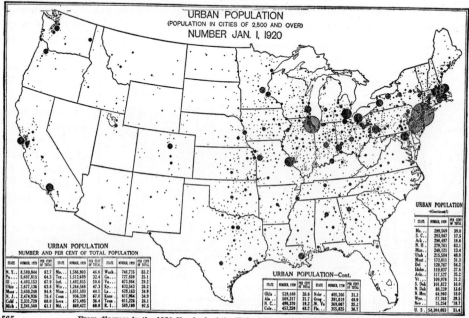

URBAN POPULATION
(POPULATION IN CITIES OF 2,500 AND OVER)
NUMBER JAN. 1, 1920

URBAN POPULATION
NUMBER AND PER CENT OF TOTAL POPULATION

STATE	NUMBER, 1920	PER CENT OF TOTAL	STATE	NUMBER, 1920	PER CENT OF TOTAL	STATE	NUMBER, 1920	PER CENT OF TOTAL
N.Y...	8,589,844	82.7	Mo...	1,586,903	46.6	Wash...	748,735	55.2
Pa...	5,607,819	64.3	Tex...	1,512,689	32.4	Ga...	727,859	25.1
Ill...	4,403,153	67.9	Ind...	1,482,855	50.6	Va...	673,984	29.2
Ohio...	3,677,136	63.8	Wis...	1,244,568	47.3	Ky...	633,543	26.2
Mass...	3,650,248	94.8	Minn...	1,051,593	44.1	La...	628,163	34.9
N.J...	2,474,936	78.4	Conn...	936,339	67.8	Kans...	617,964	34.9
Calif...	2,331,729	68.0	Iowa...	875,495	36.4	Tenn...	611,226	26.1
Mich...	2,241,560	61.1	Md...	869,422	60.0	R.I...	589,180	97.5

URBAN POPULATION (Continued)

STATE	NUMBER, 1920	PER CENT OF TOTAL
Me...	299,569	39.0
S. C...	293,987	17.5
Ark...	290,497	16.6
N. H...	279,761	63.1
Miss...	240,121	13.4
Utah...	215,584	48.0
Mont...	172,011	31.3
Del...	120,767	54.2
Idaho...	119,037	27.6
Ariz...	117,527	35.2
Vt...	109,976	31.2
S. Dak...	101,872	16.0
N. Dak...	88,239	13.6
N. Mex...	64,960	18.0
Wyo...	57,368	29.5
Nev...	15,254	19.7
U. S...	54,304,603	51.4

URBAN POPULATION—Cont.

STATE	NUMBER, 1920	PER CENT OF TOTAL	STATE	NUMBER, 1920	PER CENT OF TOTAL
Okla...	539,480	26.6	Nebr...	405,306	31.3
Ala...	509,317	21.7	Oreg...	391,019	49.9
N. C...	490,370	19.2	W. Va...	369,007	25.2
Colo...	453,259	48.2	Fla...	355,825	36.7

565   From diagram in the 1921 *Yearbook* of the United States Department of Agriculture

IMPROVED LAND AND POPULATION

THE population of the United States mounts swiftly with the passing decades. The curve goes up without a break. In spite of the passing of the frontier, food production has steadily increased with population, the fruit of the genius of the men who gave to the American husbandman the labor-saving machines and a science of agriculture. But the pace cannot be maintained. As population passes the hundred million mark and men look forward to a time, not many decades distant, when that number may be doubled, they face a fundamental problem of America's future. In 1880 for every one of America's millions, five and seven-tenths acres of improved land was cultivated. In 1920 the number had dropped to four and eight-tenths with the curve going down. In 1900 some forty-nine bushels of grain were raised for every person whom the census-takers counted. Twenty years later the figure was forty-five. During the same years the per capita food consumption in America increased. In 1920 each American farmer and farm laborer fed on the average nine of his fellow

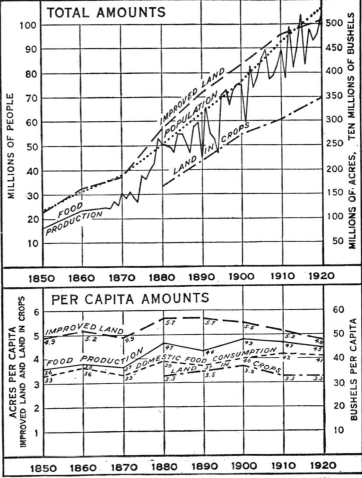

566   Diagram to Illustrate Growth of Food Production and Population, from the 1921 *Yearbook* of the United States Department of Agriculture

citizens besides himself and one person living in a foreign country. Since 1920 the average efficiency of the individual farm producer has increased. Yet the industry of agriculture suffered heavily in the readjustments that followed the World War. Rapid inflation followed by rapid deflation was one of the chief causes of a sharp agricultural depression in the years of 1920 and after. The farmer's income was reduced; husbandmen in large numbers lost all or nearly all of the hard-won savings of a lifetime. The problem of the second quarter of the twentieth century is to restore American agriculture to a healthy condition in order that the time may be postponed when a growing population shall tax the food-producing power of the nation.

567   Improved Land in a Western Valley, from a photograph by the United States Department of Agriculture

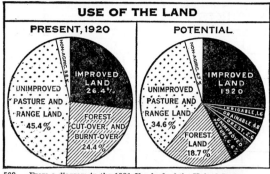

568   From a diagram in the 1921 *Yearbook* of the United States
Department of Agriculture

THE POSSIBLE INCREASE OF ARABLE LAND

FOR three centuries the Americans have chopped away the forest. The diagram (No. 569) pictures the woodland that remains. The next (No. 570) shows the wooded areas whose clearing would uncover arable land. The necessity for food would seem to condemn these timbered regions. But such may not be the case. American forests are precious, and they become more valuable as a growing demand for lumber faces diminishing reserves. These wood lots may be worth more for their timber than for the crops they would raise.

There is small reason to hope that further clearing of the forest will materially add to American food production. Yet there are other ways by which the nation's arable land can be increased. From Chesapeake Bay to the mouth of the Rio Grande the flat Atlantic coast plain is bordered by millions of acres of forested swamps. The same is true of the meandering Mississippi from the southern tip of Illinois to the sea. South of the Great Lakes stretch broad, treeless peat bogs. Much of this land may be drained, but reclamation is costly and draining will not be profitable until food prices to the farmer mount considerably higher. There remain the vast stretches of unimproved range land in the Great Plains region. The dry farmer may develop a small part, but the great mass must remain in the future as now an unimproved pasture. Of the two circles of the diagram (No. 568) the first gives the distribution of improved and unimproved land as the ratio stood in 1920, and the second shows the maximum possible increase in the productive agricultural areas of America. At best the unimproved pasture will cover more than a third of the country, while more than eighteen per cent is of no value for anything but forest. More than four per cent must be non-agricultural, the desert, the land set aside for public roads and railroads, and the ground on which the cities are built. Such are the limits which nature and civilization have set for the increasing of agricultural production by expanding the amount of soil under cultivation.

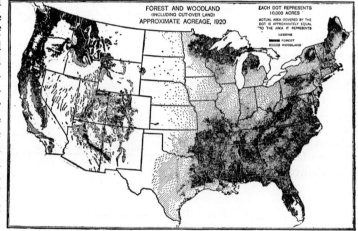

569   From a diagram in the 1921 *Yearbook* of the United States Department of Agriculture

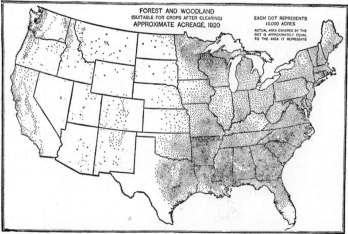

570   From a diagram in the 1921 *Yearbook* of the United States Department of Agriculture

THE FARMER CAPITALIST

WITH the passing of the frontier and free land, farming has rapidly become a capitalistic enterprise. In the forty years between 1860 and 1900, land values increased but twenty per cent. Between 1900 and 1910 they more than doubled, a greater increase than that of the entire previous history of America. From 1910 to 1920, farm lands rose some ninety per cent in value. As the American population approaches more and more

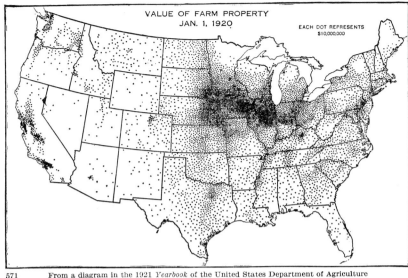

571   From a diagram in the 1921 *Yearbook* of the United States Department of Agriculture

closely to the limit of the supporting power of the environment, the curve of value seems bound to go upward. Land, however, is but a single item in the capital charges of the modern farmer. He must have a house and barns, erected in a day when building is costly. He must have cattle and horses. He must buy

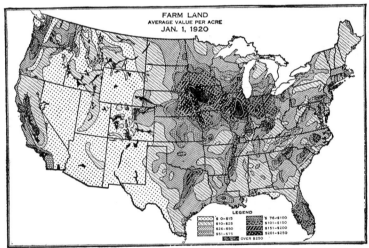

572   From a diagram in the 1921 *Yearbook* of the United States Department of Agriculture

expensive machines, plows, harrows, mowers, reapers, drills, tractors, and a host of minor tools. A glance at the diagrams will show how unevenly over the country is the distribution of value. In both the diagram of farm land values (No. 572) and that for farm property (No. 571), the Corn Belt stands out sharply with other regions of high value near the larger cities. The large black areas in the center of each map mark the greatest agricultural region in the world. But the farmer's income has not kept pace with the increase in the value of his land.

573   "A Costly Farm," from a photograph by the United States Department of Agriculture

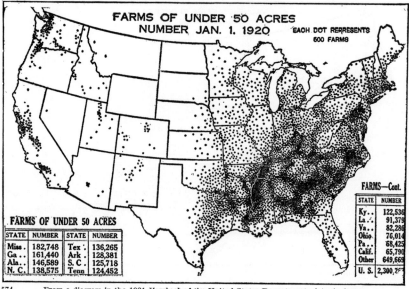

FARMS OF UNDER 50 ACRES
NUMBER JAN. 1, 1920   EACH DOT REPRESENTS
                                            500 FARMS

FARMS—Cont.

STATE	NUMBER
Ky..	122,536
La..	91,379
Va..	82,286
Ohio.	76,014
Pa..	68,425
Calif..	65,790
Other	649,669
U. S.	2,300,2...

FARMS OF UNDER 50 ACRES

STATE	NUMBER	STATE	NUMBER
Miss..	182,748	Tex .	136,265
Ga..	161,440	Ark..	128,381
Ala..	146,589	S. C.	125,718
N. C.	138,575	Tenn	124,452

574   From a diagram in the 1921 *Yearbook* of the United States Department of Agriculture

THE SMALL FARM OR THE LARGE

THE typical farm of twentieth-century America is between fifty and two hundred acres, roughly the size of the northern holdings in the heyday of the old farm. Here lives the husbandman and his family working his land with the aid of his sons or, perhaps, a hired man. The American farm is not organized like a factory; it is still a family enterprise. The hired man eats at the farmer's table, — in many cases a young man who looks forward to the time when he may aspire to ownership. Labor-saving machinery has made the farmer many times as efficient as his grandfather. High production per man has been the great achievement of American agriculture. But economic necessity, springing out of a growing population, is demanding greater production per acre. Intensive cultivation means that one man must till less soil. Perhaps the average size of farms will decrease. There is another possibility. The pressure of modern life has brought integration to industry. The great corporation, commanding large financial resources, equipped with costly machinery, and using highly trained specialists for the various phases of its work has taken a dominant place in industrial development. Will the great corporate farm some day supersede the present family organization? The fourth diagram (No. 577) shows how few comparatively are the large farms in the chief agricultural regions of America. Up to the present, the corporate farm has, in general, not prospered in America. It seems unlikely to do so in the future.

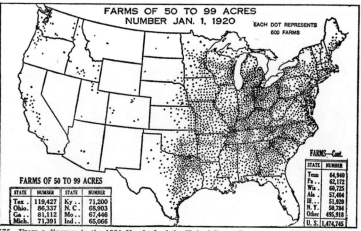

FARMS OF 50 TO 99 ACRES
NUMBER JAN. 1, 1920   EACH DOT REPRESENTS
                                            500 FARMS

FARMS—Cont.

STATE	NUMBER
Tenn.	64,940
Pa..	62,172
Wis..	60,725
Ala..	57,404
Ill..	51,920
N. Y.	50,784
Other	495,918
U. S.	1,474,745

FARMS OF 50 TO 99 ACRES

STATE	NUMBER	STATE	NUMBER
Tex .	119,427	Ky..	71,200
Ohio.	86,337	N. C.	68,903
Ga..	81,112	Mo..	67,446
Mich.	71,391	Ind..	65,066

575   From a diagram in the 1921 *Yearbook* of the United States Department of Agriculture

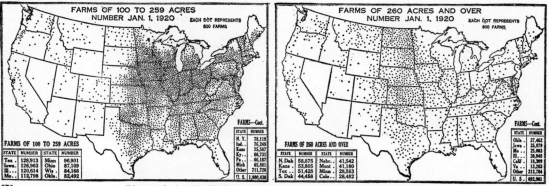

FARMS OF 100 TO 259 ACRES
NUMBER JAN. 1, 1920   EACH DOT REPRESENTS
                                            500 FARMS

FARMS—Cont.

STATE	NUMBER
N. Y.	78,119
Ind..	76,249
Kans	75,587
Ky..	66,731
Pa..	66,187
Mich	65,881
Other	711,720
U. S.	1,980,430

FARMS OF 100 TO 259 ACRES

STATE	NUMBER	STATE	NUMBER
Tex.	128,913	Minn	96,901
Iowa.	126,963	Ohio	87,109
Ill...	120,614	Wis	84,166
Mo...	112,798	Okla.	82,492

FARMS OF 260 ACRES AND OVER
NUMBER JAN. 1, 1920   EACH DOT REPRESENTS
                                            500 FARMS

FARMS—Cont.

STATE	NUMBER
Okla.	27,462
Iowa.	25,679
Mo..	25,083
Ill...	24,948
Calif.	18,309
Va..	13,253
Other	213,784
U. S.	692,561

FARMS OF 260 ACRES AND OVER

STATE	NUMBER	STATE	NUMBER
N. Dak.	58,875	Nebr..	41,542
Kans .	53,805	Mont .	41,180
Tex .	51,428	Minn .	28,563
S. Dak	44,458	Colo .	28,482

576   Diagrams in the 1921 *Yearbook* of the United States Department of Agriculture   577

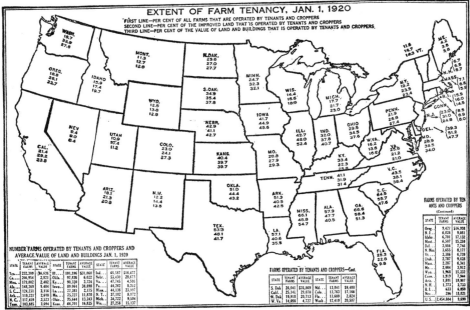

EXTENT OF FARM TENANCY, JAN. 1, 1920

FIRST LINE—PER CENT OF ALL FARMS THAT ARE OPERATED BY TENANTS AND CROPPERS
SECOND LINE—PER CENT OF THE IMPROVED LAND THAT IS OPERATED BY TENANTS AND CROPPERS
THIRD LINE—PER CENT OF THE VALUE OF LAND AND BUILDINGS THAT IS OPERATED BY TENANTS AND CROPPERS.

578   From a diagram in the 1921 *Yearbook* of the United States Department of Agriculture

THE FARM TENANT

MUCH has been written in America concerning tenant farming. In the eighteenth century the great land owners in the valley of the Hudson or in Virginia had many tenants. In that day tenancy bore some of the earmarks of feudalism. In the twentieth century the tenant is to be found in every section where agriculture exists. The retired farmer or the widow lets the farm where perhaps they have lived for the better part of their lives. This is particularly common in rich sections like Illinois, where the farm will yield sufficient income to support the owner as well as the family of the man who actually works it. In the South many a negro who has not yet developed the capacity for independent ownership must be content with the status of a tenant. In general, however, tenancy is not a sign that feudal conditions are being reproduced in twentieth-century America. It is rather the result of the rapidly mounting value of farms since the passing of the frontier and free land. In the nineteenth century the individual with but a trifling supply of capital could provide himself with a farm and become an independent landholder. In those regions where land which the homesteader a half century ago got for nothing has advanced in value to a hundred or even three hundred dollars an acre, the young farmer starting in life faces a difficult task in securing a farm. He is forced to become a tenant, to work on another man's land and to save what he can from what he produces.

If he has health and success, after a time he will earn enough capital to make a first payment on the farm he has selected for purchase. There is, generally speaking, no permanent tenant class in America; tenancy is a stage through which most men must pass on the way to ownership. To start with no capital and to become the master of a fertile and well-equipped farm requires energy, foresight, and years of self-denial. The young men who are to become the farmers of the mid-twentieth century are being trained in a hard school, one that relentlessly weeds out the unfit.

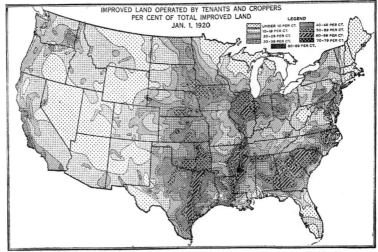

IMPROVED LAND OPERATED BY TENANTS AND CROPPERS
PER CENT OF TOTAL IMPROVED LAND
JAN. 1, 1920

579   From a diagram in the 1921 *Yearbook* of the United States Department of Agriculture

580   A South Carolina Cotton Farm, from a photograph by the United States Department of Agriculture

REBUILDING THE COTTON KINGDOM

FARM tenancy is nowhere more common than in the South. There it is a solution of the problem of the negro. The Civil War and Reconstruction left the South prostrate. Many of the old planters had made the supreme sacrifice in the conflict. Others were reduced to penury by the collapse of the Confederacy. Even where blue-coated armies had not marched, the end of the war saw arable fields growing up to weeds and underbrush and plantation buildings falling into decay. Seldom has the white race faced a problem more difficult than that which confronted the defeated Southerners when Reconstruction came to an end. With capital dissipated and their ancient labor system suddenly destroyed, they set about rebuilding the economic structure of their section on a new foundation.

Many of the old plantations were broken up; some persisted; and new ones were formed. The political control of the section slipped from the hands of the rich and aristocratic few. The numerous small farmers who had always been characteristic of the South came into power. Again the Southerner, after the food-raising period of the war, turned to his one great crop, cotton, and in special sections to rice and sugar. The South remained, as before the war, a dominantly agricultural country.

Promptly the problem of utilizing negro labor was faced. The wage system was tried, but the field hand with a little money in his pocket often refused to work until it was spent. The "standing wage" system was devised under which the laborers were not paid until the end of six months or even a year. But the negro disliked the close supervision which smacked to him of the old-time bondage. A "four day cropping system" was tried by which the negro, instead of laboring for hire, worked the farm or plantation on shares. Four days he worked for the planter and two days for himself. Land, seed, and implements were furnished by the planter, and at the end of the year the crop was divided. But even this plan did not succeed. So the system was developed which has been spread widely over the cotton country. The plantation is divided into small tracts each worked by a negro family on shares. The white owner still furnishes the stock, the seed, and the implements as well as the land and buildings. At the end of the year the crop is shared. The plan works only moderately well, but it is the best solution of the problem. The main difficulty is the shift-lessness of the negro and this is not easy to remedy.

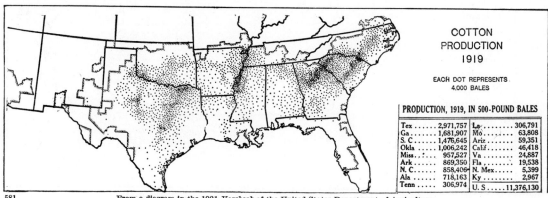

COTTON
PRODUCTION
1919

EACH DOT REPRESENTS
4,000 BALES

PRODUCTION, 1919, IN 500-POUND BALES

Tex	2,971,757	La	306,791
Ga	1,681,907	Mo	63,808
S. C	1,476,645	Ariz	59,351
Okla	1,006,242	Calif	46,418
Miss	957,527	Va	24,887
Ark	869,350	Fla	19,538
N. C	858,406	N. Mex	5,399
Ala	718,163	Ky	2,967
Tenn	306,974	U. S	11,376,130

581   From a diagram in the 1921 *Yearbook* of the United States Department of Agriculture

THE NEGRO AS A FARM OWNER

WHERE the soil of the cotton country is richest, there will be found the negro tenant. The clustered cabins of slavery days have disappeared; the tenant lives on the acres he tills. Most often with a single mule he plows the soil and "makes" the crop. Perhaps the planter supplies him with food until the fall when the crop shall be sold and the proceeds divided. Almost a quarter of the southern negro farmers own their land. But in the

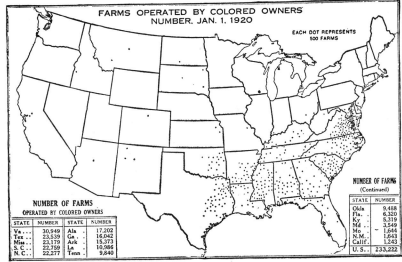

FARMS OPERATED BY COLORED OWNERS
NUMBER. JAN. 1. 1920

EACH DOT REPRESENTS 500 FARMS

NUMBER OF FARMS
OPERATED BY COLORED OWNERS

STATE	NUMBER	STATE	NUMBER
Va...	30,949	Ala .	17,202
Tex..	23,539	Ga .	16,042
Miss..	23,179	Ark .	15,373
S. C..	22,759	La .	10,986
N. C..	22,277	Tenn .	9,840

NUMBER OF FARMS
(Continued)

STATE	NUMBER
Okla	9,488
Fla..	6,320
Ky .	5,319
Md ..	3,549
Mo ..	1,644
N.M..	1,643
Calif..	1,243
U. S..	233,222

582   From a diagram in the 1921 *Yearbook* of the United States Department of Agriculture

best cotton country these owners are in a marked minority; their farms are mostly to be found in the cheap land of eastern Virginia, southeastern South Carolina, and northeastern Texas.

Side by side with the plantations and the negro farms are the smaller holdings of the whites. On these, as on the plantations worked by tenants, the husbandry is simple. The machines of the new day and a knowledge of agricultural science have only begun to make an impress on the cotton country. Even since the beginning of the present century the quality of the product raised for export has deteriorated. In the South more than elsewhere in the nation lingers that conservatism which has always been associated with husbandry. The shadow of the Civil War has not yet been fully lifted. Only a minority of farmers have money enough to pay their bills at the store while waiting for the crop. They borrow from the local bank, or obtain credit from the local merchant who, to protect himself, charges prices for credit goods that include oftentimes interest of more than nine per cent. The storekeeper and the farmer alike suffer when the crop is bad or a decline in prices spreads the shadow of depression over the cotton country. But there are influences at work which give rise to the hope that one day the South will enjoy a sounder economic life.

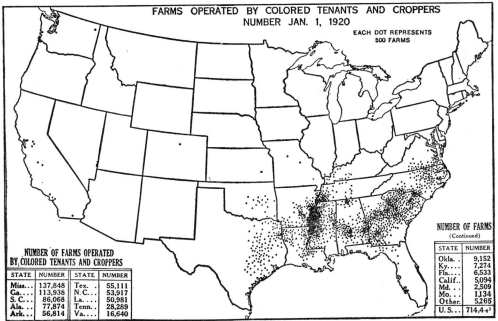

FARMS OPERATED BY COLORED TENANTS AND CROPPERS
NUMBER JAN. 1, 1920

EACH DOT REPRESENTS 500 FARMS

NUMBER OF FARMS OPERATED
BY COLORED TENANTS AND CROPPERS

STATE	NUMBER	STATE	NUMBER
Miss...	137,848	Tex. .	55,111
Ga....	113,938	N. C....	53,917
S. C...	86,068	La....	50,981
Ala...	77,874	Tenn..	28,289
Ark...	56,814	Va....	16,640

NUMBER OF FARMS
(Continued)

STATE	NUMBER
Okla..	9,152
Ky....	7,274
Fla....	6,533
Calif..	5,094
Md. .	2,509
Mo...	1,134
Other.	5,265
U. S...	714,4+1

583   From a diagram in the 1921 *Yearbook* of the United States Department of Agriculture

CROP
COMBINATIONS
IN THE
COTTON BELT

584   From a diagram in the 1921 *Yearbook* of the United States Department of Agriculture

THE NEW SOUTH

THE one-crop farmer in the South, unlike the man in almost every other calling, receives his total annual income at one time. A favorite security to the merchant who advances credit is the crop lien. So, year after year, the farmer raises cotton to pay his bills at the store. But a new day is rapidly dawning in the South. Medical and sanitary agencies are combating disease. The practices of improved husbandry are spreading throughout the countryside.

The diagram makes clear one of the fundamentals of the new agriculture of the South, greater diversity of the crops. The day of sole dependence upon cotton is passing. The South imports a small percentage of its food from other sections. Rotation is replacing the soil-destroying repetition of a single crop.

THE NEGRO

BUT the great problem of southern agriculture remains the negro. "A migrant to Mississippi, having chafed for ten years at similar experiences, wrote in 1919: 'A field negro lives in a kind of perpetual doze, a dreamy haze. . . . Nothing disturbs for any length of time the uniform and listless torpor of his existence. . . . Life moves at a low pressure; at times the wheels can barely be seen to turn.' The tether binding the two races in a single system has been broken by many individuals — negroes have set up for themselves, and whites have dispensed altogether with negro labor. But with most the tether has merely been lengthened, to the mingled gratification and regret of nearly all concerned. The rural negroes in bulk remain primitive and slack. Poverty has been a clog upon the whole southern community; and negro slackness, along with poor soil, has been the chief cause of poverty. The most common tether continues to be the plantation system, with tenancy the most widely prevalent basis . . . habitations are fixed for the year; life is lived in family units; and white folk, often of high grade, are tolerantly and affably, if patronizingly, concerned close at hand with the improvement not only of negro work but of negro life." — ULRICH B. PHILLIPS, *American Historical Review*, July, 1925.

585   Cotton Pickers, from a photograph by the United States Department of Agriculture

A NEGRO FARMER

IN 1913 this ex-slave, more than seventy-five years of age, was the owner and manager of one of the best known farms in his part of the cotton belt. When he gained his freedom, he decided to remain as a tenant on the plantation of his former owner. By thrift, hard work and good management he made enough to make a first payment on forty acres. This he increased to one hundred sixty-three. He did not attempt, alone, to cultivate this large area but concentrated his effort on two rich acres near his cabin. He heard of crop rotation and adopted it. He improved his land and won a local reputation for large yields and superior quality. He is an example of the

586   From a photograph by the United States Department of Agriculture

successful negro who is helping to make sounder the economic foundation of the South.

587   An Improved Road, from a photograph by the United States Department of Agriculture

IMPROVED COMMUNICATION

THE influences operating to ameliorate the lot of the southern farmer are active almost everywhere throughout the nation. Economic factors and racial character were responsible for the characteristics and outlook of the old farm of the North. Hand tools controlled the practices of the farmer and isolation stamped its impress on his social and intellectual life. Economic changes also have been primarily responsible for the passing of the old farm. Of these none has been more important than improved communication. The macadam highway, the automobile, the rural free delivery, and the telephone spreading rapidly in the first two decades of the twentieth century revolutionized much of rural America. Improved communication has meant the spreading out of urban civilization to the countryside. The mail carrier leaves each day in the galvanized iron mail box the metropolitan daily and with it magazines both cheap and thoughtful. From time to time he deposits the bulky catalogue of the mail-order house with its alluring illustrations.

588 Rural Free Delivery, from a photograph by the United States Department of Agriculture

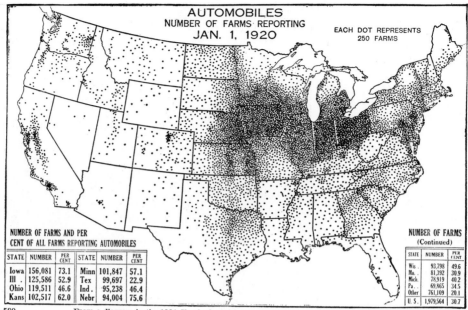

AUTOMOBILES
NUMBER OF FARMS REPORTING
JAN. 1, 1920

EACH DOT REPRESENTS
250 FARMS

NUMBER OF FARMS AND PER
CENT OF ALL FARMS REPORTING AUTOMOBILES

STATE	NUMBER	PER CENT	STATE	NUMBER	PER CENT
Iowa	156,081	73.1	Minn	101,847	57.1
Ill .	125,586	52.9	Tex	99,697	22.9
Ohio	119,511	46.6	Ind .	95,238	46.4
Kans	102,517	62.0	Nebr	94,004	75.6

NUMBER OF FARMS
(Continued)

STATE	NUMBER	PER CENT
Wis .	93,798	49.6
Mo .	81,392	30.9
Mich .	78,919	40.2
Pa .	69,865	34.5
Other	761,109	20.1
U. S.	1,979,564	30.7

589   From a diagram in the 1921 *Yearbook* of the United States Department of Agriculture

THE FARMER'S AUTOMOBILE

THE local merchant does not like the mail-order house nor is he pleased when his erstwhile farmer customer motors to the nearby city to trade.   Like other twentieth-century Americans the farmer bundles his family into the car for excursions into unknown parts.   The county boundaries, which his grandfather rarely crossed, are in a twinkling left behind.   He sees cities, villages, farming country unlike his own, and tracts of forest land.   In short, he sees, what is for him, an alien America.   He returns to the paternal acres, but a thousand subtle influences have entered his life.   They manifest themselves in his thought and speech and action.   He may be unpolished, but he can never be the rustic from whom he is descended.

590   From a photograph by the United States Department of Agriculture

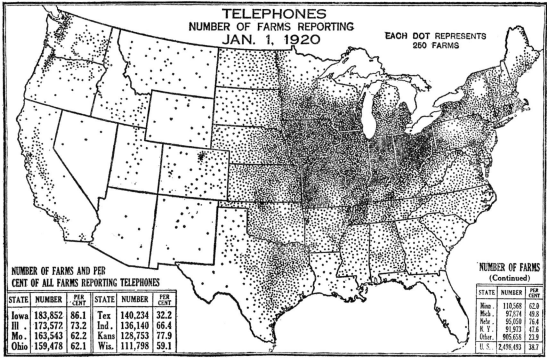

TELEPHONES
NUMBER OF FARMS REPORTING
JAN. 1, 1920

EACH DOT REPRESENTS 250 FARMS

NUMBER OF FARMS AND PER CENT OF ALL FARMS REPORTING TELEPHONES

STATE	NUMBER	PER CENT	STATE	NUMBER	PER CENT
Iowa	183,852	86.1	Tex	140,234	32.2
Ill .	173,572	73.2	Ind .	136,140	66.4
Mo.	163,543	62.2	Kans	128,753	77.9
Ohio	159,478	62.1	Wis.	111,798	59.1

NUMBER OF FARMS (Continued)

STATE	NUMBER	PER CENT
Minn .	110,568	62.0
Mich .	97,874	49.8
Nebr .	95,050	76.4
N. Y.	91,973	47.6
Other.	905,658	23.9
U. S.	2,498,493	38.7

591   From a diagram in the 1921 *Yearbook* of the United States Department of Agriculture

SPREAD OF THE TELEPHONE IN RURAL DISTRICTS

For the business man of the city the telephone has become a necessity. Its extension into the farming districts marks the break up of rural isolation. The proportion of farms possessing a telephone is indicative of the general diffusion of rural progress. "Telephones are most common on the farms of the Corn Belt and of Kansas, in which region from sixty to ninety percent, varying with the state, possess this convenience. In the Hay and Pasture, the Spring Wheat, and the Pacific Coast Regions about half the farms have telephones; in Texas and Oklahoma about one third of the farms; in the Corn and Winter Wheat Region (except Kansas), in the Great Plains and the Rocky Mountain Regions about a quarter of the farms; but in the Cotton Belt, east of Texas and Oklahoma, only from five to fifteen percent." (United States Department of Agriculture *Yearbook*, 1921.) Now the radio is broadcasting over the country districts, besides the usual program features, daily market reports for the farmers, and he can enjoy the musical programs of a distant city on a cold winter evening while sitting in his own living room beside the glowing coal stove.

592   The Farm Telephone, from a photograph by the United States Department of Agriculture

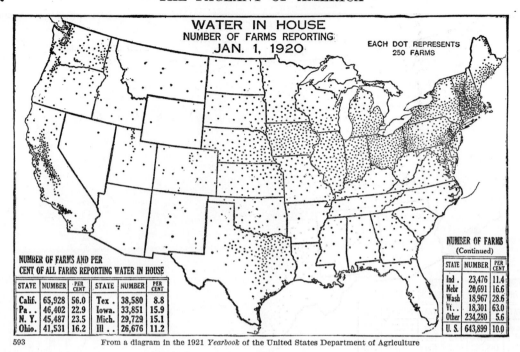

WATER IN HOUSE
NUMBER OF FARMS REPORTING
JAN. 1, 1920

EACH DOT REPRESENTS
250 FARMS

NUMBER OF FARMS AND PER CENT OF ALL FARMS REPORTING WATER IN HOUSE					
STATE	NUMBER	PER CENT	STATE	NUMBER	PER CENT
Calif.	65,928	56.0	Tex .	38,580	8.8
Pa..	46,402	22.9	Iowa.	33,851	15.9
N. Y.	45,487	23.5	Mich.	29,729	15.1
Ohio.	41,531	16.2	Ill ..	26,676	11.2

NUMBER OF FARMS (Continued)		
STATE	NUMBER	PER CENT
Ind .	23,476	11.4
Nebr	26,691	16.6
Wash	18,967	28.6
Vt..	18,301	63.0
Other	234,280	5.6
U. S.	643,899	10.0

593   From a diagram in the 1921 *Yearbook* of the United States Department of Agriculture

WOMEN'S WORK ON THE FARM

In the home still centers the life of the farm, yet the farmer's house has been the last part of his establishment to show the changes due to modern ways. Long ago the general purpose fireplace gave way to the kitchen range and the coal stove. But these last in turn have only slowly been replaced by the furnace.

594   Drawing Water on an Old-time Farm, from a photograph by Clifton Johnson

Devices to save the housewife have not been purchased with the readiness that marked the buying of machinery for the fields. This has been partly due to the lack of electric current in the country districts and partly to a need for rigid economy. The abolition of woman's ancient task of drawing and carrying water is both a measure and a symbol of the advance in country life. The scattered dots on the diagram (No. 593) should be contrasted with those on the diagram (No. 564) of farm population. Not through lack of desire for better things is the farmer's standard of living lower than that of his urban neighbor. He does not receive his fair share of the national income. ". . . the average earnings of farmers and their families for labor, risk and management, excluding the rental value of the homes in which they live, rose from $311 in 1909 to $1466 in 1919, and thereupon declined to $292 in the crop year of 1921–22, but since then have risen again to $520 in 1923–24."— Henry C. Wallace, *Our Debt and Duty to the Farmer*, 1925. At times before and since the World War the annual earnings of farm operators have fallen below the average wage paid to their farm hands. The old farm was characterized by isolation and economic self-sufficiency. The new farm is marked by inadequate return from labor and investment.

THE "BUSINESS" FARMER

In modern America has emerged the "business" farmer. He watches the market reports in the daily press or receives them by radio. Understanding the principles of farm accounting, he knows what it costs to raise his crops. He is a member of a "coöperative" like the Dairyman's League, the California Fruit Growers' Association, or the National Wool Growers' Association. He usually lives in regions where the soil is fertile. When times are good and nature friendly, he is prosperous, but he is sometimes through no fault of his own in straitened circumstances.

595   A Dairy Farmer, from a photograph by the United States Department of Agriculture

596   A Cotton Farmer, from a photograph by the United States Department of Agriculture

THE FARMER AND THE BUSINESS MAN

The "business" farmer meets the other business men of his community on a footing of equality. He joins the Rotary or the Kiwanis Club. Perhaps he is a director of the Farmers' and Merchants' Bank. He participates in movements for community betterment. He is intelligent and well read. He sends his sons and his daughters to the state university. He is a conservative in politics, distrustful of socialism and disliking labor unions and their ways. He is an individualist, prizing his independence more than money. Sometimes he travels widely within the United States, but he rarely goes abroad. He is strongly nationalistic, thoroughly American.

597   The County Agent Meets the Business Men, from a photograph by the United States Department of Agriculture

598 From *The Dayton (Ohio) Daily News*, Feb. 4, 1918, cartoon by Homer Stinson

THE FARM BUREAU FEDERATION

SINCE the World War the old dream of organizing the farmers has become a reality. The Grange has lived on as a social institution shorn of its political character and has grown in power and influence. Throughout the agricultural

THE FARMER IN THE WORLD WAR

THE World War left a deep impress on farm life. The desperate need for food production stimulated the activities of the farmers and made them more receptive to the teachings of agricultural science. The county agent, the middleman between the husbandman and the scientist, became for the first time an important figure in a vast number of rural communities. Still more, the mobilization of the resources and man power of the nation furnished a lesson in coöperation and organization that the country people took to heart. Their eyes were opened, as never before, to the responsibilities of their economic position and to its power.

599   A Farm Bureau Meeting on the Prairies, from a photograph by the United States Department of Agriculture

areas thousands of farmers' "coöperatives" have been formed for buying or selling the output of the farms. Most important of all the organizations is the Farm Bureau Federation reaching into almost every county of the nation. The individualism of the "old farm" has not been lost, but has been modified as the farmer has begun to learn to trust and to work with his neighbors. The Grange and the Farm Bureau in the twentieth century are not organizations growing out of hard times. They represent and foster the farmer's new intellectual interest in his calling, his desire for more intercourse with his fellows and his aspirations for the betterment of his neighborhood. The "Grange Hall" has become a community center.

600   A Farm Bureau Meeting in the East, from a photograph by the United States Department of Agriculture

601   Paying Dues at the Farm Bureau, from a photograph by the United States Department of Agriculture

THE ORGANIZED FARM

THE Farm Bureau originated as a county organization to coöperate with the county agent. Inevitably the county bureaus federated into state farm bureau federations. Then appeared the National Farm Bureau Federation, an organization with tremendous potential economic and political power. The effective use of this new power has presented his greatest difficulty to the farmer. He has few leaders trained in the broader national problems. His agricultural colleges teach him to produce, to manage his farm and to sell his crops.

They do not give him the liberal training in history, economics and political science which would fit him for the highest type of citizenship. The great need of the organized farmer is adequate and broad gauge national leadership.

602   "The Congressional Farm Bloc," from the Sioux City (Iowa) *Tribune*, Oct. 25, 1921, cartoon by Thiele

603   William S. Kenyon (1869–), first leader of the Farm Bloc. © Harris & Ewing

The Nonpartisan Leader

NATIONAL EDITION   MAY 30, 1921

THE USELESS MIDDLEMAN

LABOR

FARMER

604   From the *Nonpartisan Leader*, St. Paul, Minn., May 30, 1921, cartoon by Baer

THE NON-PARTISAN LEAGUE

AMERICA has had a long succession of agrarian movements. The first was that of the debtor-farmers of 1785. From 1870 to 1896 agricultural discontent again was active in the upper Mississippi valley and in the South, reaching its spectacular climax in the campaign of 1896. From 1897 through the first decade and a half of the twentieth century times were good for the American farmer. The real value of his crops was rising. The Populist party, so important in the early 'nineties, languished and died. Then among the wheat growers of the spring wheat area appeared a new agrarian revolt. In 1916 the Nonpartisan League undertook its first statewide campaign in North Dakota.

Unlike other agrarian movements the League came in a period when agriculture was relatively profitable. The wheat growers had grievances — many of the same grievances which had aroused their fathers who had participated in the Granger movement or the Alliances. They charged that freight rates were excessive, that wheat-grading at the privately owned elevators was unfair and weights untrue, that speculation in the central markets robbed the farmer of his legitimate profit, that the financial agencies in the wheat country refused to give the farmer who received his annual income at one time the form of credit which he needed. There can be no doubt that the farmer had cause for discontent. As of old he went into politics.

In 1918 the Nonpartisan League swept the state of North Dakota. The League demanded state-owned terminal elevators, flour mills, stockyards, packing houses and cold storage plants. It desired state hail insurance, the exemption of farm improvements from taxation, state inspection of docking and grading grain, and rural credit banks operated at cost. In 1919 some of these demands were enacted into law. There was, however, blundering on the part of the League leaders. During the World War sharp criticism of the National Government for the price it fixed on wheat led to the widespread conviction that the organization was unpatriotic. Moreover, some of the remedies proposed departed from American economic tradition. Most notable was the Bank of North Dakota, state-owned and state-controlled. The enemies of the League charged that it was socialistic and anti-War. With the farmer's panic of 1920 and after, a reaction occurred as the new Nonpartisan institutions felt the pressure of the times. The League lost control of the state. Then the course of the agrarian movement changed. The efforts between 1920 and 1924 to effect a political coalition between the farmer and organized labor were reminiscent of earlier attempts and earlier failures.

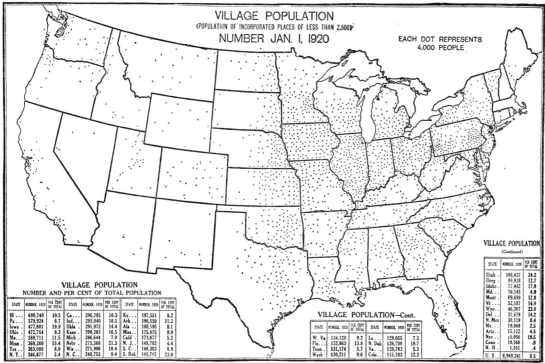

VILLAGE POPULATION
(POPULATION OF INCORPORATED PLACES OF LESS THAN 2,500)
NUMBER JAN. 1, 1920

EACH DOT REPRESENTS 4,000 PEOPLE

VILLAGE POPULATION
NUMBER AND PER CENT OF TOTAL POPULATION

STATE	NUMBER, 1920	PER CENT OF TOTAL	STATE	NUMBER, 1920	PER CENT OF TOTAL	STATE	NUMBER, 1920	PER CENT OF TOTAL
Ill ...	680,740	10.5	Ga...	296,795	10.3	Ky...	197,551	8.2
Pa...	579,924	6.7	Ind.	295,040	10.1	Ark..	196,550	11.2
Iowa.	477,801	19.9	Okla .	291,972	14.4	Ala ..	188,595	8.1
Ohio.	472,754	8.3	Kans .	290,203	16.5	Miss..	175,875	9.9
Me...	389,711	11.5	Mich .	286,644	7.9	Calif.	173,677	5.2
Minn .	368,269	15.4	Nebr.	275,568	21.3	N. J.	148,702	4.8
Tex..	363,008	8.0	Wis .	271,900	10.4	S. C.	148,303	8.8
N. Y..	346,877	3.4	N. C.	240,753	9.4	S. Dak	145,745	23.0

VILLAGE POPULATION—Cont.

STATE	NUMBER, 1920	PER CENT OF TOTAL	STATE	NUMBER, 1920	PER CENT OF TOTAL
W. Va	134,128	9.2	La...	129,055	7.3
Fla...	132,863	13.8	N. Dak	126,708	19.7
Tenn	131,174	5.7	Va...	120,783	5.3
Wash	130,211	9.6	Colo.	115,103	12.3

VILLAGE POPULATION
(Continued)

STATE	NUMBER, 1920	PER CENT OF TOTAL
Utah .	108,437	24.2
Oreg .	95,938	12.7
Idaho .	77,442	17.9
Md...	70,145	4.9
Mont .	69,699	12.8
Vt ...	52,187	14.9
Wyo..	46,267	23.8
Del ..	31,679	14.2
N. Mex	30,119	8.4
Me...	19,049	2.5
Ariz..	15,122	4.5
Nev ..	15,056	19.5
Conn .	10,568	.8
N. H .	1,551	.4
U. S ..	8,969,241	8.5

605   From a diagram in the 1921 *Yearbook* of the United States Department of Agriculture

THE COUNTRY VILLAGE TO-DAY

THE Nonpartisan League and movements like it is evidence that, in spite of improved machinery and of the new science of agriculture, all is not well with the farmer. His average income is generally but two-thirds that of the American population and his average property holdings but half the per capita holdings of the nation. In certain rich areas he is relatively well to do; but in wide stretches poverty lays a heavy hand upon the husbandman. Poverty accentuates the feature of rural life which differentiates it sharply from the city. Farms are scattered, the farmhouses sometimes from a quarter to half a mile apart. The rural village is a trading center, where perhaps the post office is located. Unlike the European village, it is not the place of residence of the active farmer. A scattered population receiving small incomes and owning property of relatively low value is rarely capable of initiating or carrying through important projects for community betterment. So very frequently the countryside lacks the improvements which are the commonplace of urban life.

606   From a photograph by the United States Department of Agriculture

607   Making Soft Soap, from a photograph by Clifton Johnson

PROBLEMS OF RURAL LIFE

In spite of the developments of the twentieth century, there is much in the rural community to give concern to the student of American life. Perhaps only in an unusually isolated or backward district will the farm woman still be found making soap, as she had been taught by her mother or grandmother. But much heavy and wearing labor remains the lot of both the housewife and her husband. It is true that improved communication and the spread of the knowledge of scientific agriculture have brought an intellectual awakening to the farmer. But in hundreds of rural centers a decaying church symbolizes the intellectual life. No public library stimulates the typical farm community. In different regions great progress has been made in making human thought accessible to the people, but for the American farm population as a whole the movement is only in its beginning. Without a developed intellectual life there can be little taste and little love of beauty. Throughout rural America many a landscape is marred by ugly, ill-kept houses and hamlets whose sole claim to distinction is the blatant false front of the general store. Sometimes religion falls back to superstition and a crass materialism makes its presence felt. Disease, the inevitable accompaniment of ignorance, lowers the physical and mental stamina of whole communities. In the South the scourge of hookworm must be combated. Even more than it needs libraries rural America needs hospitals. Here again a beginning has been made, but the full solution of the problem lies ahead. The soundness of the farm communities is of great moment for the welfare of the nation.

608   A Decadent Country Church, from a
photograph in possession of the author

609   A Rural Center, from a photograph in possession of the publishers

610   From a photograph by the United States Department of Agriculture

THE COUNTRY CHURCH

In rural America the Christian religion is in grave danger of failing. Perhaps the bald data of a survey, made by Charles O. Gill and Gifford Pinchot and published in 1920, of the rich agricultural state of Ohio, will serve best to picture a well-nigh universal situation. Some sixty-one competing Christian denominations serve the spiritual needs of the Buckeye State. More than sixty-six per cent of the six thousand, six hundred and forty-two rural churches have a membership of one hundred or less, and more than a third a membership of fifty or less. The attendance is ordinarily less than half the membership. About two-thirds of the rural churches of Ohio are without resident ministers. "The efforts of ministers are so scattered over fields more or less widely separated that much of their effectiveness is lost."

Almost five-sixths of the country churches are without the full-time services of a minister, while more than a third have one-fourth or less of a pastor's time. "Moreover, it is a rule of nearly universal application that ministers of country churches in Ohio do not remain long enough in their parishes to make effective service possible." According to the official records of the largest and one of the most efficient denominations, forty-eight per cent of its rural ministers were about to begin their first year and seventy-four per cent either their first or second year of service in the fields to which they were appointed while scarcely more than one per cent had served as long as five years. "The condition is no better in nearly all the other denominations." In the largest denomination the general average of ministers' salaries was eight hundred and fifty-seven dollars with free use of parsonage, fifty-eight per cent of the clergymen receiving less than eleven hundred dollars each. "Over considerable areas a large proportion of the ministers are uneducated. Often they are illiterate and entirely unfitted to render service acceptable to the more intelligent part of their people. In most of the State, the standard of education for ministers is low. In certain extensive areas in Ohio the country church seems to have broken down. In regions where it has been active for a century it has failed and is now failing to dispel ignorance and superstition, to prevent the spread of vice and disease, and to check the increasing production of undeveloped and abnormal individuals." The nation and the states are spending millions to increase the farmer's economic effectiveness. Here and there a dynamic religious body has built a church that molds the life of its community. Here and there competing churches have federated and so multiplied their strength. But the great Christian Church has yet to map out adequately its campaign for the spiritual regeneration of the countryside.

If the Church fails, the nation will be sorely stricken.

611   A Dynamic Rural Church, from a photograph in possession of the author

RURAL EDUCATION

RURAL education presents a situation something like that of the country church. Here again statistics and percentages serve best to tell the story. As the first quarter of the twentieth century ends, the one-room district school, where the teacher has several, often eight grades, remains the typical school of the farming regions. Nearly forty-eight per cent of America's rural schools have an enrollment of ten pupils or less, while only eight and a half per cent number twenty or more.

612 A District School, from a photograph in possession of the author

Even when the teacher has ability, the one-room school can never reach the efficiency of the graded school and the school spirit which results from numbers and organized play is largely absent. Moreover, a survey by the United States Bureau of Education has brought out that just under a third of the rural teachers in the United States have no professional training whatever, and again, just under a third have not completed high school. Only three and two-tenths per cent have received normal school diplomas.

"Here and there one finds a well-built, neatly painted, well-kept rural school, sometimes with two or three rooms, but commonly the schoolhouse is a little, one-room, weather-beaten building by a lonely roadside. A little to the rear are two out-buildings, often wretchedly cared for. The interior of the schoolhouse is generally unpainted and it is equipped with hard, straight seats and uncomfortable desks that make it anything but inviting. . . . A water pail with a tin cup, a 'volcano' stove, and a raised or lowered window generally do duty for drinking fountain, heating, and ventilation. . . . The comparative poverty of the country school district, the decentralization of our school system, and lack of central supervision and control, have been . . . important impediments to the progress of the rural school." — LLEWELLYN MACGARR, 1922.

But this situation is not universal. Much progress is being made in developing better country schools. The machines and the science of the new agriculture have given the farmers of the more progressive regions a vision of the significance of the school in farm life. Educational leaders in state and nation are aroused to

613 A Rural Consolidated School, from a photograph

the gravity of the problem. Unlike those of the church, unfortunately handicapped by sectarian divisions, they have planned their major strategy in the campaign for better schools. Undoubtedly results will be slow, but the future offers hope of ultimate success. The campaign must succeed if American husbandry is to remain in the hands of capable men and women able to apply to their work the methods and the knowledge of agricultural science. If it fails, America will the sooner reach the time when its farmers will be unable to feed its expanding population.

614   From a photograph by the United States Department of Agriculture

A FARM COMMUNITY CENTER

WHOLESOME tendencies are to be observed making for the development of community life. More and more frequently neighborhoods are building community houses, centers of intercourse and recreation. A striking feature of rural society has been the almost complete lack of sports. Golf and tennis are practically unknown and even baseball but little played. The new community centers help to fill the need for diversion.

The community house is of greater importance in the life of the women than of the men. In it is frequently housed the small public library that is bringing the country people into contact with the world of thought. In its auditorium are given lectures, concerts, theatricals on winter evenings, and dances and parties of all kinds. It is the farmer's club. The community center promises to be an important factor in that inevitable development of an American rural civilization which lies immediately ahead.

615   In a Rural Community House, from a photograph by the United States Department of Agriculture

616   The Peach Tree Carnival in Georgia.   © Wide World Photos

FARM FESTIVALS

THERE are many signs, apart from the community center, the public library, and the federated church, that the American farmers in the richer areas are awakening to a consciousness of their peculiar civilization. There is much good music in the better farm communities. The piano has replaced the family organ with its jig-saw ornamentation. In a very few communities local festivals have been developed after the fashion of the country villages of Europe. As yet the colorful and picturesque pageants or dances of the European peasants find few counterparts in America. But the future gives promise of a steady growth in the expression through the drama, of the thoughts and emotions of the people of farming regions.

617   May Day in California, from a photograph by the United States Department of Agriculture

RE-PLANNING THE RURAL VILLAGE

ONE of the movements for the betterment of rural life is that which has for its objective the lifting of the tiny country town out of the ugliness which characterized it in the nineteenth century. In the old days, the store, the blacksmith shop, the houses and a church or two were built by a community largely isolated from the intellectual life of the world, a community without artistic standards and without taste. The intellectual

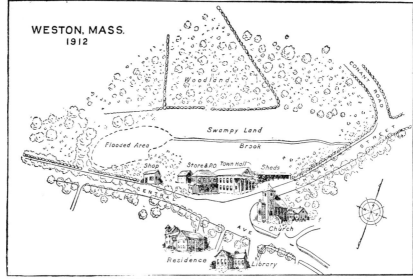

618   From *Farmers' Bulletin* No. 1441, United States Department of Agriculture, 1923

awakening of the twentieth-century farmer has made the man of the soil dissatisfied with the squalor of the old-time cross-roads hamlets. In the thoughtful magazines that the rural mail carrier brings to his door, he sees how it is possible to beautify the surroundings of human life in city and village. Traveling in his automobile on a vacation, he sees the results of an artistic ferment that is working in American life. Perhaps a man from the city builds a country retreat near his farm. These are some of the influences that are lifting the American farmer out of the carelessness of the last century, encouraging him to beautify the surroundings of his house and buildings, and sometimes even to join in re-planning the villages. The movement is not universal; it is but starting. Yet, in a sense, it is not new. Far back in the nineteenth and eighteenth centuries an artistic instinct may be found, kept alive through the generations though almost stifled by the rude conditions of country life. Perhaps the true origin of the present development may be found in the pathetic little flower bed that the overworked farm wife tended as best she could as it grew in the unmowed "front yard."

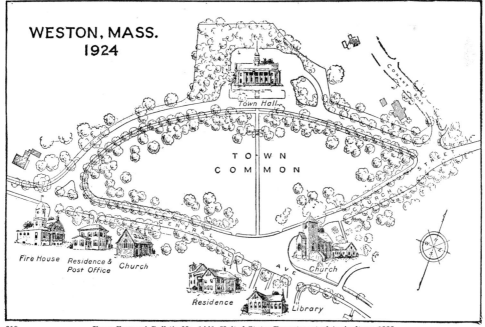

619   From *Farmers' Bulletin* No. 1441, United States Department of Agriculture, 1923

620   A Pennsylvania Farm, from a photograph by the United States Department of Agriculture

THE OLD FARM IN THE NEW DAY

FOR generations the rural folk of America have been trained in the school of the individualist. The typical farmer has been and still is his own employer and laborer. He prides himself on "being his own boss." But in the twentieth century he has come in contact with an industrial civilization based on division of labor and coöperative effort. He sees personal independence sacrificed to a certain extent for the good of the group. He is aware that these industrial groups have accumulated vast power — greater than any he can hope to attain. He considers their minute division of labor; their officers and under-officers, their foremen, and their army of laborers each specializing in a particular task. He considers his own lot. Like the unskilled laborer, he must have physical strength and endurance and, like the skilled artisan, he must be something of a mechanic. Like the executive, he must have the capacity to manage a complex enterprise. He must be a practical scientist informed of the improvements which experts are suggesting. Withal he must be a business man who watches the markets and estimates the probabilities of the future, a wise buyer and seller. Few men are capable of such many-sided development. He is in much the same position as the artisan of a century and a half ago — the days before the factory. Yet in his adjustments to the economic life of the nation he comes in contact with the intricate and powerful corporation. There is small prospect that the family type of farm will give way to the corporate type of organization. It seems likely that the rural civilization of the future will be built upon the small farm whose owner and manager must continue to be all things to all men.

621   Farmers Buying Machinery, from a photograph by the United States Department of Agriculture

622   A Homestead in Michigan, from a photograph by the United States Department of Agriculture

THE TWENTIETH–CENTURY FARM

IF the farmer still uses a type of economic organization that industry has largely discarded, his communities are repositories of much else that is old in America. Political democracy was the inevitable product of the frontier where all men were roughly equal in wealth, where there were practically no grades in social position, and where, in time of emergency, the only ranking among men resulted from their ability to fight the Indians. Twentieth-century farm communities still somewhat resemble those of the frontier. There is a rough equality of wealth; in rich sections most of the farmers are fairly well to do; in poorer regions they gravitate toward the same level of poverty. In such communities the old ideals of political democracy persist, perhaps the more strongly because the farmer fears the political power of the captain of industry and the financial giant. But the "dirt" farmer has become a minority in the nation. It is true that recently he had his way for practically a full session of Congress. But the time has come when, in general, the larger economic policies of the nation are directed by the man of the city. More than he sometimes realizes, the destiny of the nation's food-quest is in his hands.

623   A Prairie Home in Iowa, from a photograph by the United States Department of Agriculture

624   From a photograph by the United States Department of Agriculture

THE AMERICAN COUNTRYSIDE

SIDE by side with the political faith of old America lives in the countryside the religion of the nineteenth century. The majesty, the power, and the uncertainties of nature with which the farmer must deal throughout his life tend to develop his religious instincts. The Bible speaks a language which he understands, for the early Hebrews were a pastoral and an agricultural people. The farmer was taught to believe that this Bible of his fathers came out of the heart of God. About it are centered his adjustments to that vast mystery out of which he came and whither he shall return. He knows little or nothing of the investigators who are entering the secret places of nature and are revealing the ways of God. The circumstances of his life and environment have brought to most of his number but the slightest contact with the world of study and thought. That which he cannot understand, he rejects; he tenaciously clings to the old. If he loses the literally inspired Bible, he is adrift in a godless, hopeless world. His prayers sent up to the arched vault of heaven would come back to him in mockery. So the farmer over wide areas of America holds fast to the old religion. In no aspect of his life is the inherent conservatism of his calling better exemplified.

But the future must be faced. The religion of the old day with all its strength and beauty must be fused into the rural civilization of the future. The same is true of the political practices of the country districts. Upon the soundness and prosperity of rural life the ultimate welfare of the nation depends. "We must build up an ideal of an agricultural civilization. . . . Too many of our most thoughtful people assume that urbanization and civilization are the same thing. They even think that the farm population is a positive drag on the progress of the cities. They see nothing particularly worth while in generation after generation living, striving with nature, and dying on the farm. . . . It is sad but true that we have failed as yet to build up a farm community civilization which offers as many satisfactions as present-day city civilization. . . . The unattractiveness of the farm is largely because of the long hours of hard work, the lack of household conveniences, poor schools and churches, and unsatisfactory amusements. Farmers have not tried to make a living on the farm really worth while. . . . The really important thing . . . is wide acceptance by farmers of the ideal of a rural civilization which carries as much satisfaction, depth of culture, and economic stability as city civilization. To create an ideal of sufficient compelling power, thousands of well-educated farm people must think with all their heart and soul about how to give farming not only economic equality but also its full measure of human satisfaction. . . . The men of vision must arise soon if the United States is to be saved from the fate of becoming a preponderantly industrial nation in which there is not a relation of equality between agriculture and industry. They must act in the faith that it will be good for the entire Nation if agriculture from henceforth advances on terms of absolute equality with industry. . . . The problem is to clarify continually the vision of a well-rounded, self-sustaining national life in which there shall be a fair balance between industry and agriculture and in which our agriculture shall not be sacrificed to the building of cities." — HENRY C. WALLACE, *Our Debt and Duty to the Farmer*, 1925.

CHAPTER XII

THE HARVEST OF THE SEA

AS the frontier pushed westward, there were still many who remained behind. The pull of the rich lands of the interior drew hopeful frontiersmen farther and farther from the fringe of coast villages, but the pull of the sea held many others at the water's edge. In reality America had two frontiers, one working steadily across the continent and the other pushing out finally to the farthest ends of the oceans. The men and women of each knew the same hand to hand struggle with nature. The qualities of strength and independence that were bred in the forest cabins were fostered on the decks of the fishing boats and sailing ships that every year put out in larger numbers from the harbors where the first pioneers landed.

Yet there was a difference between these two frontiers. On land the rugged environment was subdued; the forest wilderness gave place to quiet, cultivated fields. But the sea remains the same forever and he who entrusts his life to the ocean must always remain, in spirit, a frontiersman. The fisherman who goes out in his open boat in summer and winter, who accepts danger and hard labor without a thought, wresting his livelihood from deep waters, keeps alive an American type that elsewhere has almost passed away. The frontiersman was the product of the nation's adventurous youth and has passed with it; the fisherman is perpetually the child of the unconquerable ocean.

One of the world's greatest fishing grounds lies off the east coast of North America from Long Island to Newfoundland. Other smaller grounds dot the shore to the south and enrich the Pacific waters. From the days of John Cabot, fishing has played a part in the destiny of America. As the nation has grown, its fishermen have increased in number. To the adventurous there still comes the call from the great waters that fringe the continent.

625 Study of a Fisherman, Provincetown, Mass., from the painting by Gerrit A. Beneker (1882-)

626   From Allain Manesson Mallet, *Description de l'Univers*, Paris, 1683

EARLY FISHING FLEETS ON THE GRAND BANKS

JOHN CABOT sailing for the English King in 1497 crossed the Atlantic and touched the North American continent. He went back with the tale that in the waters off Newfoundland "the sea is covered with fishes, which are caught not only with the net, but in baskets, a stone being tied to them in order that the baskets may sink in the water." Perhaps hardy French fishermen had before Cabot been braving the stormy north Atlantic in their annual quest for fish. At any rate, within a short time after Cabot's return, each fishing season saw the Grand Banks dotted with boats from France.

MODEL OF A SEVENTEENTH–CENTURY FISHING "SNOW"

ENGLISH fishermen soon followed the French, and London markets sold fish from the New World. The "snow" was a type of fishing vessel extensively used on the Banks. Its rig was like that of a brig with two masts. The model shown was scaled to a length of seventy-

627   From a model in the United States National Museum

two, beam of eighteen, and depth of ten feet. When on the Banks an anchor was thrown out and the current brought the ship broadside to windward. A canvas windbreak was put up to protect the fishermen from the blasts that swept the cold ocean. Just behind the canvas on the weather side stood the fishermen, each in a barrel lashed to the deck. Oilskins were, as yet, unknown, and the barrels kept the men dry as they fished with hand lines over the side. The catch was tossed onto the deck where two men busily dressed the cod and dropped them into a sluice that carried them to the salter in the hold of the vessel.

628   From a model in the United States National Museum

THE COLONIAL FISHING BOAT

BEFORE the Pilgrims came to Plymouth, fishing stations had sprung up along the New England coast. Pioneers on the edge of the forest depended upon the sea as much as upon the land for their food supply. They ventured off shore in large birch-bark canoes and dug-outs. Then, as the settlements grew and the business became established, they put to sea in larger vessels. These were mostly of the caravel type like the boats that carried Columbus on his great voyage. As the years passed the waters off New England and Newfoundland were more and more visited by these one-masted boats with boldly convex bows and high quarterdecks. The hull of the model was made after the lines of the *Sparrowhawk*, wrecked on Cape Cod in 1626, and dug from the sand in 1863. The length is only forty feet and the beam a little more than fourteen. But the boat was seaworthy and in it hardy seamen braved the toughest gales.

629   From Nicolas de Fer, *L'Atlas curieux*, Paris, 1703

COD FISHING

By the opening of the eighteenth century the handling of the cod on the Newfoundland coast was worked out in intricate detail. Nicolas de Fer put on the edge of his map of North America, published in 1703, a diagram of the process. The fisherman's habit and tackle are shown in A and B and in C the manner of fishing from barrels. D, E and F illustrate the boats and methods used in the transfer of the catch from the ship to the wharf. Under the rude shed N, the fish were cleaned and dropped into a trough G, H, I, to be carried to the salt boxes L and M. The salted fish were transported on stretcher-like devices P, first to the place of cleansing Q, and then to the drying racks V. In a press R, the cod livers were squeezed, blood and water being caught in a cask T, and the oil in a tub S. The system was primitive, but it furnished a valuable supply of food products to the people of both the Old World and the New.

AN EARLY FISHING KETCH

Fishermen and mariners busy at the Boston wharves in the late seventeenth century saw many ketches, large and small, anchored in the harbor or tied up to the docks. The ketch was originally a war vessel with the mainmast set halfway between bow and stern, and the mizzenmast further aft, leaving a long, unobstructed forward deck on which mortars were placed. But the type was found useful in peace as well as in war, and before the invention of the schooner was a favorite with the fishermen who made the journey from New England to the Banks.

630   From a model by H. C. Chester in the United States National Museum

III—20

631 From a model in the United States National Museum

OLD–STYLE FISHING SCHOONER

CONSIDERABLE interest was aroused in the little fishing village of Gloucester in the year 1713 when Captain Andrew Robinson brought to completion a fishing vessel of a new style. She had two masts but the old square sails were missing. In their place were two great fore and aft sails. An old story tells that, as she slid down the ways, an enthusiastic bystander exclaimed: "Oh, how she scoons!" "A schooner let her be,"

632 From a model in the United States National Museum

replied Captain Robinson, and the modern type of sailing vessel had been born and named. The illustration shows a schooner, known as a "heel-tapper," popular throughout the eighteenth and early nineteenth centuries. On the main deck and, in stormy weather, on the high quarter deck the fishermen stood and threw their hand lines over the side.

THE *LION*, A "CHEBACCO" BOAT

THE "heel-tappers," more than fifty feet in length, did not meet the needs of many fishermen who wanted a small craft to fish on the inshore grounds near the New England coast. Any morning in the late eighteenth-century Gloucester village might see the bright red sterns of the little "chebacco" schooners as they made for their mooring spars. Tying up, the crews threw over the hand lines and worked until boats were full or darkness drove them back to the wharves.

A "DOGBODY CHEBACCO"

A LARGER chebacco, of about seventeen tons and known as the "dogbody" from its square stern, was used for the longer sail to the Banks. Forward was a smoky little cabin where the crew slept and food was cooked in a rough fireplace. During the early years of the nineteenth century some of these little boats carried cargoes of fish to the West Indies and brought back cargoes of molasses and rum.

PROVINCETOWN IN 1838

AT Provincetown and Gloucester in the early years of the nineteenth century the beach was lined with windmills whose clumsy machinery pumped water from the ocean into

633   From a model in the United States National Museum

evaporation vats. Not only must the fisherman catch his fish but make the salt with which to cure them. The whole life of these villages centered at the shore, where the men from the fishing grounds beached their dories and prepared their catch for market. Provincetown and Gloucester were among the most important of the American fishing villages.

634   From John Warner Barber, *Historical Collections of Massachusetts*, Worcester, 1839

635   The Pinky. From a model in the United States National Museum

THE PINKY

ABOUT 1815 the chebacco gave place to the pinky, so-called because "pinked" (pointed) at both bow and stern, which remained the dominant type until 1840. The peculiarity of the pinky was the extension aft of the rail and bulwarks until they met and were fastened to a V-shaped board, like the stern of a dory. No more seaworthy boats were ever designed. These made the long trips to Newfoundland with safety. They were common on the grounds that lay close inshore. Twice the *Tiger* had desperate adventures. A sudden lifting of the fog in the Bay of Fundy disclosed to a British man-of-war the little American boat fishing in Canadian waters inside the treaty line. A gun spoke from the Englishman for the Yankee to heave to, but the *Tiger* with all sails set, the crew below decks and the captain lying flat on his back to steer the craft, was making for the open sea. When she nosed up to the home dock to tell of her adventure, two great shot holes in the canvas verified the story.

Another time the *Tiger* was frozen in the ice in Fortune Bay, Newfoundland. Hostile Newfoundlanders advanced across the ice to capture the Yankee. But the giant size and the reckless courage of the Yankee captain, whose crew was armed with a few old muskets, dissuaded them, and they left the *Tiger* to bide her time and slip out when the ice broke. Many times during the nineteenth century, to the dangers of the sea were added others arising from the competition of Canadian and Newfoundland fishermen on the north. Long negotiations between worried statesmen were necessary before peace ruled the waters.

636   The Pinky Schooner *Tiger*. From a model in the United States National Museum

ALONG THE WHARVES, GLOUCESTER, MASS.

FISHING schooners still tie up at the Gloucester wharves and fishermen put off for the Grand Banks. Time has brought change and improvement. The new boats are faster and trimmer than those of one and two centuries ago. The gas engine, which serves as auxiliary, marks the greatest difference of the new day. But they are still open boats with little cabins and the men who sail them brave the elements as did the men of old.

THE MACKEREL CATCH — FISHERMEN AT WORK

THE methods as well as the boats of the fishermen have changed with the passing years. The watch stands at the bow of the mackerel schooner keeping a lookout for the patch of broken water which marks a school. He gives the signal, "School Oh," and directs the man at the tiller as to his course. As the boat draws near, the dories are let down over the side, each with two men and a piece of the great seine aboard. Quickly the men in the boats lay the seine about the fish until the school is enclosed in a circle of floating corks. The captain from the schooner

637 © Detroit Photographic Co.

directs the work. The bottom of the net is shirred together with a rope, and the fish are left no chance of escape. The schooner tacks alongside and brings the catch aboard to be packed away in barrels of ice.

Perhaps the men are at work all night, yet they must be ready for another school at daybreak, for dawn and dusk are the best times for taking mackerel.

In both the north Atlantic and north Pacific the taking of halibut is an important industry. The halibut flourishes in the colder oceans. This great flat fish, weighing sometimes a hundred pounds, brings considerable revenue to the fishermen. Halibut, as well as mackerel and cod, account for an important share of the business of the Boston fish pier. Shipments are made to the fish markets far in the interior of the country.

638 Preparing the Nets. © Detroit Photographic Co.

639 A Cape Ann Fisherman in a Dory. © Detroit Photographic Co.

TRAWLING FROM THE DORIES

TRAWLING has been practiced since the middle of the nineteenth century. When the "Grand Banker" arrives at the fishing grounds, the dories are sent out, again with two men in a boat, one to handle the oars and the other to let out the trawl, sometimes a mile in length, which is held up at either end by buoys. Every few feet a line with hooks and bait drops from the trawl. On short winter days the trawl is barely laid down before the long process of pulling it in is begun. The fish are taken from the hooks, which are rebaited, and the great line is carefully coiled in a tub ready for use on the morrow. From early morning until late at night lasts the round of drudgery, for after the dories have returned the day's catch must be cared for.

DRYING FISH AT GLOUCESTER

SAFE ashore the fisherman no longer makes his salt but he still dries his salted catch under the open sky. It is then ready to be packed and shipped to markets all over the world.

© Detroit Publishing Co.

641   The Cod Fishing Fleet, from *Eighty Years of Progress*, Hartford, Conn., 1869

THE TRAWLER

SINCE the days of the first boats on the Grand Banks the sea has taken heavy toll of the property and lives of the fishermen. Storms have wrecked many a fishing craft or driven them, water-logged and injured by the gale, far out to sea. For the man who ventures on a trawler there is little romance. Tossed on the waves in his frail dory as he visits his trawls, at greater or less distance from his vessel, he is subject to perils unknown to the fisherman of an earlier time. His small boat rides like a shell on the sea. In experienced hands no craft is safer; but a moment of carelessness, or a slight miscalculation may cost him his life. Woe to him if the stealthy fog settles about him ere he has left his trawls and put back to the schooner. It blinds his vision, cuts off all marks to guide his course, and lets him drift he knows not where. From the earliest days the annals of the fishing ports are marked by tales of desperate adventure and tragedy. The sea still remains untamed.

642   A Dory on the Fishing Grounds, from *Harper's Weekly*, Oct. 31, 1885, after a drawing by M. J. Burns

643   From a photograph by the United States Department of Agriculture

THE FISH TRAP

On shores sloping gradually out to sea and somewhat sheltered from storms, great traps are built to take the fish that venture into shallow waters. Sometimes a school of menhaden will run into the trap followed by their enemies the bluefish, the "wolves of the ocean." The menhaden will be sold to the fishermen for bait or, if there are too many, to the oil factories or the farmers.

At other times the "pounds," as the traps are sometimes called, will be filled with weakfish, mackerel or even cod. The erection and maintenance of a trap is costly. A winter gale may loosen its posts or tear away the nets. To keep it in proper shape vigilance is required. But if it is well located in a cove or behind the sandy islands of a barrier beach, the difficulties are lessened and the profits are good.

644   © Underwood & Underwood

MENHADEN BOATS IN SOUTHERN WATERS

One of the less known of the deep sea fisheries is that of menhaden. The fish are not edible, but are used for making oil and fertilizer. They appear, after the winter season, in vast schools, and run in to the shallow shore waters to spawn. In the early years of the nineteenth century, they were caught on the coast of the north Atlantic with seines, sometimes a mile in length. Occasionally the seines may still be seen rolled up on great drums on shore. But menhaden fishing is now mostly done in the deep sea. Small steamers specially built to carry the fish search the sea watching for the roughened water above a school. When the fish have been sighted, the ship draws near and small boats lay the floating purse net in a circle around the school.

A SCHOOL OF MENHADEN

WHEN the menhaden school is encircled, the bottom of the purse net is pulled together with a rope. The steamer then draws alongside and the crew take out the catch with a scoop net. Sometimes the old menhaden schooner still sails out beside the sturdy steam-driven craft. The glistening, struggling mass of fish is transferred to the hold of the ship to be taken as rapidly as possible to the "fish factory" on shore. Here the oil is pressed out, and then fertilizer is made from the refuse.

645 © Underwood & Underwood

646 © Keystone

THE BOSTON FISH MARKET

ONE of the greatest fish markets in the world is the Boston fish pier where many schooners from the Banks tie up. The fishing industry has grown with the expansion of population and the rise in the price of meat that followed a constantly increasing demand. Refrigeration and the canning factory make the catch available to the people who live far from the sea, in the interior of the continent.

ALONG THE BOSTON FISH PIER

To pass through the archways on either side of the Boston fish pier and to see the forests of masts rising above the water outside is to appreciate the magnitude of the deep-sea fishing industry of America. As in agriculture, the corporation has made little progress in the fisheries of the Banks. Like the farmer, the fisherman who owns his schooner and his nets or trawls is independent and an individualist. The risks of his calling and the constant battle with nature have developed a hardy and self-reliant type. The fisherman must know the sea and its ways and must meet the inevitable emergencies with courage and sure judgment.

648   The Clammer. From a photograph by Clifton Johnson

649   A Cape Cod Fisherman.   From a photograph by
            Rudolf Eickemeyer

THE FISHERMAN — A LITTLE CHANGING TYPE

Accustomed to the risks of the sea in an open boat, the fisherman has learned to face the ups and downs of his calling with equanimity; the joys and cares of each day are sufficient and the morrow may look out for itself. Money comes "easy" when the season is good, and as easily goes when the season is done. But the pride of wealth once his still lingers. Known to have made many dollars a day on the water, he will rarely stoop to labor for a daily wage on land.

The shore dweller may be a scalloper, or a digger of clams, or he may go out each morning to pull up his lobster pots, or in southern waters he may participate in the great business of taking shrimp. Whatever his special work, he is a fisherman stamped with the mark of his calling. Poor but independent, living from hand to mouth, rugged and weatherbeaten, the type changes little in a swiftly moving age.

650   From a photograph by the United States Department of Agriculture

THE OYSTERMAN WITH HIS TONGS

FIRST cousin to the fisherman is the oysterman. Here and there along the Atlantic coast are areas where conditions of water and temperature make it possible for oysters to live and propagate. Long Island Sound and Chesapeake Bay are the most important but there are many others. During the latter eighteenth and early nineteenth centuries oystermen worked these natural beds from rowboats. Off Blue Point on the Long Island shore or in Chesapeake Bay during the season, fleets of boats could have been seen, each with a man standing or seated in it, slowly lifting the oysters from the bottom with his primitive tongs.

651   From a photograph by the United States Department of Agriculture

THE OYSTER SCHOONER

THE business of taking oysters grew. The tongs were replaced by a drag net which the oystermen call a "dredge." The schooner replaced the rowboat and beat slowly back and forth over the bed dragging a dredge on either side. On the rich grounds the fleet of oyster boats increased and the bay bottoms were dragged so often that the oysters began to give out. In the latter half of the nineteenth century the oystermen along the Atlantic coast began to suffer. They faced a radical change in their methods or a destruction of their business.

652   © Keystone

OYSTER SHELLS FOR OYSTER "FARMING"

GREAT piles of shells beside the oyster "shucking houses" were the measure of the attack upon the natural beds. When these began to give out, oyster farming began. Bay bottoms where oysters would not propagate but where they would live and grow were leased to private persons. The oyster farmer "plants" a part of his "farm" each spring with tiny embryo oysters. Before he puts the "seed" in the water, he covers the bottom with oyster shells.

THE OYSTER STEAMER

SAILING craft proved clumsy to handle in dragging the dredges over the restricted acres of the oyster farms, slow in coming about and useless when the wind died away. Small steamers became the means by which the nineteenth-century oysterman cultivated his farm. The twentieth century has brought a vast expansion. The primitive oysterman has evolved into a capitalist.

653   From a photograph by the United States Department of Agriculture

INDIAN METHOD OF DRYING SALMON, ALASKA

VASTLY different from the oyster business is the salmon fishing of the Pacific coast. Early explorers in Puget Sound and the Columbia River found the summer streams full of salmon running up to spawn. In July the waters of the Columbia were lashed with the leaping of fish moving rapidly and steadily inland. Indians living in the region

654 © Keystone

had become dependent upon the salmon for their food. They shot the fish with bows and arrows; they gaffed them with spears in the rapids. Some had devised elaborate fish traps which they built in protected tidewater regions. They dried the catch on the shore after the method which still persists on the Alaskan coast. Dried salmon served for food during the long winter months when the fish had left the rivers to feed in the deep sea.

655 © Keystone

HAULING A SALMON SEINE IN THE COLUMBIA

As Oregon and Washington filled with settlers, white men took the place of the Indians in the salmon fishing. When the transcontinental railroads linked the Pacific coast with the markets of the East, salmon canneries preserved the fish for far distant consumers. Salmon fishing grew rapidly into a business of great importance. The primitive methods of the early days gave way to modern devices. One of the most effective of these is the great seine which is used where the river shoals on a sand bar. The net is towed out by boats in a broad semicircle. Horses are attached to either end and a shining, leaping mass of fish is hauled ashore.

656   © Keystone

657   © Keystone

THE COLUMBIA RIVER FISH WHEEL

BESIDES seines, gill nets, and hand lines, the salmon fisheries make use of a wheel carrying two or three dip nets. The river current turns the wheel slowly round, bringing up the dip nets full of salmon which fall into a trough and slide into the bottom of the boat or into the receptacle which takes them to the cannery. The stationary wheels are placed in the channels where the fish are known to run. The floating wheels move out into midstream and anchor where the salmon happen to be running best.

A BARGE CATCH OF SALMON

THOUSANDS of fish are brought each year to the wharves of the canneries. The supply seems inexhaustible. And yet already ominous signs point to a lessening of the runs. Laws have thus far only imperfectly protected the salmon. It remains for the future to solve the problem of saving the rich food supply of Pacific waters.

THE NEW YORK STATE FISH HATCHERY

THE twentieth century has seen the rapid development of fish conservation throughout the United States. The danger of the extinction of brook trout early led to the artificial propagation of this and other fresh water fish and the restocking of the lakes and streams which the anglers frequent. Fish hatcheries have been established where schools of brood fish supply the necessary millions of eggs. These are fertilized and hatched, and the tiny fry are given a start in life under conditions as well adapted as possible to the maximum production of fish.

658 © Underwood & Underwood

659 © Underwood & Underwood

PLANTING TOMCOD FRY IN A LONG ISLAND HARBOR

SALT water as well as fresh water fish are produced in the hatcheries to make good the catches of the fishermen. Salmon, smelt, shad, herring and cod are but a few of the varieties that the national and state governments are seeking to guard against the inroads made by the vast fishing operations that characterize the twentieth century. How little the colonial fisherman of New England would have thought that the fish which he found so abundant off his coasts could ever need artificial replenishing.

660   From D. P. De Vries, *Reyse in Neuwe Welt*, Amsterdam, 1655

AN EARLY WHALING PICTURE

THE greatest of the fishermen were the old-time whalers. From time immemorial men had seen great spouting monsters in the ocean and had occasionally found their carcasses washed up on the beach. Almost as soon as the New England settlements in America were established the pioneers began to utilize the products of the stranded whales.

WHALING OFF LONG ISLAND

THE stranding of a whale brought busy days to the little seventeenth-century villages along the north Atlantic coast. In 1644, within four years after its founding, the men of Southampton, Long Island, divided the villagers into four groups, each group to take charge of the drift whales cast ashore in its ward. Whenever one was washed up, lots were promptly cast and two persons from each group selected to cut it up. The bounty of the sea was shared by all alike save the cutters, who received a double portion for their labor. When the work was done, the watchful Indians, by right of treaty, were allowed to carry off the "fynnes and tails." Whaling began as a community enterprise. The picture represents a scene in the late nineteenth century, after the great days of whaling had passed, and when an occasional cast-up whale brought the shore community to the beach as it had two hundred years before.

661   From *Harper's Weekly*, Jan. 31, 1885, after a drawing by W. P. Bodfish

662   © Asahel Curtis

INDIANS CUTTING UP A WHALE AT NEAH BAY, WASHINGTON

EVEN now a Pacific whale, nosing in close to shore, is sometimes caught in a storm and washed up on the beach. The modern Indians of the coast profit, as their forefathers for centuries profited, by the happy accident.

SHERBURNE, THE WHALING PORT OF NANTUCKET, IN 1811

THE early colonists were not long content to wait upon fortune. Watchmen were planted on the tops of the highest sand dunes and when a black, spouting mass was discerned in gray inshore waters, the village rushed as one man to the shore. Crude harpoons clattered on the bottoms of small boats hastily pushed off to join in the chase. If the whale were killed, the carcass was guided to the beach and the villagers had work for days. First came the cutting up. Then the oil was tried out. When "oyle" passed as currency at some of the local trade exchanges at the rate of one pound ten shillings per barrel, people gave little heed to the risks of the chase. But whaling from small boats soon gave place to ships seeking prey in the open sea as the eighteenth century advanced. Ports like Sherburne sent more and more ships each year in search of the treasure-laden monsters.

663

From *The Port Folio*, 1811, after a drawing by J. Sansom

664   From a photograph in the collection of the Old Dartmouth Historical Society,
New Bedford, Mass.

WHARVES AT NEW BEDFORD

WHALING, well established in the eighteenth century, suffered heavily from the seven years of the American Revolution. After the war the industry revived, only to be again struck down in the second war with England. When the treaty of Ghent brought peace to the Atlantic, the whale fishery entered upon its "golden era." During the 'thirties, 'forties and 'fifties a great American whaling fleet scoured the seven seas. At the docks of many harbors in New England and Long Island tied up the sturdy sailing vessels engaged in the greatest of the fisheries. Most important of the whaling ports was the little town of New Bedford. The whole life of the village, as of the neighboring island of Nantucket, was centered in the business of taking whales.

THE WHALING VESSEL

ALTHOUGH ships were constantly coming and going, the departure of a whaling vessel was an event in the life of the port. The crowd of friends and relatives, gathered at the wharf to wave good-bye, saw a vessel of four hundred or five hundred tons rigged for seaworthiness rather than for speed. Just forward of the mainmast and embedded in brick was the huge boiler for trying out oil. In their blocks hung the curved whaleboats, twenty-eight feet in length. On the decks below could be seen the captain and one or two mates supervising the departure. Here and everywhere on the vessel scurried the crew. Among these were a few specialists, a cook, a steward, a carpenter, a blacksmith, a cooper, a doctor, and one boat-steerer for each of the whaleboats. In addition were enough common seamen to bring the total to about thirty men. When the last rope had been cast off and the ship stood out to sea, no one could foretell when or under what circumstances she would return. The crowd at the dock, scattering to shops or homes, hoped that the whaler would return from a lucky trip with coffers full of hard money.

665   From a model of the Bark *Sea Fox*, in the Peabody Museum, Salem, Mass.

666   From a lithograph, 1838, in the collection of Allan Forbes, Boston, from the painting by Thomas Birch after a sketch by C. B. Hulsart

WHALING OFF HAWAII, 1833

A FAVORITE voyage of the 'forties was to touch at the Azores, follow down the west coast of Africa and, rounding the Cape of Good Hope, cross the Indian Ocean to Australia. Here the whaler turned his prow northward. Sometimes he went to the whaling grounds in the Bering Sea, sometimes to the "offshore" grounds in the central Pacific. Many times he stopped at one of the Polynesian Islands to barter with the natives for supplies. On the homeward journey, the skipper rounded Cape Horn and a second time turned north. It might be three years after she had set sail that the weather-beaten whaling ship tacked into the familiar waters of the home port, perhaps a fortune in oil and bone in her and tales of adventure a-plenty.

As the incoming ship was sighted in the distance, excitement stirred the whaling town. Anxious eyes straining through telescopes finally made out the name of the home-comer. The news ran through the streets and the people crowded down to the dock for the welcome.

WHALEBOATS FOLLOWING A SPERM WHALE

WHEN a whale was located, the whaleboats were lowered away. An old whaler, Captain Davis, has described the craft which brought the seamen to close quarters with their prey. "For lightness and form; for carrying capacity as compared with its weight and sea-going qualities; for speed and facility of movement at the word of command; for the placing of the men at the best advantage in the exercise of their power by the nicest adaptation of the varying length of the oar to its position in the boat; and, lastly, for a simplicity of construction, which renders repairs practicable on board ship, the whale boat is simply as perfect as the combined skill of the million men who have risked life and limb in service could make it." — ALEXANDER STARBUCK, *History of the American Whale Fishery,* 1878.

667   From a lithograph, 1859, in the collection of Allan Forbes, after a sketch by A. Van Best and R. S. Gifford

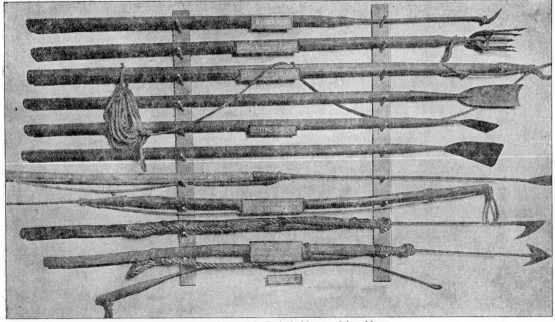

668   From the collection of the Peabody Museum, Salem, Mass.

669 From *The Century Illustrated Monthly Magazine*, August, 1870, engraving by
J. W. Evans after a drawing by W. Taber; by permission of The Century Co.

WHALING TOOLS

In the bow of the whaleboat stood the captain or the mate armed with harpoon. Near him lay the long, slender lance used to kill the exhausted whale. The other tools were in the ship awaiting the carcass to be brought alongside — cutting spades and implements for handling the blubber. The ship itself with its device for trying out the oil was the only expensive equipment which the whaler needed. His tools were simple, hand implements, depending for their efficiency upon the skill of the user.

"FAST TO A WHALE"

Whales were not easy to catch. The whaleboats made their way stealthily towards the black, floating mass. When striking distance had been reached, the captain or mate in the bow threw the harpoon and "fastened" the whale to the boat. As the maddened beast rushed through the water, the boat was not seldom carried so far away that the distant ship was but a spot on the horizon. When the rush slackened, the boat maneuvered into position for thrusting the lance into a vital spot.

THE ATTACK

"In 1850, Captain Cook, of the bark *Parker Cook* of Provincetown, lowered two boats for a full sperm whale. The nearest boat met him head on, and, when abreast of the hump, the boat-steerer put two irons into him. Before the boat could be brought head on, the whale broached half out of water and capsized her, the line fouling the boat-steerer's leg, almost severing it from the body. With great presence of mind he cut the line, and the other boat picked up

670   From a lithograph, in the collection of Allan Forbes, from the painting by William Page after a drawing by C. B. Hulsart

the upset crew, and returned to the bark. But the whale was not satisfied with his victory over the boat . . . making for the bark he struck her a tremendous blow, prostrating the men on deck and burying the cut-water and stern up to the planking in his head. A second time he struck the vessel, but with much less force. In the meantime, Captain Cook got his bomb-lance ready and lowered another boat. Three times within eight yards of him, the captain fired the lance into his body, and eventually made him spout blood, though with every piercing of the lance he rushed open-mouthed at the boat, requiring the utmost skill and coolness to avoid him. One hundred and three barrels of oil was the reward of the captors." — Alexander Starbuck, *History of the American Whale Industry*, 1878.

THE CAPTURE

Sometimes a sperm whale, maddened by pain, would rush the whaleboat and grind it to bits between his great teeth. A right whale, powerful and quick, would dart about, lashing the water with his tremendous tail and flukes, a blow from which would throw a boat into the air. There were times when lives hung on the skill and nerve of the boat-steerer in the stern. He must be strong and quick. He must foresee possible emergencies. He must guide his small craft, carried swiftly along the surface, in such a manner that it would

not ship a load of water. He must be ever ready for a sudden change of course on the part of the frenzied whale. However great the danger, few captains would willingly let their prey escape. The prize was worth too much. Brave without recklessness, resolute and resourceful, self-reliant and self-possessed, guarding the lives of his men and the safety of his ship, the captain of a whaler was one of the finest types America has produced.

671   From a lithograph in the collection of Allan Forbes, after drawings by A. Van Best and R. S. Gifford

672   Bark *Kathleen* Hit by a Whale, 1902.   From the painting by E. T. Russell in the collection of Allan Forbes

THE RISKS OF THE CHASE

In 1902 the bark *Kathleen* was struck and sunk by a whale. Such accidents were very rare. In 1850 the *Anne Alexander* was struck by a wounded whale and sunk in the offshore ground of the Pacific. Eleven men with little food and water were left adrift but had the fortune soon to meet a passing sail. Among the grim tales of the old whaling days is that of the *Essex* of Nantucket. In 1819, in mid-Pacific, the ship, surrounded by a school of whales, was struck by an enraged monster who tore a hole in her bottom. Before she went down the crew salvaged some food and water and a few nautical instruments and had time to build up the gunwales of the open boats and fit them with masts and sails. On November 22 they started in their open boats on a thousand-mile journey to the coast of South America. Weeks passed. A barren island was reached and abandoned, but a spring replenished their water. Three men at their own request were left on this bit of land. Finally the boats became separated, one never to be heard of again. In the remaining craft the feebler men died, and their bodies became food for the despairing survivors. On the first of February desperate necessity forced the four occupants of the captain's boat to draw lots to see who should die and who should be the executioner. One boat was picked up on the seventeenth of February and the other, with but two occupants, on the twenty-third after three months at sea.

The story of the *Essex* told by the emaciated survivors sent a shudder through the whaling towns. There were other whaling boats separated from the ship by some accident that succeeded in making prodigious journeys across the oceans. How many tried and failed, and were reported "lost at sea" no one will ever know. The memories of the *Essex* made doubly poignant the dread suspense of those who waited for loved ones who perhaps would never return.

673   *Whaling in the South Pacific.*   From the painting, 1837, by Benjamin F. West (1818–54), in the Peabody Museum, Salem, Mass.

A GAME OF CHANCE

WHALING, like all fishing, was a game of chance. Occasionally a ship made as much as a hundred thousand dollars on a single voyage but more often the profit was moderate and many times the voyage stood the owners a heavy loss. The uncertainty and the opportunity for big profits lured to the whaling fleet many of the best men who sailed the sea. After the excitement of the chase came the heavy work of cutting up and "trying-out" the oil.

674   From a lithograph, 1859, in the collection of Allan Forbes, from the painting by J. Cole

WHALERS "TRYING OUT"

"BESIDES her hoisted boats, an American whaler is outwardly distinguished by her try-works. She presents the curious anomaly of the most solid masonry joining with oak and hemp in constituting the completed ship. It is as if from the open field a brick-kiln were transported to her planks. The try-works are planted between the foremast and mainmast, the most roomy part of the deck. The timbers beneath are of a peculiar strength, fitted to sustain the weight of an almost solid mass of brick and mortar, some ten feet by eight square, and five in height. The foundation does not penetrate the deck, but the masonry is firmly secured

675 From *The Century Illustrated Monthly Magazine*, August, 1890, after a sketch by J. O. Davidson; by permission of The Century Co.

to the surface by ponderous knees of iron bracing it on all sides, and screwing it down to the timbers. On the flanks it is cased with wood, and at top completely covered by a large, sloping, battened hatchway. Removing this hatch we expose the great try-pots, two in number, and each of several barrels' capacity. When not in use, they are kept remarkably clean. . . .

"Here be it said that in a whaling voyage the first fire in the try-works has to be fed for a time with wood. After that no wood is used, except as a means of quick ignition to the staple fuel. In a word, after being tried out, the crisp, shriveled blubber, now called scraps or fritters, still contains considerable of its unctuous properties. These fritters feed the flames. Like a plethoric burning martyr, or a self-consuming misanthrope, once ignited, the whale supplies his own fuel and burns by his own body. Would that he consumed his own smoke! for his smoke is horrible to inhale, and inhale it you must, and not only that, but you must live in it for the time. It has an unspeakable, wild, Hindoo odor about it, such as may lurk in the vicinity of funereal pyres. It smells like the left wing of the day of judgment; it is an argument for the pit." — HERMAN MELVILLE, *Moby Dick*, 1899.

676   From a lithograph, 1862, in the collection of Allan Forbes, after a drawing by Benjamin Russell (1804–85)

THE STONE FLEET OF NEW BEDFORD

THE Civil War brought heavy losses to the Atlantic whaling fleet. Confederate privateers and commerce raiders captured and destroyed many of them. Some ships were sold and many were laid up. A large number of the Pacific fleet sailed under the Hawaiian flag. The Federal government bought forty old whalers which formed the larger part of the two famous stone fleets that were sunk in 1861 off Charleston and Savannah to block the ports.

677   From the painting by William Bradford (1827–92), photograph by Gramstorff Bros., Inc.

THE ARCTIC WHALER

AFTER the Civil War, whaling never recovered its former vigor. Whales were becoming scarce and wary. Longer voyages and more expensive equipment were required. Each summer a fleet worked its way in among the ice floes of the Bering Sea. To the usual dangers of the sea were added the risks of the frozen North.

678   The Abandoned Whalers.   From a lithograph, 1872, in the Bostonian Society Collections

THE LOSS OF THE ARCTIC FLEET IN 1871

In the fall of 1871 from port to port along the Atlantic coast ran the story of the loss of thirty-seven of the Arctic fleet. The captains had stayed too long on whaling grounds. The ice floes had closed about them and no friendly gale had opened a passage to the ocean. The crews abandoned the ships and made their way, dragging the whaleboats across eighty miles of wind-swept ice to the point where the remainder of the fleet awaited them. In a heavy sea twelve hundred survivors were distributed among the seven vessels outside the floes, and the voyage to Honolulu began. The dangers of the Arctic fishing in the north Pacific proved a serious deterrent. Few ships returned from the Bering Sea without showing heavy scars from contacts with the ice. Many were wrecked in foggy weather or drawn on shore by gales. The summer of 1872 after the wreck of the Arctic fleet found, however, twenty-seven ships busy in the treacherous Arctic waters.

679   Making for the Rescue Fleet.   From a lithograph, 1872, in the Bostonian Society Collections

680   From a lithograph, 1862, in the Bostonian Society Collections, after a drawing by Benjamin Russell

A WHALE SHIP ON THE NORTHWEST COAST CUTTING IN HER
LAST RIGHT WHALE

THE days of the old whaler are now numbered. The products from the new petroleum, introduced before
the Civil War and spreading rapidly after the conflict ended, ate into and sharply limited the market for
whale oil. One by one the whaling ships hauled up after the last voyage and their masters turned to other
callings. The whaling ships and the sail-driven packets and clippers of the old merchant marine passed from
the sea together.

BOMB EXPLODING IN A WHALE

BUT whaling has not entirely passed away. Whalers still ply the waters of the northern oceans or strike out
into the broad Pacific. Every summer they may be seen north of Newfoundland hastily taking advantage
of the short season. The steamship has replaced the old sailing vessel. Many of the risks of the old whale
chase have passed with the development of new devices. A small gun from the bow of the modern ship
shoots the harpoon into the whale and an exploding bomb does the work of the lance. The business still calls for
hardihood. But with the passing of the old-time whaling captain America lost one of the best expressions of its
sturdy frontier spirit.

681   From a photograph in the collection of the Old Dartmouth Historical Society, New Bedford, Mass.

NOTES ON THE PICTURES

4. The sub-title of Pyne's work states that his figures and landscapes are "accurately drawn from Nature" and "for the embellishment of the landscape." The Print Room, British Museum, has some of his originals. Pyne also published *The Costumes of Great Britain*, 1808, *Rudiments of Landscape Drawing*, 1812, and *Etchings of Rustic Figures for the Embellishment of the Landscape*, 1815.

5, 6. Markham was a voluminous writer. "He is equally at home in expounding the best methods of tillage, the treatment of live stock, the subtleties of hawking, the secrets of angling, or the most approved recipe for the housewife; there is little indeed, in the whole range of country pleasures, and duties, upon which he did not discourse with ease, enthusiasm, and authority." — *Cambridge History of English Literature*, IV, 364–77.

9. Cut taken from *Art Journal*, London, 1878, article "Art Among the Ballad Mongers." "It doubtless has reference," says the writer, "to the parable of the sower, and is interesting as showing not only the mediæval harrow but the sower's bag or wallet instead of a basket. In reference to this the Rev. J. W. Ebsworth . . . informs me that the 'Men of Kent' still in sowing occasionally use the wallet, as here represented, and not the basket."

10. Painter of miniature not known, but evidently one of the most skillful of the 14th century. The Psalter, a bulky volume of 319 leaves, illuminated by hand in gold, blue, vermilion, carmine and black, with initials in gold on colored ground, the pictures being mostly of Biblical scenes with separate pictures of rural life as headings for a calendar. Miniature is a technical term for a picture in an illuminated MS.

11. Accurate view by David Loggan (1635–1700), artist and engraver, born in Danzig. Engaged on illustrations for *Cantabrigia Illustrata* for nearly twelve years, using a workroom provided for him in Trinity College. Also illustrated *Oxonia Illustrata*, being appointed, 1699, engraver to the University of Oxford.

12. See 10.

13. Comenius, a famous 17th-century educator, published the first child's picture-book. Engravings made by Michael Endter of Nuremberg.

15. See 11.

17. See 13.

18. See 10.

23. See 13.

26, 27, 29, 30. Joseph Nash (1809–78), water-color painter and lithographer, student of architecture under Augustus Charles Pugin (1762–1832), a Frenchman who prepared a large illustrated series of works on Gothic buildings of England. Nash's picturesque views of late Gothic buildings were accompanied by figures to illustrate manners and customs of the time. He strove for picturesque effects rather than for correct structural detail.

28. Essentially accurate, copied from early prints.

31. See 26.

32. See 4.

33. By Johannes Kip (1653–1722), Dutch draftsman and engraver who settled at Westminster, England, where he did most of his work and where he died. Engravings are of historical interest since many of the houses portrayed have been altered and some have been demolished.

36. Original in Sloane Collection, British Museum, contains marginal notes and other memoranda in handwriting of John Winthrop. Draftsman of map not known. Names of towns, rivers and ponds written in a small, plain hand, not Winthrop's. Map believed to have been sent to England in 1637 or 1638. See Winsor, Vol. III, p. 380, for outline of the whole sketch, with comment by editor.

41. Group planned by and executed under the direction of Hobart Nichols, who painted the background; foreground by Albert E. Butler and W. B. Peters; animals mounted by Coloman Jonas, of Denver, Col.

42. Foreground planned and executed by Albert E. Butler; background painted by Hobart Nichols after a sketch by Courtney Brandreth.

45. Group prepared under the direction of J. D. Figgins; background by Bruce Horsfall; accessories by J. D. Figgins; birds mounted by H. C. Denslow.

46. By former member of the staff of the American Museum of Natural History. (See also Vol. I., p. 26.)

47. Engraving after the original drawing by John White, 1585, who was with the first Raleigh expedition to Roanoke. (See *Notes on the Pictures*, Vol. I, 7.)

48, 49, 50, 52, 54, 64. Artist specializes on American history and life.

51. Essentially accurate.

61, 62, 63. Sketches by Italian traveler in United States, Count Luigi Castiglioni. Visited all seaboard states to study flora and fauna. Elected member of the American Philosophical Society. Introduced into Europe various American trees.

64–66. See 48.

67, 68. The record of earmarks is taken from "Eleazer Hawkins, Jr. Liber eius. Made by David Willets the 12th day of the 2d Month New Stile Annoque Domini 1752." Hawkins was a resident of Brookhaven, L. I. Record books of cattle marks were commonly kept in the colonial period.

72. Conjectural view, topography correct.

75. The Meeker house was located in village called Lyons Farms, near Newark, N. J. Built in 1674 by Benjamin Meeker and occupied continuously by his descendants until its demolition in 1913. Sketch made by descendant of the original owner.

76. Reconstruction under supervision of George Francis Dow.

80, 81. The two maps are the result of exhaustive research by Leonard W. Labaree, instructor in history, Yale University.

83. Miller was chaplain to His Majesty's forces and lived in the Fort at New York. He says, in speaking of preparing his book "and also taken draughts of all the cities, towns, forts and churches. . . . I was obliged to cause them all to be thrown overboard [after having been taken as a prisoner by a French privateer. He rewrote the history] through God's assistance and the help of my memory and certain knowledge I had of things."

84. By the leading American illustrator of his day, whose many drawings on American history and life are essentially accurate.

85. A reconstruction.

90. Drawing shows internal evidence of accurate knowledge.

92. Artist painted pictures on Maryland life and history.

93. Detail from engraving after drawing by Jacques Le Moyne, 1565, who came to America with the Laudonnière expedition. See Vol. I, *Notes on the Pictures*, 7, 292.

94. Cut copied from 1574 edition of Monardes (1493–1588), a Spanish physician who probably made drawing of tobacco plant brought from America to Spain.

99. Artist's conception correct in its general details; buildings on the wharf improbable at this date.

101. Map drawn by Augustine Herrmann (*ca.* 1605–86) from his own survey, engraved by William Faithorne. Herrmann, agent for Dutch merchants at New Amsterdam, transported a colony to Maryland in 1660, and in 1662 in return for making a map of Virginia and Maryland received from Lord Baltimore a patent for Bohemia Manor, afterwards in-

creasing holdings to 30,000 acres. The following is inscribed on the map itself: "Virginia and Maryland As it is Planted and Inhabited this present Year 1670 Surveyed and Exactly drawne by the Only Labour and Endeavour of Augustine Herrmann . . . Published by Authority of his Majesty's Royal Licence . . . to Augustine Herrmann and Thomas Withinbrook . . . 1673 . . . W. Faithorne, Sculpt."

102. Pyle's picture is merely illustrative; the horse has the appearance of a nineteenth-century thoroughbred, a type not known in Virginia at this time.

103. Artist, Virginia born, and educated in art abroad, was frequent illustrator of books and magazines. Many of his oil paintings are preserved in the Confederate Museum, Richmond.

104. Artist was a Virginian, and student of southern life and ways. See 303, 348.

108. Sketched by officer of the Royal Navy, who visited America in 1827 and 1828, traveling through Atlantic coast states and Ohio and Mississippi valleys; sketches were published with his own descriptions. See 311.

114. Latrobe a distinguished American architect. See Vol. XIII.

116. Picture copied from Guiliemus Piso, . . . *De Braziliensi*, Amsterdam, 1648, original in color.

119. Sketched by an English traveler in America.

120. Annotation at top of map is in George Washington's handwriting.

124. Artist, Swedish born, produced many first-rate paintings and illustrations for magazines and books during an active career of over fifty years. Painted a series on Civil War battle scenes, originals now in the Seventh Regiment Armory, New York. See Vol. I, *Notes on the Pictures*, 643.

125. Artist a native of Baltimore, studied at Paris; painter of 18th-century life, chiefly in the South. Also painted pictures on the Revolution.

126, 127. Artist a pupil of Gérôme, whose influence he shows; has painted over fifty canvases on American history. His work is marked by sentimentalism and rich color effects. See *Notes on the Pictures*, Vol. I, 409, for other examples of his work.

129. See 125.

130, 131. See 124.

132. Accurate in spirit, by well-known painter of American historical pictures.

133. See 126.

137. Accurate view, from sketch by J. W. Barber, whose illustrations of American towns and scenes were from sketches on the spot.

138. See 119.

139. Artist one of America's great landscape painters, educated abroad.

142. By engraver of remarkable versatility and prolific production, sometimes called the "Father of American engraving." Originally influenced by the Englishman Bewick, whose work he copied. See 148, 158, 160, 161, 164, 165.

145. Original owner, John Curtis, of Boxford, Mass., left his plow to respond to call for men at Lexington.

148. See 142.

152. Early example of the work of a noted American painter.

153. See 139.

155. Artist best known for his paintings of American life in rural communities, mid-nineteenth century, the scenes mostly on Long Island, where he was born and died. See 259, 266, 295.

158. See 142.

159. Accurate view of Housatonic River, by well-known painter of landscape.

160, 161, 164. See 142.

168. By American painter of reputation, educated at Düsseldorf, at Paris and in Holland, known for his many careful studies of rural and of negro life, represented in many collections. See 260.

169. From drawing when artist was 23, and student at night school of the National Academy of Design. Later was painter of typically American *genre* pictures, Civil War and Virginia (negro) studies, and of marine pictures. See 279, 296, 334, 335, 339.

173. Accurate view by English miniaturist who settled in Philadelphia in 1794. Engraved a series of plates of views around Philadelphia, and of country seats in the United States.

174. See 84.

176, 177. The painter, a native of Connecticut, was chiefly known for his landscapes and pictures of farming and sporting scenes. See 246.

179. Artist, a pupil of Howard Pyle, has specialized on American history and life.

180. Artist's work shows sympathetic knowledge of American life and character; many of his pictures will help to preserve typical features of a phase of rural civilization that has almost disappeared. See 242, 264, 297.

183. Artist an observant interpreter of the rugged side of life in rural communities, painting American types and manners as he saw them. See 268, 271, 273, 290, 312.

186. Sketch by an English traveler on the American frontier, early nineteenth century.

189. Sketched from observation by a British traveler.

190. Collot traveled widely in remote sections of the United States; illustration drawn from observation.

191. By an English painter whose many sympathetic studies of early New England life have had a wide vogue in the form of engravings.

195. See 142.

241. Artist, an Englishman, visited the United States and Canada four times between 1836 and 1852; illustrations appeared in *American Scenery*, 1840, and *Canadian Scenery*, 1842.

242. See 180.

246. See 176.

259. See 155.

260. See 168.

261. Artist a versatile and clever portrayer of the life of the plain people of America, with an eye for humorous situations and small-town character studies. See 267, 272, 275, 277, 283, 285, 299, 341.

264. See 180.

266. See 155.

267. See 261.

268. See 183.

269. Artist studied at Düsseldorf and at Paris. Painted landscape and rural life.

271. See 183.

272. See 261.

273. See 183.

275. See 261.

276. By a leading illustrator of the eighteen seventies.

277. See 261.

279. See 169.

283–285. See 261.

286. By a pupil of Howard Pyle, illustrator for magazines.

289. Early example of illustration for woodcut engravings, done by American who became a notable painter.

290. See 183.

295. See 155.

296. See 169.

297. See 180.

298. Artist, born in South Carolina, studied abroad; illustration is after his first important picture, 1876. A prolific and versatile painter of American *genre*, marked by humor and insight.

299. See 261.

300. See 180.

303. See 104.

305. Artist traveled extensively in mid-nineteenth century through middle and western states; sketches simple but accurate. See 316.

311. See 108.

312. See 183.

318, 319, 320, 321, 323, 324. Drawn from observation.

326. Drawn by a well-known illustrator of the period.

327. Drawn from author's description of scene when on tour of the South.

329. From "an original sketch." Artist a well-known illustrator of his day.

330. Scene is in Virginia, "from a sketch by our special artist."

334, 335, 339. Artist spent some time in Virginia, studying negro types. See 169.

348. See 104, 303.

353. Artist visited upper Missouri region, painting Indian portraits and life about 1834. For other examples of his work, see Vol. I, *Notes on the Pictures*, 62, 63, 64, 66, 67, etc.

358. By German artist who visited Indian country about 1845.

362. Artist spent eight years among western Indians, 1832 to 1840; painted many canvases on Indian manners and customs; originals, now in the United States National Museum, are faithful representations of a day long gone. For other examples of his work, see Vol. I, *Notes on the Pictures*, 68, 72, 75, 76, 86, 87, etc.

366. See 358.

370. Artist, born at St. Louis, has painted many realistic studies of the life of the Northwest where he has lived; he is sometimes called the "cowboy artist." See 382, 395.

371. Artist, graduate of Yale School of Fine Arts, spent several years on western plains, studying Indian, cowboy and army life; painted many pictures of note, marked by dashing vigor of style.

378. By a California artist, self-taught; specialized on scenery of mountain and desert, Indian and cowboy life. See 400.

379. See 371, 388.

380. By a western artist, pupil of LaFarge; specializing on mural paintings on western history.

382. See 370.

383. Artist born in Colorado; pupil of Howard Pyle, painter of mural decorations for banks and public buildings, on western history and life.

392, 393. See 383.

394. Artist specialized on sporting scenes and pictures of wild life and adventure.

395. See 370.

400. See 378.

404. See 84.

436. Drawn for the publication issued by the United States Patent Office, 1892, Benjamin Butterworth, Commissioner, to illustrate the progressive development of mechanical invention.

459. Reconstruction, based on accurate knowledge.

480, 481. See 436.

551. The cartoonist was famous in his generation for his scathing exposures of political corruption.

553, 555, 556. Gillam was a leading cartoonist of his day, with leanings to the Republican side.

559. See 553.

604. Cartoonist, elected to Congress, served 1917–21.

625. Artist, member of the Provincetown (Mass.) colony, has specialized on pictures of American workmen in large plants, also on fishermen types.

629. De Fer was geographer to the then King of France. Picture essentially accurate.

630. Model shows distinctly Dutch influence.

633. The name "Chebacco" comes from the name of the place where this type of vessel was first built, then part of the present town of Essex, Mass.

634. See 137.

660. Fanciful, used as an embellishment for a map.

666. Birch, an Englishman who settled in Philadelphia in 1794, painted marine pictures and naval battles of the War of 1812, in which field he was notably good. Original sketch was made by Hulsart, who was on board one of the vessels at the time.

667. Legend on lithograph says the picture was "corrected by Benj. Russell," said by Allan Forbes to have been the "best known sketcher and painter of whaling scenes and whaling vessels of his time."

671. See 667.

678, 679. Published by Benjamin Russell, New Bedford, Mass., and probably his own work.

INDEX

Titles of books under author are in italics; titles of illustrations under producer are in quotation marks.

Pests, to pioneer farmers, 57, 74, 78, 93; on Great Plains, 193; protection against, 249, 251, 252, 255.

Peters, Richard, and agricultural reform, 100, 101; portrait, 100.

Philadelphia, port, 83; grain trade, 83.

Philadelphia Society for Promoting Agriculture, 100, 101; *Address*, 100; motto, 100; prizes and medal, 101; *Memoirs*, 101.

Phillips, Ulrich B., on master and slaves, 150; on negro labor problem, 278.

Pickering, Timothy, and agricultural reform, 101.

Picturesque America, 36, 82, 147, 188, 192.

Pigs. *See* Swine.

Pilgrims. *See* Plymouth.

Pinchot, Gifford, on rural religion, 289.

Pinkerton, John, *General Collection of Voyages*, 83.

Pinky schooner, 302.

Pitch marks, 37.

Pitt's thresher, 230.

Pittsfield, Mass., agricultural society, 104.

Plans. *See* Maps and plans.

Plantations, development of system, 1, 49; and slavery, 51; colonial Virginia, 52, 53, 61; financial system of colonial, English agent, 54; rice, in South Carolina, 55–58; mansions, 60, 150, 163; colonial life and customs, 60, 63–66; ideal arrangement of buildings, 62; in New York, 70; and politics, 142, 149; sugar, 154; later aristocracy, 163; barbecue, 164; travel and society, 165; end of system, 165, 276. *See also* Cotton; Slavery.

Pleasant Hill Academy, 242.

Pleuro-pneumonia in cattle, 108.

Plough Boy, first number, 110.

Plows and plowing, early English, 10; early colonial, 36; eighteenth-century, 73; fall plowing, 80; later, 119; improvement, iron, 207–209; for prairie sod, steel, 210, 211; early steam, 211; gang, 212, 214; disc, tractors, 213, 214.

Plymouth, first planting, 32.

Pocumtuck Valley Memorial Association, Deerfield, material from, 38.

Politics, colonial farmer and, 85, 89; later rural, 118, 134, 283; southern antebellum, 142, 149. *See also* Agrarian movements.

Poor whites, lowland, 147–149.

Population, rural and urban (1920), 270; and food production, 271.

Populist Party, demands, 5, 265, 266; campaign of 1896, 267.

Port Folio, 315.

Post office, country, 127; rural free delivery, 279.

Poultry clubs, 257.

Powderly, Terence V., 265.

Prairie Farmer, 260.

Prairies, railroad grants and settlers, 167; soil, 167; breaking, plows, 167, 210; farms, 168; wheat culture, 199. *See also* Great Plains.

Preparedness, rural attitude, 132.

Priestley, Joseph, and agricultural science, 243.

Progressive Farmer, on Knapp, 255.

Prothero, Rowland E., on English villagers, 16; *English Farming*, 16, 21; on English ladies, 21.

Provincetown, Mass., fishing center, view, 301.

Public lands, railroad grants and settlers, 167; land sharks, 172; and extensive culture, 206, 239; grant for agricultural schools, 244, 245; passing of era, 268. *See also* Homesteads.

Public Record Office, London, material from, 15.

Public utilities. *See* Transportation.

Pugh, Evan, portrait, 242; and agricultural education, 242.

Pyle, Howard, "First Slaves in Virginia," 51; "Wharf of Virginia Plantation," 53; "Virginia Planter," 67.

Pyne, William Henry, *Microcosm*, 10, 11.

QUEEN MARY'S PSALTER, 11, 12, 15.

Quoits, pitching, 132.

RADIO, influence, 281.

Railroads, early, effect on rural life, 140; village depot, 140; western advance, 166, 167, 173; land grants and settlers, 167, 168; and cattle industry, 177; Granger agitation and regulation, 263.

Rakes, mechanic, 224.

Raleigh, Sir Walter, and tobacco, 50.

Ramsay, David, *South Carolina*, 55.

Reaper, Hussey's, 217; McCormick's, 218; his factories, 219; improvements, 219–221; trials, 220; self-binder, 221; headers, 222; present use, 223.

Reclamation, desert before, 234; pioneer irrigation, 234; natural reservoirs, 235; Carey Act, 235; federal works, dams, 235; distribution of water, 236–238; revolving fund, 237; results, 238; map of irrigated districts, 268; drainage, 272.

Records of Massachusetts Bay, 37.

Redfield, Edward W., "Sleighing," 86.

Refrigeration, and cattle industry, 183.

Religion, English peasant, 15; Sabbath at English manor, 18; former rural conditions, 136, 137; negro, 158, 162; cowboy, 186; present-day rural, 288, 289; rural fundamentalism, 296. *See also* Churches.

Remington, Frederic, "Bronco Buster," 176; "Stampede by Lightning," 180; "Cattle in a Corn Corral," 184.

Rensselaerswyck, manor houses, 44, 97; manor, 45.

Reservation, Indians on, 5, 166, 185.

Revivals, 136.

Reynolds, Sir Joshua, "Robert Carter," 63.

Rice, J. E., "Lawrence, Kansas," 169.

Rice, colonial crop, 49; beginning of culture, 55; lands, 55, 56; method of culture, 56, 57; threshing, 57; husking, 58.

Riley, James Whitcomb, on fiddler, 117; *Neghborly Poems*, 117, 118; on rural independence, 118.

Roads, turnpikes, 3, 112, 113, 233; colonial Virginia, 49; country, and covered bridges, 122; antebellum southern, 147, 149, 154; dirt, 232; early care, 233; planked, 233; modern improved, 233, 234, 279. *See also* Communication; Transportation.

Robinson, Andrew, schooner, 300.

Rogers, W. A., "On the Oregon Trail," 170; Trail Across a Stream," 170; "First Season in Oregon," 171; "Cowboys breaking Camp," 179; "Jerked Down," 181.

Rolfe, John, and tobacco, 51.

Rolling tobacco, 53.

Rollins, Philip A., *The Cowboy*, 178, 186.

Rotation of crops, manorial and later English, 9, 22; Bordley's condemnation, 100; lack in western wheat culture, 199, 200; present-day, in South, 278. *See also* Soil.

Round-up in cattle country, 179–181.

Royal Ontario Museum of Archæology, Toronto, material from, 172, 173.

Rube, 117.

Rural betterment, first movement, 3, 90, 98–100. *See also* Agricultural education; Agricultural societies; Communication; Community life; Education; Health; Social conditions.